ARMY LETTERS
FROM AN OFFICER'S WIFE

FRANCES M. A. ROE AND HER DOG, HAL.

ARMY LETTERS
FROM AN OFFICER'S WIFE

1871–1888

BY

FRANCES M. A. ROE

INTRODUCTION BY
SANDRA L. MYRES

ILLUSTRATED BY I. W. TABER
FROM CONTEMPORARY PHOTOGRAPHS

UNIVERSITY OF NEBRASKA PRESS
LINCOLN AND LONDON

First Bison Book printing: 1981
Most recent printing indicated by first digit below:
3   4   5   6   7   8   9   10

Library of Congress Cataloging in Publication Data

Roe, Frances Marie Antoinette Mack, Mrs.
  Army letters from an officer's wife, 1871–1888.

  Reprint. Originally published: New York: D. Appleton, 1909.
  Includes bibliographical references.
  1. Frontier and pioneer life—West (U.S.) 2. United States. Army—
Military life. 3. West (U.S.)—Description and travel—1860–1880. 4.
West (U.S.)—Description and travel—1880–1950. 5. Roe, Frances
Marie Antoinette Mack, Mrs. 6. West (U.S.)—Biography. 7. Army
wives—West (U.S.)—Correspondence. I. Taber, I. West. II. Title.
F596.R68   1981   355.1'2'0978   81–7571
ISBN 0–8032–3859–2   AACR2
ISBN 0–8032–8905–7 (pbk.)

Reprinted from the first edition published by D. Appleton and
Company, 1909.

∞

TO

MY COMRADE

"FAYE"

INTRODUCTION

by Sandra L. Myres

Among the most popular and informative descriptions of life in the nineteenth-century West are the many accounts written by the officers and men of the United States Army. These range from official journals of expeditions and campaigns and formal histories of various units to diaries, books, and personal memoirs published by generals, captains, lieutenants, and even an occasional enlisted man. Although uneven in quality and information, these narratives give an added dimension to our view of western military life, and the better ones, such as Captain John G. Bourke's *On the Border with Crook*, are found in almost every western bibliography.

Ranking along with their husbands as chroniclers of life in the West were the army wives whose articles and books one historian has correctly labeled minor frontier classics.[1] Indeed the "ladies of the army" were among the most perceptive observers of western life, and their journals, diaries, and reminiscences provide one of the richest, and until recently one of the least known and appreciated, sources of information on life in the West during the last years of the American frontier. Far from home, confined to often inadequate and uncomfortable quarters in what seemed to many of them a barren, inhospitable land, the women presented a picture of western life very different from that of their husbands. The wives were understandably more concerned with the difficulties of making a home and raising a family than they were with military strategy or campaigns against hostile Indians. Their narratives tend to concentrate on events of home and garrison life, or, as Elizabeth Custer phrased it, "the domestic life of an army family . . . [and] the trifling perplexities and events which went to fill up the sum of our existence."[2] But the army women were also educated, curious, and eager to learn what they could of the Great American West, and their books are filled with their observations on the land and its people. The army wives offered comment and insights into western life which, if not as exciting as the hordes of bloodthirsty savages, armed desperadoes, death-defying heroes, and delicate heroines of the popular press nor as elegant in literary tone as the books produced by professional writers, still give a vivid and detailed view of western life.

Although many of the army wives kept diaries, journals, or notes on their experiences, most were never intended for publication. The women wrote out of boredom, frustration, loneliness, and occasionally fear, confiding to paper the thoughts and impressions they would not or could not mention to their often overworked and certainly underpaid husbands. Some of the women later prepared their reminiscences for their children and grandchildren or published stories of their army life in order to supplement small pensions or retirement pay. In retrospect, the literary production of the army wives was prodigious in relation to their numbers. The post–Civil War frontier army was never large, and the entire officer corps numbered no more than two thousand at any one time. Many of the officers did not marry or left their wives and families in the East. Yet, from the relatively small group of army wives who did accompany their husbands west, a surprising number of journals and reminiscences appeared in print in either article or book-length form prior to 1920. Beginning with Teresa Griffin Vielé's *"Following the Drum": A Glimpse of Frontier Life* in 1858, ten additional book-length accounts, many published in more than one edition, had appeared by 1910.[3] These published recollections can add to our knowledge and understanding of the nineteenth-century frontier, and Frances Roe's *Army Letters from an Officer's Wife* is an excellent example of this genre of western literature.

Frances Marie Antoinette Mack Roe was born in Orleans, Jefferson County, New York, the daughter of Ralph Gilbert Mack and Mary Coulton Mack. Mack, a farmer, and his wife both traced their families to Revolutionary soldiers, and Frances was proud of her ancestry. She was educated at a private school in Elmira, New York, where she met Fayette Washington Roe, a young Virginian whose father, Francis Asbury Roe, was a naval commander (and later admiral) widely acclaimed for his services during the Mexican and Civil wars. Fayette evidently considered a naval career. After his graduation from Brooklyn Polytechnic Institute and a year's study at Burlington College, he served as a captain's clerk on the steamer *Michigan* during 1865. However, he must have decided that a life at sea was not for him. In 1867, he entered the United States Military Academy at West Point. He graduated in June 1871 and was commissioned a second lieutenant in the United States Infantry. In August, Frances and Fayette were married and almost immediately started westward so Fayette could join his regiment, then stationed at Fort Lyon, Colorado, where Mrs. Roe's sprightly account of their frontier life begins.

Like other army wives, Frances was enthralled by the natural beauty of much of the western landscape, and her narrative includes detailed descriptions of particularly impressive western scenes. Although less flowery and romantic in her descriptions than many other western writers, she appreciated the natural environment and was very much an outdoorswoman. She was fond of fishing and hunting; she described in detail many gay expeditions to well-known fishing streams and the excitement of her first buffalo hunt, and she often boasted of her skill with fishing pole and firearms. She loved horses and was proud of her ability as a rider. "Since I have been with the Army," she bragged, "I have ridden twenty-two horses that had never been ridden by a woman before! . . . [and] I was never unseated, not once!" Indeed, Roe's love of the West and the outdoor life is evident throughout her narrative. Like many other army wives, she recognized the economic potential of the West, but she also mourned the "progress" which she feared would spoil much of its scenic grandeur. At one point, she wrote, "We hear that a railroad will soon be built through that cañon [Prickley-Pear Canyon, Montana], but we hope not. It would be positively wicked to ruin anything so grand."

Much of Roe's book, like those of other army wives, consists of long accounts of the problems and pleasures of life at western posts. She bemoaned her often inadequate quarters and described the indignity of being "ranked out," a common practice in the frontier army. She also commented on servants, sand, and shortages; the snakes, spiders, and venomous insects; and the dirt-covered and cold accommodations she was forced to endure at Fort Supply, Indian Territory. Like most army families, the Roes had to contend with the low pay and the economies necessary to make ends meet, the lack of schools, churches, and recreational facilities, and the difficulty of finding adequate furnishings for their often crude quarters.[4]

But Frances did not dwell on such matters. Like the other wives, she described the parties and dances, the amateur theatricals, colorful parades, and band concerts, the fancy dinners for visiting dignitaries, and the occasional wedding or special holiday celebration that enlivened garrison life. Most officers' wives had at least one servant, either brought from the East or recruited from the enlisted men in their husband's command, and few had more than minimal household duties to perform. They spent their days visiting, reading, writing long letters to relatives and friends, sewing, drawing, or, like Frances, riding, fishing, and hunting.[5]

Frances could well afford the time to pursue her outdoor interests because she had few home responsibilities, and she and Fayette had no children. Whether this was due to some physical disability (perhaps related to Faye's chronic illness) or whether, like other army couples, they decided that the exigencies of army life—the mobile existence, the lack of adequate medical and educational facilities at western posts—precluded a family, is not clear. Frances clearly devoted to her pets much of the love and affection which she might have given to children. Most officers and some enlisted men had an assorted collection of pets, and western garrisons were populated by a variety of horses, cats, dogs, birds, and occasionally more unusual animals such as raccoons, armadillos, and other wild creatures.[6] Frances wrote fondly not only of her favorite mounts and her close companion, the greyhound Hal, but of her squirrels and chickens and of other post pets. It is clear that sometimes she preferred the company of her animals to that of human companions.

Indeed, Roe, like the other army women, was less than impressed with the uncouth, ill-mannered, profane, and often violent people to be found in the West. The dress, manners, and language of some western frontiersfolk were particularly appalling to the army wives raised in the East, and most penned at least one derogatory comment about western society. Lydia Lane, whose husband served at a number of southwestern posts, best summed up the women's feelings when she remarked, "We are told to take in the stranger, as by so doing we 'may entertain an angel unawares,' but I do not think that class of guests often travelled in Texas and New Mexico . . . and if they did . . . their disguise was complete."[7]

In addition to their comments on western white society, all of the army wives made a point of discussing the Indian peoples they encountered. Most had read both the romanticized literature of Cooper and the McGuffey school texts and the accounts of Indian atrocities, real and imagined, in the popular press, and they went west with a good many preconceptions and great curiosity about the Native Americans. Some of their preconceptions and prejudices vanished as they observed and studied the Indians at first hand, and a few were openly sympathetic to the "plight of the red race." Most, like their husbands, were ambivalent, viewing the Indians, as one historian has pointed out, with "fear, distrust, loathing, contempt, and condescension, on the one hand; curiosity, admiration, sympathy, and even friendship, on the other."[8]

In her own comments on the Indians, Roe was less charitable than most of the army women. Although she described at length many of her encounters with Indians and occasionally recognized some hint of kindness or friendliness in their manner, she offered no expression of understanding or sympathy. Her attitude is clearly summed up in the early pages of her book when she describes the Indians not as the "real noble red men" she had hoped to meet but as "simply and only painted, dirty, and nauseous-smelling savages!" Nor did her ideas change. Toward the end of her account, as she mourns the changing nature of the West and "the passing of the buffalo and other game," she adds that she has no regrets for the passing of the Indians, for "there are still too many of them!"[9]

Roe was equally derogatory in her much briefer remarks about the Chinese, Mexicans, and Negroes she met. Although her racist attitudes are unacceptable today, they were not unusual among nineteenth-century women of her background and education. Whatever her prejudices, Roe generally enjoyed her army life and left the frontier with some regret. On leaving Montana for headquarters duty in Omaha in 1888, Frances expressed the ambivalence typical of many army women who longed for "civilization" and yet were reluctant to leave their Western homes. Roe was sure, she wrote, that she would be "wretched . . . cooped up in a noisy city" and that if she ever returned to "the old army life of the West" she would find everything changed and "a new condition of things." But she was pleased that Faye had been promoted to a staff position and confessed that she looked forward to the refinements of city life and to meeting "people of culture."

Despite the happy, almost carefree tone of Mrs. Roe's

account of her army days, her life had a tragic ending. As her book details, the Roes served at a number of western posts between 1871 and 1888, when Faye was named aide-de-camp to General John R. Brooke, commanding general of the Department of the Platte. Roe's fitness reports indicated that he was a competent, but not a brilliant, officer. Most of his life, apparently, he languished in the shadow of his respected and successful father. In any event, Fayette performed well on Brooke's staff and served as adjutant general, judge advocate, and inspector general as well as in several other staff positions. In 1898, on Brooke's recommendation, Roe was named lieutenant colonel of staff and judge advocate of the First Army Corps and transferred to Mobile, Alabama. He had suffered for many years from chronic gastritis and severe headaches, and his new duties and the hot, humid climate placed additional strains on his health. According to one friend, Roe felt himself "incompetent to perform as judge advocate," and his feelings of inadequacy, along with his heavy work load, brought on a complete mental and physical collapse. In December, he requested retirement, and after treatment at the Hot Springs, Arkansas, Army and Navy Hospital, he and Frances moved to Port Orange, Florida, where they hoped the warm climate and quiet life would restore Faye's health.

For the next sixteen years the couple lived quietly in Port Orange. Frances prepared her reminiscences for publication, and the volume appeared in 1909 under the D. Appleton and Company imprint. Although the book received favorable critical comment in several national periodicals,[10] it was certainly not a best seller or a great financial success. Nor were other "army books" by officers' wives much more popular. As one military historian has pointed out, the frontier army had "no strong constituency or interest group in the East." Except for reports of the Indian wars and accounts of sensational events such as the Custer "massacre" and the fight at Wounded Knee there was little interest in western military affairs. Most readers of western literature preferred the stories of Bret Harte and Mary Hallock Foote or the lurid and exciting accounts of Indian warfare in the popular press to the books by officers and their wives who wrote realistically and sympathetically of army life.

Despite Frances's devoted nursing, Fayette's health did not improve, and Frances herself grew increasingly frail and ill. Frances's failing health, his own physical condition, and his lack of success in gaining a long-sought promotion to major preyed on Faye's mind. On September 28, 1916, he shot and killed himself. Frances wrote at the time to an army comrade that "he thought his life to be at an end, feeling that he could not live after I had gone. We had been good comrades forty-five years, and now it seems as though I was breaking faith with him to live on."[12] Fayette was buried in Arlington Cemetery. Frances was too ill to attend the services, although she lived another three and a half years. She died on May 6, 1920, and was buried in Arlington next to her "faithful comrade."

Notes

1. Robert M. Utley, "Arizona Vanquished," *American West* 6 (November 1969): 16.

2. Elizabeth B. Custer, *"Boots and Saddles"; or, Life in Dakota*

with General Custer, reprint edition, ed. Jane R. Stewart (Norman: University of Oklahoma Press, 1961), p. xxix.

3. Teresa (Griffin) Vielé, *"Following the Drum": A Glimpse of Frontier Life* (New York: Rudd and Carleton, 1858; reprint editions 1859, 1864); Margaret I. Carrington, *Ab-sa-ro-ka: Home of the Crows* (Philadelphia: J. B. Lippincott & Co., 1868; reprint editions 1869, 1878, 1879, 1890, 1896); Elizabeth B. Custer, *"Boots and Saddles"; or, Life in Dakota with General Custer* (New York: Harper & Brothers, 1885; reprint editions 1885 [2d and 3d editions], 1899, 1902); Elizabeth B. Custer, *Tenting on the Plains; or General Custer in Kansas and Texas* (New York: C. L. Webster & Co., 1887; reprint editions 1889, 1893, 1895); Elizabeth B. Custer, *Following the Guidon* (New York: Harper & Brothers, 1890; reprint edition 1899); Mrs. Orsemus B. Boyd, *Cavalry Life in Tent and Field* (New York: J. S. Tait & Sons, 1894); Ellen M. Biddle, *Reminiscences of a Soldier's Wife* (Philadelphia: J. B. Lippincott Co., 1907); Martha Summerhayes, *Vanished Arizona: Recollections of My Army Life* (Philadelphia: J. P. Lippincott & Co., 1908; reprint edition 1911); Frances M. A. Roe, *Army Letters from an Officer's Wife, 1871–1888* (New York and London: D. Appleton & Co., 1909); Mrs. Lydia S. Lane, *I Married a Soldier; or, Old Days in the Old Army* (Philadelphia: J. B. Lippincott Co., 1910).

4. For the views of other army wives, see Sandra L. Myres, "The Ladies of the Army—Views of Western Life," in *The American Military on the Frontier: Proceedings of the Seventh Military History Symposium, USAF Academy, 1976* (Washington, D.C.: Office of Air Force History, 1978), pp. 137–39; Forrest R. Blackburn, "Families on the Frontier," *Military Review* 49 (October 1969): 19–24; Patricia Y. Stallard, *Glittering Misery: Dependents of the Indian Fighting Army* (Fort Collins, Colo.: Old Army Press, 1978), pp. 15–42.

5. Myres, "The Ladies of the Army," p. 139; Blackburn, "Families on the Frontier," pp. 24–26, and Stallard, *Glittering Misery,* pp. 42–52, also discuss the recreational activities and social life of the army wives.

6. Sprightly accounts of army pets are found in W. S. Nye,

Carbine and Lance: The Story of Old Fort Sill (Norman: University of Oklahoma Press, 1937), pp. 285, 291, and Custer, *Following the Guidon*, reprint edition (Norman: University of Oklahoma Press, 1966), pp. 112–30.

7. Lane, *I Married a Soldier*, reprint edition (Albuquerque: Horn & Wallace, 1964), pp. 146–47.

8. Robert M. Utley, *Frontier Regulars: The United States Army and the Indian, 1866–1891* (New York: Macmillan, 1973), p. 45.

9. See Myres, "The Ladies of the Army," pp. 140–43, for other army wives' views of the Native Americans.

10. Reviews appeared in *American Library Association Booklist* 6 (November 1909): 83; *Dial* 47 (November 16, 1909): 390; *Literary Digest* 39 (November 6, 1909): 787; *Nation* 89 (November 25, 1909): 518; and the *New York Times*, December 25, 1909. Myres, "The Ladies of the Army," pp. 146–49 discusses the publication history and reviews of other army women's books.

11. Utley, *Frontier Regulars*, p. 59.

12. Quoted from Fayette Roe's obituary in *Annual Report of the Association of Graduates* (West Point, N.Y., June 12, 1917), p. 71.

PREFACE

PERHAPS it is not necessary to say that the events mentioned in the letters are not imaginary—perhaps the letters themselves tell that! They are truthful accounts of experiences that came into my own life with the Army in the far West, whether they be about Indians, desperadoes, or hunting—not one little thing has been stolen. They are of a life that has passed— as has passed the buffalo and the antelope—yes, and the log and adobe quarters for the Army. All flowery descriptions have been omitted, as it seemed that a simple, concise narration of events as they actually occurred, was more in keeping with the life, and that which came into it.

FRANCES M. A. ROE.

LIST OF ILLUSTRATIONS

LIST OF ILLUSTRATIONS

ARMY LETTERS

FROM AN OFFICER'S WIFE

KIT CARSON, COLORADO TERRITORY,
October, 1871.

IT is late, so this can be only a note—to tell you that
we arrived here safely, and will take the stage for
Fort Lyon to-morrow morning at six o'clock. I am
thankful enough that our stay is short at this terrible
place, where one feels there is danger of being murdered any minute. Not one woman have I seen here,
but there are men—any number of dreadful-looking
men—each one armed with big pistols, and leather
belts full of cartridges. But the houses we saw as
we came from the station were worse even than the
men. They looked, in the moonlight, like huge cakes
of clay, where spooks and creepy things might be
found. The hotel is much like the houses, and ap-
pears to have been made of dirt, and a few drygoods
boxes. Even the low roof is of dirt. The whole place
is horrible, and dismal beyond description, and just
why anyone lives here I cannot understand.

I am all upset! Faye has just been in to say that
only one of my trunks can be taken on the stage with
us, and of course I had to select one that has all sorts

of things in it, and consequently leave my pretty dresses here, to be sent for—all but the Japanese silk which happens to be in that trunk. But imagine my mortification in having to go with Faye to his regiment, with only two dresses. And then, to make my shortcomings the more vexatious, Faye will be simply fine all the time, in his brand new uniform!

Perhaps I can send a long letter soon—if I live to reach that army post that still seems so far away.

FORT LYON, COLORADO TERRITORY,
October, 1871.

AFTER months of anticipation and days of weary travel we have at last got to our army home! As you know, Fort Lyon is fifty miles from Kit Carson, and we came all that distance in a funny looking stage coach called a " jerkey," and a good name for it, too, for at times it seesawed back and forth and then sideways, in an awful breakneck way. The day was glorious, and the atmosphere so clear, we could see miles and miles in every direction. But there was not one object to be seen on the vast rolling plains—not a tree nor a house, except the wretched ranch and stockade where we got fresh horses and a perfectly uneatable dinner.

It was dark when we reached the post, so of course we could see nothing that night. General and Mrs. Phillips gave us a most cordial welcome—just as though they had known us always. Dinner was served soon after we arrived, and the cheerful dining room, and the table with its dainty china and bright silver, was such a surprise—so much nicer than anything we had expected to find here, and all so differ-

"It seesawed back and forth and then sideways, in an awful breakneck way."

ent from the terrible places we had seen since reaching the plains. It was apparent at once that this was not a place for spooks! General Phillips is not a real general—only so by brevet, for gallant service during the war. I was so disappointed when I was told this, but Faye says that he is very much afraid that I will have cause, sooner or later, to think that the grade of captain is quite high enough. He thinks this way because, having graduated at West Point this year, he is only a second lieutenant just now, and General Phillips is his captain and company commander.

It seems that in the Army, lieutenants are called "Mister" always, but all other officers must be addressed by their rank. At least that is what they tell me. But in Faye's company, the captain is called general, and the first lieutenant is called major, and as this is most confusing, I get things mixed sometimes. Most girls would. A soldier in uniform waited upon us at dinner, and that seemed so funny. I wanted to watch him all the time, which distracted me, I suppose, for once I called General Phillips "Mister!" It so happened, too, that just that instant there was not a sound in the room, so everyone heard the blunder. General Phillips straightened back in his chair, and his little son gave a smothered giggle—for which he should have been sent to bed at once. But that was not all! That soldier, who had been so dignified and stiff, put his hand over his mouth and fairly rushed from the room so he could laugh outright. And how I longed to run some place, too—but not to laugh, oh, no!

These soldiers are not nearly as nice as one would suppose them to be, when one sees them dressed up in

2

their blue uniforms with bright brass buttons. And they can make mistakes, too, for yesterday, when I asked that same man a question, he answered, " Yes, sorr! " Then I smiled, of course, but he did not seem to have enough sense to see why. When I told Faye about it, he looked vexed and said I must never laugh at an enlisted man—that it was not dignified in the wife of an officer to do so. And then I told him that an officer should teach an enlisted man not to snicker at his wife, and not to call her " Sorr," which was disrespectful. I wanted to say more, but Faye suddenly left the room.

The post is not at all as you and I had imagined it to be. There is no high wall around it as there is at Fort Trumbull. It reminds one of a prim little village built around a square, in the center of which is a high flagstaff and a big cannon. The buildings are very low and broad and are made of adobe—a kind of clay and mud mixed together—and the walls are very thick. At every window are heavy wooden shutters, that can be closed during severe sand and wind storms. A little ditch—they call it *acéquia*—runs all around the post, and brings water to the trees and lawns, but water for use in the houses is brought up in wagons from the Arkansas River, and is kept in barrels.

Yesterday morning—our first here—we were awakened by the sounds of fife and drum that became louder and louder, until finally I thought the whole Army must be marching to the house. I stumbled over everything in the room in my haste to get to one of the little dormer windows, but there was nothing to be seen, as it was still quite dark. The drumming

became less loud, and then ceased altogether, when a
big gun was fired that must have wasted any amount
of powder, for it shook the house and made all the
windows rattle. Then three or four bugles played a
little air, which it was impossible to hear because of
the horrible howling and crying of dogs—such howls
of misery you never heard—they made me shiver.
This all suddenly ceased, and immediately there were
lights flashing some distance away, and dozens of men
seemed to be talking all at the same time, some of
them shouting, " Here! " " Here! " I began to think
that perhaps Indians had come upon us, and called
to Faye, who informed me in a sleepy voice that it
was only reveille roll-call, and that each man was an-
swering to his name. There was the same performance this morning, and at breakfast I asked General
Phillips why soldiers required such a beating of drums,
and deafening racket generally, to awaken them in the
morning. But he did not tell me—said it was an old
army custom to have the drums beaten along the
officers' walk at reveille.

Yesterday morning, directly after guard-mounting,
Faye put on his full-dress uniform—epaulets, beautiful scarlet sash, and sword—and went over to the
office of the commanding officer to report officially.
The officer in command of the post is lieutenant
colonel of the regiment, but he, also, is a general by
brevet, and one can see by his very walk that he ex-
pects this to be remembered always. So it is apparent
to me that the safest thing to do is to call everyone
general—there seem to be so many here. If I make
a mistake, it will be on the right side, at least.

Much of the furniture in this house was made by

soldier carpenters here at the post, and is not only
very nice, but cost General Phillips almost nothing,
and, as we have to buy everything, I said at dinner
last evening that we must have some precisely like it,
supposing, of course, that General Phillips would feel
highly gratified because his taste was admired.   But
instead of the smile and gracious acquiescence I had
expected, there was another straightening back in the
chair, and a silence that was ominous and chilling.
Finally, he recovered sufficient breath to tell me that
at present, there were no good carpenters in the company.   Later on, however, I learned that only captains and officers of higher rank can have such things.
The captains seem to have the best of everything, and
the lieutenants are expected to get along with smaller
houses, much less pay, and much less everything else,
and at the same time perform all of the disagreeable
duties.

Faye is wonderfully amiable about it, and assures
me that when he gets to be a captain I will see that it is
just and fair.   But I happen to remember that he told
me not long ago that he might not get his captaincy
for twenty years.   Just think of it—a whole long life-
time—and always a Mister, too—and perhaps by that
time it will be " just and fair " for the lieutenants to
have everything!

We saw our house yesterday—quarters I must
learn to say—and it is ever so much nicer than we
had expected it to be.   All of the officers' quarters
are new, and this set has never been occupied.   It has
a hall with a pretty stairway, three rooms and a large
shed downstairs, and two rooms and a very large hall
closet on the second floor.   A soldier is cleaning the

windows and floors, and making things tidy generally. Many of the men like to cook, and do things for officers of their company, thereby adding to their pay, and these men are called strikers.

There are four companies here—three of infantry and one troop of cavalry. You must always remember that Faye is in the infantry. With the cavalry he has a classmate, and a friend, also, which will make it pleasant for both of us. In my letters to you I will disregard army etiquette, and call the lieutenants by their rank, otherwise you would not know of whom I was writing—an officer or civilian. Lieutenant Baldwin has been on the frontier many years, and is an experienced hunter of buffalo and antelope. He says that I must commence riding horseback at once, and has generously offered me the use of one of his horses. Mrs. Phillips insists upon my using her saddle until I can get one from the East, so I can ride as soon as our trunks come. And I am to learn to shoot pistols and guns, and do all sorts of things.

We are to remain with General and Mrs. Phillips several days, while our own house is being made habitable, and in the meantime our trunks and boxes will come, also the colored cook. I have not missed my dresses very much—there has been so much else to think about. There is a little store just outside the post that is named "Post Trader's," where many useful things are kept, and we have just been there to purchase some really nice furniture that an officer left to be sold when he was retired last spring. We got only enough to make ourselves comfortable during the winter, for it seems to be the general belief here that these companies of infantry will be ordered to Camp Supply, Indian Territory, in the spring. It must be a most dreadful place—with old log houses built in the hot sand hills, and surrounded by almost every tribe of hostile Indians.

It may not be possible for me to write again for several days, as I will be very busy getting settled in the house. I must get things arranged just as soon as I can, so I will be able to go out on horseback with Faye and Lieutenant Baldwin.

FORT LYON, COLORADO TERRITORY,
October, 1871.

WHEN a very small girl, I was told many wonderful tales about a grand Indian chief called Red Jacket, by my great-grandmother, who, you will remember, saw him a number of times when she, also, was a small girl. And since then—almost all my life—I have wanted to see with my very own eyes an Indian—a real noble red man—dressed in beautiful skins embroidered with beads, and on his head long, waving feathers.

Well, I have seen an Indian—a number of Indians —but they were not Red Jackets, neither were they noble red men. They were simply, and only, painted, dirty, and nauseous-smelling savages! Mrs. Phillips says that Indians are all alike—that when you have seen one you have seen all. And she must know, for she has lived on the frontier a long time, and has seen many Indians of many tribes.

We went to Las Animas yesterday, Mrs. Phillips, Mrs. Cole, and I, to do a little shopping. There are several small stores in the half-Mexican village, where curious little things from Mexico can often be found, if one does not mind poking about underneath the trash and dirt that is everywhere. While we were in the largest of these shops, ten or twelve Indians dashed up to the door on their ponies, and four of them, slipping down, came in the store and passed on quickly to the counter farthest back, where the ammunition is kept. As they came toward us in their imperious way, never once looking to the right or to the left, they seemed like giants, and to increase in size and numbers with every step.

Their coming was so sudden we did not have a chance to get out of their way, and it so happened that Mrs. Phillips and I were in their line of march, and when the one in the lead got to us, we were pushed aside with such impatient force that we both fell over on the counter. The others passed on just the same, however, and if we had fallen to the floor, I presume they would have stepped over us, and otherwise been oblivious to our existence. This was my introduction to an Indian—the noble red man!

As soon as they got to the counter they demanded powder, balls, and percussion caps, and as these things were given them, they were stuffed down their muzzle-loading rifles, and what could not be rammed down the barrels was put in greasy skin bags and hidden under their blankets. I saw one test the sharp edge of a long, wicked-looking knife, and then it, also, disappeared under his blanket. All this time the other Indians were on their ponies in front, watching every move that was being made around them.

There was only the one small door to the little adobe shop, and into this an Indian had ridden his piebald pony; its forefeet were up a step on the sill and its head and shoulders were in the room, which made it quite impossible for us three frightened women to run out in the street. So we got back of a counter, and, as Mrs. Phillips expressed it, " midway between the devil and the deep sea." There certainly could be no mistake about the " devil " side of it!

It was an awful situation to be in, and one to terrify anybody. We were actually prisoners—penned in with all those savages, who were evidently in an ugly mood, with quantities of ammunition within their reach, and only two white men to protect us. Even the few small windows had iron bars across. They could have killed every one of us, and ridden far away before anyone in the sleepy town found it out.

Well, when those inside had been given, or had helped themselves to, whatever they wanted, out they all marched again, quickly and silently, just as they had come in. They instantly mounted their ponies, and all rode down the street and out of sight at race speed, some leaning so far over on their little beasts that one could hardly see the Indian at all. The pony that was ridden into the store door was without a bridle, and was guided by a long strip of buffalo skin which was fastened around his lower jaw by a slip-knot. It is amazing to see how tractable the Indians can make their ponies with only that one rein.

The storekeeper told us that those Indians were Utes, and were greatly excited because they had just heard there was a small party of Cheyennes down the river two or three miles. The Utes and Cheyennes are bitter enemies. He said that the Utes were very cross—ready for the blood of Indian or white man— therefore he had permitted them to do about as they pleased while in the store, particularly as we were there, and he saw that we were frightened. That young man did not know that his own swarthy face was a greenish white all the time those Indians were in the store! Not one penny did they pay for the things they carried off. Only two years ago the entire Ute nation was on the warpath, killing every white person they came across, and one must have much faith in Indians to believe that their " change of heart " has been so complete that these Utes have learned to love the white man in so short a time.

No! There was hatred in their eyes as they approached us in that store, and there was restrained murder in the hand that pushed Mrs. Phillips and me over. They were all hideous—with streaks of red or green paint on their faces that made them look like fiends. Their hair was roped with strips of bright-colored stuff, and hung down on each side of their shoulders in front, and on the crown of each black head was a small, tightly plaited lock, ornamented at the top with a feather, a piece of tin, or something fantastic. These were their scalp locks. They wore blankets over dirty old shirts, and of course had on long, trouserlike leggings of skin and moccasins. They were not tall, but rather short and stocky. The odor of those skins, and of the Indians themselves, in that stuffy little shop, I expect to smell the rest of my life!

We heard this morning that those very savages rode out on the plains in a roundabout way, so as to get in advance of the Cheyennes, and then had hidden themselves on the top of a bluff overlooking the trail they knew the Cheyennes to be following, and had fired upon them as they passed below, killing two and wounding a number of others. You can see how treacherous these Indians are, and how very far from noble is their method of warfare! They are so disappointing, too—so wholly unlike Cooper's red men.

We were glad enough to get in the ambulance and start on our way to the post, but alas! our troubles were not over. The mules must have felt the excitement in the air, for as soon as their heads were turned toward home they proceeded to run away with us. We had the four little mules that are the special pets of the quartermaster, and are known throughout the garrison as the " shaved-tails," because the hair on their tails is kept closely cut down to the very tips, where it is left in a square brush of three or four inches. They are perfectly matched—coal-black all over, except their little noses, and are quite small. They are full of mischief, and full of wisdom, too, even for government mules, and when one says, " Let's take a sprint," the others always agree—about that there is never the slightest hesitation.

Therefore, when we first heard the scraping of the brake, and saw that the driver was pulling and sawing at the tough mouths with all his strength, no one was surprised, but we said that we wished they had waited until after we had crossed the Arkansas River. But we got over the narrow bridge without meeting more than one man, who climbed over the railing and seemed less anxious to meet us than we were to meet him. As soon as we got on the road again, those mules, with preliminary kicks and shakes of their big heads, began to demonstrate how fast they could go. We had the best driver at the post, and the road was good and without sharp turns, but the ambulance was high, and swayed, and the pace was too fast for comfort.

The little mules ran and ran, and we held ourselves on our seats the best we could, expecting to be tipped over any minute. When we reached the post they made a wonderful turn and took us safely to the government corral, where they stopped, just when they got ready. One leader looked around at us and commenced to bray, but the driver was in no mood for such insolence, and jerked the poor thing almost down.

Three tired, disheveled women walked from the corral to their homes; and very glad one of them was to get home, too! Hereafter I shall confine myself to horseback riding—for, even if John is frisky at times, I prefer to take my chances with the one horse, to four little long-eared government mules! But I have learned to ride very well, and have a secure seat now. My teachers, Faye and Lieutenant Baldwin, have been most exacting, but that I wanted. Of course I ride the army way, tight in the saddle, which is more difficult to learn. Any attempt to "rise" when on a trot is ridiculed at once here, and it does look absurd after seeing the splendid and graceful riding of the officers. I am learning to jump the cavalry hurdles and ditches, too. I must confess, however, that taking a ditch the first time was more exciting than enjoyable. John seemed to like it better than I did.

FORT LYON, COLORADO TERRITORY,
November, 1871.

IN many of my letters I have written about learning
to ride and to shoot, and have told you, also, of
having followed the greyhounds after coyotes and rabbits with Faye and Lieutenant Baldwin. These hunts
exact the very best of riding and a fast horse, for
coyotes are very swift, and so are jack-rabbits, too,
and one look at a greyhound will tell anyone that he
can run—and about twice as fast as the big-eared fox-
hounds in the East. But I started to write you about
something quite different from all this—to tell you
of a really grand hunt I have been on—a splendid
chase after buffalo!

A week or so ago it was decided that a party of enlisted men should be sent out to get buffalo meat for
Thanksgiving dinner for everybody—officers and enlisted men—and that Lieutenant Baldwin, who is an experienced hunter, should command the detail. You
can imagine how proud and delighted I was when
asked to go with them, Lieutenant Baldwin saying
that the hunt would be worth seeing, and well repay
one for the fatigue of the hard ride.

So, one morning after an early breakfast, the horses
were led up from the stables, each one having on a
strong halter, and a coiled picket rope with an iron pin
fastened to the saddle. These were carried so that
if it should be found necessary to secure the horses
on the plains, they could be picketed out. The bachelors' set of quarters is next to ours, so we all got
ready together, and I must say that the deliberate way
in which each girth was examined, bridles fixed, rifles
fastened to saddles, and other things done, was most

exasperating. But we finally started, about seven
o'clock, Lieutenant Baldwin and I taking the lead, and
Faye and Lieutenant Alden following.

The day was very cold, with a strong wind blowing,
so I wore one of Faye's citizen caps, with tabs tied
down over my ears, and a large silk handkerchief
around my neck, all of which did not improve my
looks in the least, but it was quite in keeping with the
dressing of the officers, who had on buckskin shirts,
with handkerchiefs, leggings, and moccasins. Two
large army wagons followed us, each drawn by four
mules, and carrying several enlisted men. Mounted
orderlies led extra horses that officers and men were
to ride when they struck the herd.

Well, we rode twelve miles without seeing one living thing, and then we came to a little adobe ranch
where we dismounted to rest a while. By this time
our feet and hands were almost frozen, and Faye
suggested that I should remain at the ranch until they
returned; but that I refused to do—to give up the
hunt was not to be thought of, particularly as a
ranchman had just told us that a small herd of buffalo had been seen that very morning only two miles
farther on. So, when the horses were a little rested,
we started, and, after riding a mile or more, we came
to a small ravine, where we found one poor buffalo,
too old and emaciated to keep up with his companions,
and who, therefore, had been abandoned by them, to
die alone. He had eaten the grass as far as he could
reach, and had turned around and around until the
ground looked as though it had been spaded.

He got up on his old legs as we approached him,
and tried to show fight by dropping his head and

throwing his horns to the front, but a child could have pushed him over. One of the officers tried to persuade me to shoot him, saying it would be a humane act, and at the same time give me the *prestige* of having killed a buffalo! But the very thought of pointing a pistol at anything so weak and utterly helpless was revolting in the extreme. He was such an object of pity, too, left there all alone to die of starvation, when perhaps at one time he may have been leader of his herd. He was very tall, had a fine head, with an uncommonly long beard, and showed every indication of having been a grand specimen of his kind.

We left him undisturbed, but only a few minutes later we heard the sharp report of a rifle, and at once suspected, what we learned to be a fact the next day, that one of the men with the wagons had killed him. Possibly this was the most merciful thing to do, but to me that shot meant murder. The pitiful bleary eyes of the helpless old beast have haunted me ever since we saw him.

We must have gone at least two miles farther before we saw the herd we were looking for, making fifteen or sixteen miles altogether that we had ridden. The buffalo were grazing quietly along a meadow in between low, rolling hills. We immediately fell back a short distance and waited for the wagons, and when they came up there was great activity, I assure you. The officers' saddles were transferred to their hunters, and the men who were to join in the chase got their horses and rifles ready. Lieutenant Baldwin gave his instructions to everybody, and all started off, each one going in a different direction so as to form a *cordon,*

Faye said, around the whole herd. Faye would not join in the hunt, but remained with me the entire day. He and I rode over the hill, stopping when we got where we could command a good view of the valley and watch the run.

It seemed only a few minutes when we saw the buffalo start, going from some of the men, of course, who at once began to chase them. This kept them running straight ahead, and, fortunately, in Lieutenant Baldwin's direction, who apparently was holding his horse in, waiting for them to come. We saw through our field glasses that as soon as they got near enough he made a quick dash for the herd, and cutting one out, had turned it so it was headed straight for us.

Now, being on a buffalo hunt a safe distance off, was one thing, but to have one of those huge animals come thundering along like a steam engine directly upon you, was quite another. I was on one of Lieutenant Baldwin's horses, too, and I felt that there might be danger of his bolting to his companion, Tom, when he saw him dashing by, and as I was not anxious to join in a buffalo chase just at that time, I begged Faye to go with me farther up the hill. But he would not go back one step, assuring me that my horse was a trained hunter and accustomed to such sights.

Lieutenant Baldwin gained steadily on the buffalo, and in a wonderfully short time both passed directly in front of us—within a hundred feet, Faye said. Lieutenant Baldwin was close upon him then, his horse looking very small and slender by the side of the grand animal that was taking easy, swinging strides, apparently without effort and without speed, his tongue lolling at one side. But we could see that the pace was really terrific—that Lieutenant Baldwin was freely using the spur, and that his swift thoroughbred was stretched out like a greyhound, straining every muscle in his effort to keep up. He was riding close to the buffalo on his left, with revolver in his right

" My horse behaved very well."

hand, and I wondered why he did not not shoot, but Faye said it would be useless to fire then—that Lieutenant Baldwin must get up nearer the shoulder, as a buffalo is vulnerable only in certain parts of his body, and that a hunter of experience like Lieutenant Baldwin would never think of shooting unless he could aim at heart or lungs.

My horse behaved very well—just whirling around a few times—but Faye was kept busy a minute or two by his, for the poor horse was awfully frightened, and lunged and reared and snorted; but I knew that he could not unseat Faye, so I rather enjoyed it, for you know I had wanted to go back a little!

Lieutenant Baldwin and the buffalo were soon far away, and when our horses had quieted down we recalled that shots had been fired in another direction, and looking about, we saw a pathetic sight. Lieutenant Alden was on his horse, and facing him was an immense buffalo, standing perfectly still with chin drawn in and horns to the front, ready for battle. It was plain to be seen that the poor horse was not enjoying the meeting, for every now and then he would try to back away, or give a jump sideways. The buffalo was wounded and unable to run, but he could still turn around fast enough to keep his head toward the horse, and this he did every time Lieutenant Alden tried to get an aim at his side.

There was no possibility of his killing him without assistance, and of course the poor beast could not be abandoned in such a helpless condition, so Faye decided to go over and worry him, while Lieutenant Alden got in the fatal shot. As soon as Faye got there I put my fingers over my ears so that I would not hear the report of the pistol. After a while I looked across, and there was the buffalo still standing, and both Faye and Lieutenant Alden were beckoning for me to come to them. At first I could not understand what they wanted, and I started to go over, but it finally dawned upon me that they were actually waiting for me to come and kill that buffalo! I saw no glory in shooting a wounded animal, so I turned my

3

horse back again, but had not gone far before I heard the pistol shot.

Then I rode over to see the huge animal, and found Faye and Lieutenant Alden in a state of great excitement.   They said he was a magnificent specimen —unusually large, and very black—what they call a blue skin—with a splendid head and beard.   I had been exposed to a bitterly cold wind, without the warming exercise of riding, for over an hour, and my hands were so cold and stiff that I could scarcely hold the reins, so they jumped me up on the shoulders of the warm body, and I buried my hands in the long fur on his neck.   He fell on his wounded side, and looked precisely as though he was asleep—so much so that I half expected him to spring up and resent the indignity he was being subjected to.

Very soon after that Faye and I came on home, reaching the post about seven o'clock.   We had been in our saddles most of the time for twelve hours, on a cold day, and were tired and stiff, and when Faye tried to assist me from my horse I fell to the ground in a heap.   But I got through the day very well, considering the very short time I have been riding—that is, really riding.   The hunt was a grand sight, and something that probably I will never have a chance of seeing again—and, to be honest, I do not want to see another, for the sight of one of those splendid animals running for his life is not a pleasant one.

The rest of the party did not come in until several hours later; but they brought the meat and skins of four buffalo, and the head of Lieutenant Alden's, which he will send East to be mounted.   The skin he intends to take to an Indian camp, to be tanned by the squaws. Lieutenant Baldwin followed his buffalo until he got in the position he wanted, and then killed him with one shot. Faye says that only a cool head and experience could have done that. Much depends upon the horse, too, for so many horses are afraid of a buffalo, and lunge sideways just at the critical moment.

Several experienced hunters tell marvelous tales of how they have stood within a few yards of a buffalo and fired shot after shot from a Springfield rifle, straight at his head, the balls producing no effect whatever, except, perhaps, a toss of the head and the flying out of a tuft of hair. Every time the ball would glance off from the thick skull. The wonderful mat of curly hair must break the force some, too. This mat, or cushion, in between the horns of the buffalo Lieutenant Alden killed, was so thick and tangled that I could not begin to get my fingers in it.

FORT LYON, COLORADO TERRITORY,
December, 1871.

OUR first Christmas on the frontier was ever so pleasant, but it certainly was most vexatious not to have that box from home. And I expect that it has been at Kit Carson for days, waiting to be brought down. We had quite a little Christmas without it, however, for a number of things came from the girls, and several women of the garrison sent pretty little gifts to me. It was so kind and thoughtful of them to remember that I might be a bit homesick just now. All the little presents were spread out on a table, and in a way to make them present as fine an appearance as possible. Then I printed in large letters, on a piece of cardboard, " One box—contents unknown!" and stood it up on the back of the table. I did this to let everyone know that we had not been forgotten by home people. My beautiful new saddle was brought in, also, for although I had had it several weeks, it was really one of Faye's Christmas gifts to me.

They have such a charming custom in the Army of going along the line Christmas morning and giving each other pleasant greetings and looking at the pretty things everyone has received. This is a rare treat out here, where we are so far from shops and beautiful Christmas displays. We all went to the bachelors' quarters, almost everyone taking over some little remembrance—homemade candy, cakes, or something of that sort.

I had a splendid cake to send over that morning, and I will tell you just what happened to it. At home we always had a large fruit cake made for the holidays, long in advance, and I thought I would have one this year as near like it as possible. But it seemed that the only way to get it was to make it. So, about four weeks ago, I commenced. It was quite an undertaking for me, as I had never done anything of the kind, and perhaps I did not go about it the easiest way, but I knew how it should look when done, and of course I knew precisely how it should taste. Eliza makes delicious every-day cake, but was no assistance whatever with the fruit cake, beyond encouraging me with the assurance that it would not matter in the least if it should be heavy.

Well, for two long, tiresome days I worked over that cake, preparing with my own fingers every bit

of the fruit, which I consider was a fine test of per-
severance and staying qualities. After the ingre-
dients were all mixed together there seemed to be
enough for a whole regiment, so we decided to make
two cakes of it. They looked lovely when baked, and
just right, and smelled so good, too! I wrapped
them in nice white paper that had been wet with
brandy, and put them carefully away—one in a stone
jar, the other in a tin box—and felt that I had done
a remarkably fine bit of housekeeping. The bachelors
have been exceedingly kind to me, and I rejoiced at
having a nice cake to send them Christmas morning.
But alas! I forgot that the little house was fragrant
with the odor of spice and fruit, and that there was
a man about who was ever on the lookout for good
things to eat. It is a shame that those cadets at West
Point are so starved. They seem to be simply famished for months after they graduate.

It so happened that there was choir practice that
very evening, and that I was at the chapel an hour
or so. When I returned, I found the three bachelors
sitting around the open fire, smoking, and looking
very comfortable indeed. Before I was quite in the
room they all stood up and began to praise the cake.
I think Faye was the first to mention it, saying it was
a " great success "; then the others said " perfectly
delicious," and so on, but at the same time assuring
me that a large piece had been left for me.

For one minute I stood still, not in the least grasping their meaning; but finally I suspected mischief,
they all looked so serenely contented. So I passed on
to the dining room, and there, on the table, was one
of the precious cakes—at least what was left of it, the

very small piece that had been so generously saved for me. And there were plates with crumbs, and napkins, that told the rest of the sad tale—and there was wine and empty glasses, also. Oh, yes! Their early Christmas had been a fine one. There was nothing for me to say or do—at least not just then—so I went back to the little living-room and forced myself to be halfway pleasant to the four men who were there, each one looking precisely like the cat after it had eaten the canary! The cake was scarcely cold, and must have been horribly sticky—and I remember wondering, as I sat there, which one would need the doctor first, and what the doctor would do if they were all seized with cramps at the same time. But they were not ill—not in the least—which proved that the cake was well baked. If they had discovered the other one, however, there is no telling what might have happened.

At half after ten yesterday the chaplain held service, and the little chapel was crowded—so many of the enlisted men were present. We sang our Christmas music, and received many compliments. Our little choir is really very good. Both General Phillips and Major Pierce have fine voices. One of the infantry sergeants plays the organ now, for it was quite too hard for me to sing and work those old pedals. Once I forgot them entirely, and everybody smiled —even the chaplain!

From the chapel we—that is, the company officers and their wives—went to the company barracks to see the men's dinner tables. When we entered the dining hall we found the entire company standing in two lines, one down each side, every man in his best inspection uniform, and every button shining. With eyes to the front and hands down their sides they looked absurdly like wax figures waiting to be " wound up," and I did want so much to tell the little son of General Phillips to pinch one and make him jump. He would have done it, too, and then put all the blame upon me, without loss of time.

The first sergeant came to meet us, and went around with us. There were three long tables, fairly groaning with things upon them: buffalo, antelope, boiled ham, several kinds of vegetables, pies, cakes, quantities of pickles, dried " apple-duff," and coffee; and in the center of each table, high up, was a huge cake thickly covered with icing. These were the cakes that Mrs. Phillips, Mrs. Barker, and I had sent over that morning. It is the custom in the regiment for the wives of the officers every Christmas to send the enlisted men of their husbands' companies large plum cakes, rich with fruit and sugar. Eliza made the cake I sent over, a fact I made known from its very beginning, to keep it from being devoured by those it was not intended for.

The hall was very prettily decorated with flags and accoutrements, but one missed the greens. There are no evergreen trees here, only cottonwood. Before coming out, General Phillips said a few pleasant words to the men, wishing them a " Merry Christmas " for all of us. Judging from the laughing and shuffling of feet as soon as we got outside, the men were glad to be allowed to relax once more.

At six o'clock Faye and I, Lieutenant Baldwin, and Lieutenant Alden dined with Doctor and Mrs. Wilder. It was a beautiful little dinner, very delicious, and served in the daintiest manner possible. But out

here one is never quite sure of what one is eating, for
sometimes the most tempting dishes are made of almost nothing. At holiday time, however, it seems
that the post trader sends to St. Louis for turkeys,
celery, canned oysters, and other things. We have no
fresh vegetables here, except potatoes, and have to
depend upon canned stores in the commissary for a
variety, and our meat consists entirely of beef, except
now and then, when we may have a treat to buffalo
or antelope.

The commanding officer gave a dancing party Friday evening that was most enjoyable. He is a wid-
ower, you know. His house is large, and the rooms
of good size, so that dancing was comfortable. The
music consisted of one violin with accordion accompaniment. This would seem absurd in the East, but
I can assure you that one accordion, when played well
by a German, is an orchestra in itself. And Doos
plays very well. The girls East may have better music
to dance by, and polished waxed floors to slip down
upon, but they cannot have the excellent partners one
has at an army post, and I choose the partners!

The officers are excellent dancers—every one of
them—and when you are gliding around, your chin,
or perhaps your nose, getting a scratch now and then
from a gorgeous gold epaulet, you feel as light as
a feather, and imagine yourself with a fairy prince.
Of course the officers were in full-dress uniform Friday night, so I know just what I am talking about,
scratches and all. Every woman appeared in her
finest gown. I wore my nile-green silk, which I am
afraid showed off my splendid coat of tan only too
well.

The party was given for Doctor and Mrs. Anderson, who are guests of General Bourke for a few days. They are *en route* to Fort Union, New Mexico. Mrs. Anderson was very handsome in an elegant gown of London-smoke silk. I am to assist Mrs. Phillips in receiving New Year's day, and shall wear my pearl-colored Irish poplin. We are going out now for a little ride.

FORT LYON, COLORADO TERRITORY,
January, 1872.

WHEN we came over on the stage from Kit Carson last fall, I sat on top with the driver, who told me of many terrible experiences he had passed through during the years he had been driving a stage on the plains, and some of the most thrilling were of sand storms, when he had, with great difficulty, saved the stage and perhaps his own life. There have been ever so many storms, since we have been here, that covered everything in the houses with dust and sand, but nothing at all like those the driver described. But yesterday one came—a terrific storm—and it so happened that I was caught out in the fiercest part of it.

As Faye was officer of the day, he could not leave the garrison, so I rode with Lieutenant Baldwin and Lieutenant Alden. The day was glorious—sunny, and quite warm—one of Colorado's very best, without a cloud to be seen in any direction. We went up the river to the mouth of a pretty little stream commonly called " The Picket Wire," but the real name of which is La Purgatoire. It is about five miles from the post and makes a nice objective point for a short ride, for the clear water gurgling over the stones, and the trees and bushes along its banks, are always attractive in this treeless country.

The canter up was brisk, and after giving our horses the drink from the running stream they always beg for, we started back on the road to the post in unusually fine spirits. Almost immediately, however, Lieutenant Baldwin said, " I do not like the looks of that cloud over there!" We glanced back in the direction he pointed, and seeing only a streak of dark gray low on the horizon, Lieutenant Alden and I paid no more attention to it. But Lieutenant Baldwin was very silent, and ever looking back at the queer gray cloud. Once I looked at it, too, and was amazed at the wonderfully fast way it had spread out, but just then John shied at something, and in managing the horse I forgot the cloud.

When about two miles from the post, Lieutenant Baldwin, who had fallen back a little, called to us, " Put your horses to their best pace—a sand storm is coming!" Then we knew there was a possibility of much danger, for Lieutenant Baldwin is known to be a keen observer, and our confidence in his judgment was great, so, without once looking back to see what was coming after us, Lieutenant Alden and I started our horses on a full run.

Well, that cloud increased in size with a rapidity you could never imagine, and soon the sun was obscured as if by an eclipse. It became darker and darker, and by the time we got opposite the post trader's there could be heard a loud, continuous roar, resembling that of a heavy waterfall.

Just then Lieutenant Baldwin grasped my bridle rein on the right and told Lieutenant Alden to ride close

"I was almost swept from my saddle."

on my left, which was done not a second too soon, for as we reached the officers' line the storm struck us, and with such force that I was almost swept from my saddle. The wind was terrific and going at hurricane speed, and the air so thick with sand and dirt we could not see the ears of our own horses. The world seemed to have narrowed to a space that was appalling! You will think that this could never have been—that I was made blind by terror—but I can assure you that the absolute truth is being written.

Lieutenant Baldwin's voice sounded strange and far, far away when he called to me, "Sit tight in your saddle and do not jump!" And then again he fairly yelled, " We must stay together—and keep the horses from stampeding to the stables!" He was afraid they would break away and dash us against the iron supports to the flagstaff in the center of the parade ground. How he could say one word, or even open his mouth, I do not understand, for the air was thick with gritty dirt. The horses were frantic, of course, whirling around each other, rearing and pulling, in their efforts to get free.

We must have stayed in about the same place twenty minutes or longer, when, just for one instant, there was a lull in the storm, and I caught a glimpse of the white pickets of a fence! Without stopping to think of horse's hoofs and, alas! without calling one word to the two officers who were doing everything possible to protect me, I shut my eyes tight, freed my foot from the stirrup, and, sliding down from my horse, started for those pickets! How I missed Lieutenant Alden's horse, and how I got to that fence, I do not know. The force of the wind was terrific, and besides, I was obliged to cross the little *acéquia*. But I did get over the fifteen or sixteen feet of ground without falling, and oh, the joy of getting my arms around those pickets!

The storm continued for some time; but finally the atmosphere began to clear, and I could see objects around me. And then out of the dust loomed up Lieutenant Baldwin. He was about halfway down the line and riding close to the fence, evidently looking for me. When he came up, leading my horse, his face was black with more than dirt. He reminded me of having told me positively not to jump from my horse, and asked if I realized that I might have been knocked down and killed by the crazy animals. Of course I had perceived all that as soon as I reached safety, but I could not admit my mistake at that time without breaking down and making a scene. I was nervous and exhausted, and in no condition to be scolded by anyone, so I said: " If you were not an old bachelor you would have known better than to have told a woman not to do a thing—you would have known that, in all probability, that would be the very thing she would do first!" That mollified him a little, but we did not laugh—life had just been too serious for that.

The chaplain had joined us, and so had Lieutenant Alden. The fence I had run to was the chaplain's, and when the good man saw us he came out and assisted me to his house, where I received the kindest care from Mrs. Lawton. I knew that Faye would be greatly worried about me, so as soon as I had rested a little—enough to walk—and had got some of the dust out of my eyes, the chaplain and I hurried down to our house to let him know that I was safe.

At every house along the line the heavy shutters were closed, and not one living thing was to be seen, and the post looked as though it might have been long abandoned. There was a peculiar light, too, that made the most familiar objects seem strange. Yes, we saw a squad of enlisted men across the parade ground, trying with immense ropes to get back in place the heavy roof of the long commissary building which had been partly blown off.

We met Faye at our gate, just starting out to look for us. He said that when the storm first came up he was frightened about me, but when the broad adobe house began to rock he came to the conclusion that I was about as safe out on the plains as I would be in a house, particularly as I was on a good horse, and with two splendid horsemen who would take the very best care of me. My plait of hair was one mass of dirt and was cut and torn, and is still in a deplorable condition, and my face looks as though I had just recovered from smallpox. As it was Monday, the washing of almost every family was out on lines, about every article of which has gone to regions unknown. The few pieces that were caught by the high fences were torn to shreds.

FORT LYON, COLORADO TERRITORY,
January, 1872.

OUR little party was a grand success, but I am still wondering how it came about that Mrs. Barker and I gave it together, for, although we are all in the same company and next-door neighbors, we have seen very little of each other. She is very quiet, and seldom goes out, even for a walk. It was an easy matter to arrange things so the two houses could, in a way, be connected, as they are under the same long roof, and the porches divided by a railing only, that was removed for the one evening. The dancing was in our house, and the supper was served at the Barkers'. And that supper was a marvel of culinary art, I assure you, even if it was a fraud in one or two things. We were complimented quite graciously by some of the older housekeepers, who pride themselves upon knowing how to make more delicious little dishes out of nothing than anyone else. But this time it was

North and South combined, for you will remember
that Mrs. Barker is from Virginia.

The chicken salad—and it was delicious—was made
of tender veal, but the celery in it was the genuine
article, for we sent to Kansas City for that and a few
other things. The turkey galantine was perfect, and
the product of a resourceful brain from the North, and
was composed almost entirely of wild goose! There
was no April fool about the delicate Maryland bis-
cuits, however, and other nice things that were set
forth. We fixed up cozily the back part of our hall
with comfortable chairs and cushions, and there punch
was served during the evening. Major Barker and
Faye made the punch. The orchestra might have
been better, but the two violins and the accordion
gave us music that was inspiring, and gave us noise,
too, and then Doos, who played the accordion, kept
us merry by the ever-pounding down of one govern-
ment-shod foot.

Everyone in the garrison came—even the chaplain
was here during the supper. The officers were in
full-dress uniform, and the only man in plain evening
dress was Mr. Dunn, the post trader, and in comparison to the gay uniforms of the officers he did
look so sleek, from his shiny black hair down to the
toes of his shiny black pumps! Mrs. Barker and I
received, of course, and she was very pretty in a
pink silk gown entirely covered with white net, that
was caught up at many places by artificial pink roses.
The color was most becoming, and made very pronounced the rich tint of her dark skin and her big
black eyes.

Well, we danced before supper and we danced after

supper, and when we were beginning to feel just a
wee bit tired, there suddenly appeared in our midst a
colored woman—a real old-time black mammy—in a
dress of faded, old-fashioned plaids, with kerchief,
white apron, and a red-and-yellow turban tied around
her head. We were dancing at the time she came in,
but everyone stopped at once, completely lost in amazement, and she had the floor to herself. This was what
she wanted, and she immediately commenced to dance
wildly and furiously, as though she was possessed,
rolling her big eyes and laughing to show the white
teeth. Gradually she quieted down to a smooth, rhyth-
mic motion, slowly swaying from side to side, sometimes whirling around, but with feet always flat on
the floor, often turning on her heels. All the time her
arms were extended and her fingers snapping, and
snapping also were the black eyes. She was the personification of grace, but the dance was weird—made
the more so by the setting of bright evening dresses
and glittering uniforms. One never sees a dance of
this sort these days, even in the South, any more than
one sees the bright-colored turban. Both have passed
with the old-time darky.

Of course we recognized Mrs. Barker, more because
there was no one else in our small community who
could personify a darky so perfectly, than because
there was any resemblance to her in looks or gesture.
The make-up was artistic, and how she managed the
quick transformation from ball dress to that of the
plantation, with all its black paint and rouge, Mrs.
Barker alone knows, and where on this earth she got
that dress and turban, she alone knows. But I imagine she sent to Virginia for the whole costume. At

all events, it was very bright in her to think of this unusual *divertissement* for our guests when dancing was beginning to lag a little. The dance she must have learned from a mammy when a child. I forgot to say that during the time she was dancing our fine orchestra played old Southern melodies. And all this was arranged and done by the quietest woman in the garrison!

Our house was upset from one end to the other to make room for the dancing, but the putting of things in order again did not take long, as the house has so very little in it. Still, I always feel rebellious when anything comes up to interfere with my rides, no matter how pleasant it may be. There have been a great many antelope near the post of late, and we have been on ever so many hunts for them. The greyhounds have not been with us, however, for following the hounds when chasing those fleet animals not only requires the fastest kind of a horse and very good riding, but is exceedingly dangerous to both horse and rider because of the many prairie-dog holes, which are terrible death traps. And besides, the dogs invariably get their feet full of cactus needles, which cause much suffering for days.

So we have been flagging the antelope, that is, taking a shameful advantage of their wonderful curiosity, and enticing them within rifle range. On these hunts I usually hold the horses of the three officers and my own, and so far they have not given me much trouble, for each one is a troop-trained animal.

The antelope are shy and wary little creatures, and possess an abnormal sense of smell that makes it absolutely necessary for hunters to move cautiously to

4

leeward the instant they discover them. It is always
an easy matter to find a little hill that will partly
screen them—the country is so rolling—as they creep
and crawl to position, ever mindful of the dreadful
cactus. When they reach the highest point the flag
is put up, and this is usually made on the spot, of a
red silk handkerchief, one corner run through the ram-

"Off the whole band will streak."

mer of a Springfield rifle. Then everyone lies down
flat on the ground, resting on his elbows, with rifle in
position for firing.

Antelope always graze against the wind, and even
a novice can tell when they discover the flag, for they
instantly stop feeding, and the entire band will whirl
around to face it, with big round ears standing straight
up, and in this way they will remain a second or
two, constantly sniffing the air. Failing to discover

anything dangerous, they will take a few steps forward, perhaps run around a little, giving quick tossings of the head, and sniffing with almost every breath, but whatever they do the stop is always in the same position—facing the flag, the strange object they cannot understand. Often they will approach very slowly, making frequent halts after little runs, and give many tossings of the head as if they were actually coquetting with death itself! Waiting for them to come within range of the rifle requires great patience, for the approach is always more or less slow, and frequently just as they are at the right distance and the finger is on the trigger, off the whole band will streak, looking like horizontal bars of brown and white! I am always so glad when they do this, for it seems so wicked to kill such graceful creatures. It is very seldom that I watch the approach, but when I do happen to see them come up, the temptation to do something to frighten them away from those murderous guns is almost irresistible.

But never once are they killed for mere pleasure! Their meat is tender and most delicious after one has learned to like the " gamey " flavor. And a change in meat we certainly do need here, for unless we can have buffalo or antelope now and then, it is beef every day in the month—not only one month, but every month.

The prairie-dog holes are great obstacles to following hounds on the plains, for while running so fast it is impossible for a horse to see the holes in time to avoid them, and if a foot slips down in one it means a broken leg for the horse and a hard throw for the rider, and perhaps broken bones also. Following these English greyhounds—which have such wonderful speed and keenness of sight—after big game on vast plains, is very different from running after the slow hounds and foxes in the East, and requires a very much faster horse and quite superior riding. One has to learn to ride a horse—to get a perfect balance that makes it a matter of indifference which way the horse may jump, at any speed—in fact, one must become a part of one's mount before these hunts can be attempted.

Chasing wolves and rabbits is not as dangerous, for they cannot begin to run as fast as antelope. And it is great fun to chase the big jack-rabbits. They know their own speed perfectly and have great confidence in it. When the hounds start one he will give one or two jumps high up in the air to take a look at things, and then he commences to run with great bounds, with his enormously long ears straight up like sails on a boat, and almost challenges the dogs to follow. But the poor hunted thing soon finds out that he must do better than that if he wishes to keep ahead, so down go the ears, flat along his back, and stretching himself out very straight, goes his very fastest, and then the real chase is on.

But Mr. Jack-Rabbit is cunning, and when he sees that the long-legged dogs are steadily gaining upon him and getting closer with every jump, he will invariably make a quick turn and run back on his own tracks, often going right underneath the fast-running dogs that cannot stop themselves, and can only give vicious snaps as they jump over him. Their stride—often fifteen and twenty feet—covers so much more ground than the rabbit's, it is impossible for them to

"The long-legged dogs are steadily gaining upon him."

make as quick turns, therefore it is generally the slow dog of the pack that catches the rabbit. And frequently a wise old rabbit will make many turns and finally reach a hole in safety.

The tail of a greyhound is his rudder and his brake, and the sight is most laughable when a whole pack of them are trying to stop, each tail whirling around like a Dutch windmill. Sometimes, in their frantic efforts to stop quickly, they will turn complete somersaults and roll over in a cloud of dust and dirt. But give up they never do, and once on their feet they start back after that rabbit with whines of disappointment and rage. Many, many times, also, I have heard the dogs howl and whine from the pain caused by the cactus spines in their feet, but not once have I ever seen any one of them lag in the chase.

But the pack here is a notoriously fine one. The leader, Magic, is a splendid dog, dark brindle in color, very swift and very plucky, also most intelligent. He is a sly rascal, too. He loves to sleep on Lieutenant Baldwin's bed above all things, and he sneaks up on it whenever he can, but the instant he hears Lieutenant Baldwin's step on the walk outside, down he jumps, and stretching himself out full length in front of the fire, he shuts his eyes tight, pretends to be fast asleep, and the personification of an innocent, well-behaved dog! But Lieutenant Baldwin knows his tricks now, and sometimes, going to the bed, he can feel the warmth from his body that is still there, and if he says, " Magic, you old villain," Magic will wag his tail a little, which in dog language means, " You are pretty smart, but I'm smart, too! "

With all this outdoor exercise, one can readily perceive that the days are not long and tiresome. Of course there are a few who yawn and complain of the monotony of frontier life, but these are the stay-at-homes who sit by their own fires day after day and let cobwebs gather in brain and lungs. And these, too, are the ones who have time to discover so many faults in others, and become our garrison gossips! If they would take brisk rides on spirited horses in this wonderful air, and learn to shoot all sorts of guns in all sorts of positions, they would soon discover that a frontier post can furnish plenty of excitement. At least, I have found that it can.

Faye was very anxious for me to become a good shot, considering it most essential in this Indian coun-

try, and to please him I commenced practicing soon
after we got here. It was hard work at first, and I
had many a bad headache from the noise of the guns.
It was all done in a systematic way, too, as though
I was a soldier at target practice. They taught me
to use a pistol in various positions while standing;
then I learned to use it from the saddle. After that
a little four-inch bull's-eye was often tacked to a tree
seventy-five paces away, and I was given a Spencer
carbine to shoot (a short magazine rifle used by the
cavalry), and many a time I have fired three rounds,
twenty-one shots in all, at the bull's-eye, which I was
expected to hit every time, too.

Well, I obligingly furnished amusement for Faye
and Lieutenant Baldwin until they asked me to fire a
heavy Springfield rifle—an infantry gun. After one
shot I politely refused to touch the thing again. The
noise came near making me deaf for life; the big
thing rudely "kicked" me over on my back, and the
bullet—I expect that ball is still on its way to Mars
or perhaps the moon. This earth it certainly did not
hit! Faye is with the company almost every morning, but after luncheon we usually go out for two or
three hours, and always come back refreshed by the
exercise. And the little house looks more cozy, and
the snapping of the blazing logs sounds more cheerful
because of our having been away from them.

FORT LYON, COLORADO TERRITORY,
April, 1872.

SOME of the most dreadful things have occurred
since I wrote you last, and this letter will make
you unhappy, I know. To begin with, orders have

actually come from Department Headquarters at Leavenworth for two companies of infantry here—General Phillips' and Captain Giddings'—to go to Camp Supply! So that is settled, and we will probably leave this post in about ten days, and during that time we are expected to sell, give away, smash up, or burn about everything we possess, for we have already been told that very few things can be taken with us. I do not see how we can possibly do with less than we have had since we came here.

Eliza announced at once that she could not be induced to go where there are so many Indians—said she had seen enough of them while in New Mexico. I am more than sorry to lose her, but at the same time I cannot help admiring her common sense. I would not go either if I could avoid it.

You will remember that not long ago I said that Lieutenant Baldwin was urging me to ride Tom, his splendid thoroughbred, as soon as he could be quieted down a little so I could control him. Well, I was to have ridden him to-day for the first time! Yesterday morning Lieutenant Baldwin had him out for a long, hard run, but even after that the horse was nervous when he came in, and danced sideways along the officers' drive in his usual graceful way. Just as they got opposite the chaplain's house, two big St. Bernard dogs bounded over the fence and landed directly under the horse, entangling themselves with his legs so completely that when he tried to jump away from them he was thrown down on his knees with great force, and Lieutenant Baldwin was pitched over the horse's head and along the ground several feet.

He is a tall, muscular man and went down heavily,

breaking three ribs and his collar bone on both sides!
He is doing very well, and is as comfortable to-day as
can be expected, except that he is grieving piteously
over his horse, for the poor horse—beautiful Tom—
is utterly ruined! Both knees have been sprung, and
he is bandaged almost as much as his master.

The whole occurrence is most deplorable and distressing. It seems so dreadful that a strong man
should be almost killed and a grand horse completely
ruined by two clumsy, ill-mannered dogs. One belongs to the chaplain, too, who is expected to set a
model example for the rest of us. Many, many times
during the winter I have ridden by the side of Tom,
and had learned to love every one of his pretty ways,
from the working of his expressive ears to the graceful movement of his slender legs. He was a horse
for anyone to be proud of, not only for his beauty
but as a hunter, too, and he was Lieutenant Baldwin's
delight and joy.

It does seem as if everything horrible had come all
at once. The order we have been expecting, of course,
as so many rumors have reached us that we were to
go, but all the time there has been hidden away a little
hope that we might be left here another year.

I shall take the greyhound puppy, of course. He is
with Blue, his mother, at Captain Richardson's quarters, but he is brought over every day for me to see.
His coat is brindled, dark brown and black—just
like Magic's—and fine as the softest satin. One foot is
white, and there is a little white tip to his tail, which,
it seems, is considered a mark of great beauty in a
greyhound. We have named him Harold.

Nothing has been done about packing yet, as the

orders have just been received. The carpenters in the
company will not be permitted to do one thing for us
until the captain and first lieutenant have had made
every box and crate they want for the move. I am
beginning to think that it must be nice to be even a
first lieutenant. But never mind, perhaps Faye will
get his captaincy in twenty years or so, and then it
will be all " fair and square."

FORT LYON, COLORADO TERRITORY,
May, 1872.

EVERYTHING is packed or disposed of, and we
are ready to start to-morrow on the long march
to Camp Supply. Two large army wagons have been
allowed to each company for the officers' baggage, but
as all three officers are present with the company Faye
is in, and the captain has taken one of the wagons for
his own use, we can have just one half of one of those
wagons to take our household goods to a country
where it is absolutely impossible to purchase one
thing! We have given away almost all of our furniture, and were glad that we had bought so little when
we came here. Our trunks and several boxes are to
be sent by freight to Hays City at our own expense,
and from there down to the post by wagon, and if
we ever see them again I will be surprised, as Camp
Supply is about one hundred and fifty miles from the
railroad. We are taking only one barrel of china—
just a few pieces we considered the most necessary—
and this morning Faye discovered that the first lieutenant had ordered that one barrel to be taken from
the wagon to make more room for his own things.
Faye ordered it to be put back at once, and says it

will stay there, too, and I fancy it will! Surely we are entitled to all of our one half of the wagon—second choice at that.

I am to ride in an ambulance with Mrs. Phillips, her little son and her cook, Mrs. Barker and her small son. There will be seats for only four, as the middle seat has been taken out to make room for a comfortable rocking-chair that will be for Mrs. Phillips's exclusive use! The dear little greyhound puppy I have to leave here. Faye says I must not take him with so many in the ambulance, as he would undoubtedly be in the way. But I am sure the puppy would not be as troublesome as one small boy, and there will be two small boys with us. It would be quite bad enough to be sent to such a terrible place as Camp Supply has been represented to us, without having all this misery and mortification added, and all because Faye happens to be a second lieutenant!

I have cried and cried over all these things until I am simply hideous, but I have to go just the same, and I have made up my mind never again to make myself so wholly disagreeable about a move, no matter where we may have to go. I happened to recall yesterday what grandmother said to me when saying good-by: " It is a dreadful thing not to become a woman when one ceases to be a girl!" I am no longer a girl, I suppose, so I must try to be a woman, as there seems to be nothing in between. One can find a little comfort, too, in the thought that there is no worse place possible for us to be sent to, and when once there we can look forward to better things sometime in the future. I do not mind the move as much as the unpleasant experiences connected with it.

But I shall miss the kind friends, the grand hunts and delightful rides, and shall long for dear old John, who has carried me safely so many, many miles.

Lieutenant Baldwin is still ill and very depressed, and Doctor Wilder is becoming anxious about him. It is so dreadful for such a powerful man as he has been to be so really broken in pieces. He insists upon being up and around, which is bad, very bad, for the many broken bones.

I will write whenever I find an opportunity.

OLD FORT ZARAH, KANSAS,
April, 1872.

OUR camp to-night is near the ruins of a very old fort, and ever since we got here, the men have been hunting rattlesnakes that have undoubtedly been holding possession of the tumble-down buildings, many snake generations. Dozens and dozens have been killed, of all sizes, some of them being very large. The old quarters were evidently made of sods and dirt, and must have been dreadful places to live in even when new.

I must tell you at once that I have the little greyhound. I simply took matters in my own hands and got him! We came only five miles our first day out, and after the tents had been pitched that night and the various dinners commenced, it was discovered that many little things had been left behind, so General Phillips decided to send an ambulance and two or three men back to the post for them, and to get the mail at the same time. It so happened that Burt, our own striker, was one of the men detailed to go, and

when I heard this I at once thought of the puppy I
wanted so much. I managed to see Burt before he
started, and when asked if he could bring the little
dog to me he answered so heartily, " That I can,
mum," I felt that the battle was half won, for I knew
that if I could once get the dog in camp he would
take care of him, even if I could not.

Burt brought him and kept him in his tent that
night, and the little fellow seemed to know that he
should be good, for Burt told me that he did not whim-
per once, notwithstanding it was his first night from
his mother and little companions. The next morning,
when he was brought to me, Faye's face was funny,
and after one look of astonishment at the puppy he
hurried out of the tent—so I could not see him laugh,
I think. He is quite as pleased as I am, now, to have
the dog, for he gives no trouble whatever. He is fed
condensed milk, and I take care of him during the
day and Burt has him at night. He is certainly much
better behaved in the ambulance than either of the
small boys who step upon our feet, get into fierce
fights, and keep up a racket generally. The mothers
have been called upon to settle so many quarrels between their sons, that the atmosphere in the ambulance has become quite frigid.

The day we came from the post, while I was grieving for the little greyhound and many other things
I had not been permitted to bring with me, and the
rocking-chair was bruising my ankles, I felt that it
was not dignified in me to submit to the treatment I
was being subjected to, and I decided to rebel. Mrs.
Barker and her small son had been riding on the back
seat, and I felt that I was as much entitled to a seat

there as the boy, nevertheless I had been sitting on the seat with Mrs. Phillips's servant and riding backward. This was the only place that had been left for me at the post that morning. After thinking it all over I made up my mind to take the small boy's seat, but just where he would sit I did not know.

When I returned to the ambulance after the next rest—I was careful to get there first—I sat down on the back seat and made myself comfortable, but I must admit that my heart was giving awful thumps, for Mrs. Barker's sharp tongue and spitfire temper are well known. My head was aching because of my having ridden backward, and I was really cross, and this Mrs. Barker may have noticed, for not one word did she say directly to me, but she said much to her son—much that I might have resented had I felt inclined. The small boy sat on his mother's lap and expressed his disapproval by giving me vicious kicks every few minutes.

Not one word was said the next morning when I boldly carried the puppy to that seat. Mrs. Barker looked at the dog, then at me, with great scorn, but she knew that if she said anything disagreeable Mrs. Phillips would side with me, so she wisely kept still. I think that even Faye has come to the conclusion that I might as well have the dog—who lies so quietly in my lap—now that he sees how I am sandwiched in with rocking-chairs, small boys, and servants. The men march fifty minutes and halt ten, each hour, and during every ten minutes' rest Harold and I take a little run, and this makes him ready for a nap when we return to the ambulance. From this place on I am to ride with Mrs. Cole, who has her own ambulance. This will be most agreeable, and I am so delighted that she should have thought of inviting me.

Camping out is really very nice when the weather is pleasant, but the long marches are tiresome for everybody. The ambulances and wagons are driven directly back of the troops, consequently the mules can never go faster than a slow walk, and sometimes the dust is enough to choke us. We have to keep together, for we are in an Indian country, of course. I feel sorry for the men, but they always march "rout" step and seem to have a good time, for we often hear them laughing and joking with each other.

We are following the Arkansas River, and so far the scenery has been monotonous—just the same rolling plains day after day. Leaving our first army home was distressing, and I doubt if other homes and other friends will ever be quite the same to me. Lieutenant Baldwin was assisted to the porch by his faithful Mexican boy, so he could see us start, and he looked white and pitifully helpless, with both arms bandaged tight to his sides. One of those dreadful dogs is in camp and going to Camp Supply with us, and is as frisky as though he had done something to be proud of.

This cannot be posted until we reach Fort Dodge, but I intend to write to you again while there, of course, if I have an opportunity.

FORT DODGE, KANSAS,
May, 1872.

IT was nearly two o'clock yesterday when we arrived at this post, and we go on again to-day about eleven. The length of all marches has to be regulated by water and wood, and as the first stream on the road to Camp Supply is at Bluff Creek, only ten miles from here, there was no necessity for an early start. This gives us an opportunity to get fresh supplies for our mess chests, and to dry things also.

There was a terrific rain and electric storm last evening, and this morning we present anything but a military appearance, for around each tent is a fine array of bedding and clothing hung out to dry. Our camp is at the foot of a hill a short distance back of the post, and during the storm the water rushed down with such force that it seemed as though we were in danger of being carried on to the Arkansas River.

We had just returned from a delightful dinner with Major and Mrs. Tilden, of the cavalry, and Faye had gone out to mount the guard for the night, when, without a moment's warning, the storm burst upon us. The lightning was fierce, and the white canvas made it appear even worse than it really was, for at each flash the walls of the tent seemed to be on fire. There was no dark closet for me to run into this time, but there was a bed, and on that I got, taking the little dog with me for company and to get him out of the wet. He seemed very restless and constantly gave little whines, and at the time I thought it was because he, too, was afraid of the storm. The water was soon two and three inches deep on the ground under the tent, rushing along like a mill race, giving little gurgles as it went through the grass and against the tent pins. The roar of the rain on the tent was deafening.

The guard is always mounted with the long steel bayonets on the rifles, and I knew that Faye had on his sword, and remembering these things made me almost scream at each wicked flash of lightning, fearing that he and the men had been killed. But he came to the tent on a hard run, and giving me a long waterproof coat to wrap myself in, gathered me in his arms and started for Mrs. Tilden's, where I had been urged to remain overnight. When we reached a narrow board walk that was supposed to run along by her side fence, Faye stood me down upon it, and I started to do some running on my own account. Before I had taken two steps, however, down went the walk and down I went in water almost to my knees, and then splash—down went the greyhound puppy! Up to that instant I had not been conscious of having the little dog with me, and in all that rain and water Faye had been carrying me and a fat puppy also.

The walk had been moved by the rushing water, and was floating, which we had no way of knowing, of course. I dragged the dog out of the water, and we finally reached the house, where we received a true army welcome—a dry one, too—and there I remained until after breakfast this morning. But sleep during the night I did not, for until long after midnight I sat in front of a blazing fire holding a very sick puppy. Hal was desperately ill and we all expected him to die at any moment, and I was doubly sorrowful, because I had been the innocent cause of it. Ever since I have had him he has been fed condensed milk only—perhaps a little bread now and then; so when we got here I sent for some fresh milk, to give him a treat. He drank of it greedily and seemed to enjoy it so much, that I let him have all he wanted during the afternoon. And it was the effect of the milk that

5

made him whine during the storm, and not because he was afraid of the lightning. He would have died, I do believe, had it not been for the kindness of Major Tilden who knows all about greyhounds. They are very delicate and most difficult to raise. The little dog is a limp bunch of brindled satin this morning, wrapped in flannel, but we hope he will soon be well.

A third company joined us here and will go on to Camp Supply. Major Hunt, the captain, has his wife and three children with him, and they seem to be cultured and very charming people. Mrs. Hunt this moment brought a plate of delicious spice cake for our luncheon. There is a first lieutenant with the company, but he is not married.

There is only one mail from here each week, so of course there will be only one from Camp Supply, as that mail is brought here and then carried up to the railroad with the Dodge mail. It is almost time for the tents to be struck, and I must be getting ready for the march.

CAMP SUPPLY, INDIAN TERRITORY,
May, 1872.

THIS place is quite as dreadful as it has been rep- resented to us. There are more troops here than at Fort Lyon, and of course the post is very much larger. There are two troops of colored cavalry, one of white cavalry, and three companies of infantry. The infantry companies that have been stationed here, and which our three companies have come to relieve, will start in the morning for their new station, and will use the transportation that brought us down. Con- sequently, it was necessary to unload all the things from our wagons early this morning, so they could be turned over to the outgoing troops. I am a little curious to know if there is a second lieutenant who will be so unfortunate as to be allowed only one half of a wagon in which to carry his household goods.

Their going will leave vacant a number of officers' quarters, therefore there will be no selection of quarters by our officers until to-morrow. Faye is next to the junior, so there will be very little left to select from by the time his turn comes. The quarters are really nothing more than huts built of vertical logs plastered in between with mud, and the roofs are of poles and mud! Many of the rooms have only sand floors. We dined last evening with Captain and Mrs. Vincent, of the cavalry, and were amazed to find that such wretched buildings could be made so attractive inside. But of course they have one of the very best houses on the line, and as company commander, Captain Vincent can have done about what he wants. And then, again, they are but recently married, and all their furnishings are new and handsome. There is one advantage in being with colored troops—one can always have good servants. Mrs. Vincent has an excellent colored soldier cook, and her butler was thoroughly trained as such before he enlisted. It did look so funny, however, to see such a black man in a blue uniform.

The march down from Fort Dodge was most uncomfortable the first two days. It poured and poured rain, and then poured more rain, until finally everybody and everything was soaked through. I felt so sorry for the men who had to march in the sticky mud. Their shoes filled fast with water, and they were compelled constantly to stop, take them off, and pour out

the water. It cleared at last and the sun shone warm
and bright, and then there was another exhibition in
camp one afternoon, of clothing and bedding drying
on guy ropes.

All the way down I was on the lookout for Indians, and was laughed at many a time for doing so,
too. Every time something unusual was seen in the

"Two soldiers . . . shot in the back."

distance some bright person would immediately ex-
claim, "Oh, that is only one of Mrs. Rae's Indians!" I said very little about what I saw during the
last day or two, for I felt that the constant teasing
must have become as wearisome to the others as it
had to me. But I am still positive that I saw the
black heads of Indians on the top of ever so many
hills we passed. When they wish to see and not be

seen they crawl up a hill on the side farthest from
you, but only far enough up to enable them to look
over, and in this position they will remain for hours,
perfectly motionless, watching your every movement.
Unless you notice the hill very carefully you will
never see the black dot on top, for only the eyes and
upper part of the head are exposed. I had been told
all this many times; also, that when in an Indian
country to be most watchful when Indians are not
to be seen.

Camp Supply is certainly in an Indian country, for
it is surrounded by Comanches, Apaches, Kiowas,
Cheyennes, and Arapahoes—each a hostile tribe, except
the last. No one can go a rod from the garrison without an escort, and our weekly mail is brought down in
a wagon and guarded by a corporal and several privates. Only last week two couriers—soldiers—who
had been sent down with dispatches from Fort Dodge,
were found dead on the road, both shot in the back,
probably without having been given one chance to
defend themselves.

We are in camp on low land just outside the post,
and last night we were almost washed away again by
the down-pouring rain, and this morning there is mud
everywhere. And this is the country that is supposed
never to have rain! Mrs. Vincent invited me most cordially to come to her house until we at least knew
what quarters we were to have, and Captain Vincent
came early to-day to insist upon my going up at once,
but I really could not go. We have been in rain and
mud so long I feel that I am in no way fit to go to
anyone's house. Besides, it would seem selfish in me
to desert Faye, and he, of course, would not leave

the company as long as it is in tents. We are delighted at finding such charming people as the Vincents at this horrid place.

CAMP SUPPLY, INDIAN TERRITORY,
June, 1872.

WE are in our own house now and almost settled. When one has only a few pieces of furniture it does not take long to get them in place. It is impossible to make the rooms look homelike, and I often find myself wondering where in this world I have wandered to! The house is of logs, of course, and has a pole and dirt roof, and was built originally for an officers' mess. The dining room is large and very long, a part of which we have partitioned off with a piece of canvas and converted into a storeroom. We had almost to get down on our knees to the quartermaster before he would give us the canvas. He is in the quartermaster's department and is most arrogant; seems to think that every nail and tack is his own personal property and for his exclusive use.

Our dining room has a sand floor, and almost every night little white toadstools grow up all along the base of the log walls. All of the logs are of cottonwood and have the bark on, and the army of bugs that hide underneath the bark during the day and march upon us at night is to be dreaded about as much as a whole tribe of Indians!

I wrote you how everyone laughed at me on the march down because I was positive I saw heads of Indians on the sand hills so many times. Well, all that has ceased, and the mention of " Mrs. Rae's Indians " is carefully avoided! There has been sad proof that the Indians were there, also that they were

" Watching us closely."

watching us closely and kept near us all the way down from Fort Dodge, hoping for a favorable opportunity to steal the animals. The battalion of the —th Infantry had made only two days' march from here, and the herders had just turned the horses and mules out to graze, when a band of Cheyenne Indians swooped down upon them and stampeded every animal, leaving the companies without even one mule! The poor things are still in camp on the prairie, waiting for something, anything, to move them on. General Phillips is mightily pleased that the Indians did not succeed in getting the animals from his command, and I am pleased that they cannot tease me any more.

My ride with Lieutenant Golden, Faye's classmate, this morning was very exciting for a time. We started directly after stable call, which is at six o'clock. Lieutenant Golden rode Dandy, his beautiful thoroughbred, that reminds me so much of Lieutenant Baldwin's Tom, and I rode a troop horse that had

never been ridden by a woman before. As soon as he
was led up I noticed that there was much white to be
seen in his eyes, and that he was restless and ever
pawing the ground. But the orderly said he was not
vicious, and he was sure I could ride him. He did not
object in the least to my skirt, and we started off in
fine style, but before we reached the end of the line he
gave two or three pulls at the bit, and then bolted!
My arms are remarkably strong, but they were like a
child's against that hard mouth. He turned the corner sharply and carried me along back of the laundress' quarters, where there was a perfect network of
clothes lines, and where I fully expected to be swept
from the saddle. But I managed to avoid them by
putting my head down close to the horse's neck, Indian fashion. He was not a very large horse, and
lowered himself, of course, by his terrific pace. He
went like the wind, on and up the hill in front of the
guard house. There a sentry was walking post, and
on his big infantry rifle was a long bayonet, and the
poor man, in his desire to do something for me, ran
forward and held the gun horizontally right in front
of my horse, which caused him to give a fearful
lunge to the right and down the hill. How I managed to keep my seat I do not know, and neither do
I know how that mad horse kept right side up on
that down jump. But it did not seem to disturb him
in the least, for he never slackened his speed, and
on we went toward the stables, where the cavalry
horses were tied to long picket ropes, and close together, getting their morning grooming.

All this time Lieutenant Golden had not attempted
to overtake me, fearing that by doing so he might

make matters worse, but when he saw that the horse was running straight for his place on the line, he pushed forward, and grasping my bridle rein, almost pulled the horse on his haunches. He said later that I might have been kicked to death by the troop horses if I had been rushed in among them. We went on to the stables, Lieutenant Golden leading my horse, and you can fancy how mortified I was over that performance, and it was really unnecessary, too. Lieutenant Golden, also the sergeant, advised me to dismount and try another horse, but I said no! I would ride that one if I could have a severer bit and my saddle girths tightened. Dismount before Lieutenant Golden, a cavalry officer and Faye's classmate, and all those staring troopers—I, the wife of an infantry officer? Never! It was my first experience with a runaway horse, but I had kept a firm seat all the time—there was some consolation in that thought.

Well, to my great relief and comfort, it was discovered that the chin chain that is on all cavalry bits had been left off, and this had made the curb simply a straight bit and wholly ineffective. The sergeant fastened the chain on and it was made tight, too, and he tightened the girths and saw that everything was right, and then Lieutenant Golden and I started on our ride the second time. I expected trouble, as the horse was then leaving his stable and companions, but when he commenced to back and shake his head I let him know that I held a nice stinging whip, and that soon stopped the balking. We had to pass three long picket lines of horses and almost two hundred troopers, every one of whom stared at me with both eyes. It was embarrassing, of course, but I was glad to let the

whole line of them see that I was capable of managing
my own horse, which was still very frisky. I knew
very well, too, that the sergeant's angry roar when he
asked, " Who bridled this horse? " had been heard by
many of them. Our ride was very delightful after
all its exciting beginning, and we are going again to-

"A band of Cheyenne Indians swooped down upon them."

morrow morning. I want to let those troopers see that
I am not afraid to ride the horse they selected for me.

I shall be so glad when Hal is large enough to go
with me. He is growing fast, but at present seems
to be mostly legs. He is devoted to me, but I regret
to say that he and our old soldier cook are not the dearest friends. Findlay is so stupid he cannot appreciate
the cunning things the little dog does. Hal is fed
mush and milk only until he gets his second teeth, and
consequently he is wild about meat. The odor of a
broiling beefsteak the other day was more than he

could resist, so he managed to get his freedom by slipping his collar over his head, and rushing into the kitchen, snatched the sizzling steak and was out again before Findlay could collect his few wits, and get across the room to stop him. The meat was so hot it burned his mouth, and he howled from the pain, but drop it he did not until he was far from the cook. This I consider very plucky in so young a dog! Findlay ran after the little hound, yelling and swearing, and I ran after Findlay to keep him from beating my dog. Of course we did not have beefsteak that day, but, as I told Faye, it was entirely Findlay's fault. He should have kept watch of things, and not made it possible for Hal to kill himself by eating a whole big steak!

Yesterday, Lieutenant Golden came in to luncheon, and when we went in the dining room I saw at once that things were wrong, very wrong. A polished table is an unknown luxury down here, but fresh table linen we do endeavor to have. But the cloth on the table yesterday was a sight to behold, with big spots of dirt all along one side and dirt on top. Findlay came in the room just as I reached the table, and I said, " Findlay, what has happened here? " He gave one look at the cloth where I pointed, and then striking his knuckles together, almost sobbed out, " Dot tamn dog, mum! " Faye and Lieutenant Golden quickly left the room to avoid hearing any more remarks of that kind, for it was really very dreadful in Findlay to use such language. This left me alone, of course, to pacify the cook, which I found no easy task. Old Findlay had pickled a choice buffalo tongue with much care and secrecy, and had served it for luncheon yesterday as a great surprise and treat. There was the platter on the table, but there could be no doubt of its having been licked clean. Not one tiny piece of tongue could be seen any place.

The window was far up, and in vain did I try to convince everyone that a strange dog had come in and stolen the meat, that Hal was quite too small to have reached so far; but Findlay only looked cross and Faye looked hungry, so I gave that up. Before night, however, there was trouble and a very sick puppy in the house, and once again I thought he would die. And every few minutes that disagreeable old cook would come in and ask about the dog, and say he was afraid he could not get well—always with a grin on his face that was exasperating. Finally, I told him that if he had served only part of the tongue, as he should have done, the dog would not have been so ill, and we could have had some of it. That settled the matter—he did not come in again. Findlay has served several enlistments, and is regarded as an old soldier, and once upon a time he was cook for the colonel of the regiment, therefore he sometimes forgets himself and becomes aggressive. I do not wonder that Hal dislikes him.

And Hal dislikes Indians, too, and will often hear their low mumbling and give little growls before I dream that one is near. They have a disagreeable way of coming to the windows and staring in. Sometimes before you have heard a sound you will be conscious of an uncomfortable feeling, and looking around you will discover five or six Indians, large and small, peering at you through the windows, each ugly nose pressed flat against the glass! It is enough to drive one mad. You never know when they are about, their tread is so stealthy with their moccasined feet.

Faye is officer of the guard every third day now. This sounds rather nice; but it means that every third day and night—exactly twenty-four hours—he has to spend at the guard house, excepting when making the rounds, that is, visiting sentries on post, and is permitted to come to the house just long enough to eat three hurried meals. This is doing duty, and would be all right if there were not a daily mingling of white and colored troops which often brings a colored sergeant over a white corporal and privates. But the most unpleasant part for the officer of the guard is that the partition in between the officer's room and guard room is of logs, unchinked, and very open, and the weather is very hot! and the bugs, which keep us all in perpetual warfare in our houses, have full sway there, going from one room to the other.

The officers say that the negroes make good soldiers and fight like fiends. They certainly manage to stick on their horses like monkeys. The Indians call them "buffalo soldiers," because their woolly heads are so much like the matted cushion that is between the horns of the buffalo. We had letters from dear old Fort Lyon yesterday, and the news about Lieutenant Baldwin is not encouraging. He is not improving and Doctor Wilder is most anxious about him. But a man as big and strong as he was must certainly get well in time.

IT seems as if I had to write constantly of unpleasant occurrences, but what else can I do since unpleasant occurrences are ever coming along? This time I must tell you that Faye has been turned out of quarters—" ranked out," as it is spoken of in the Army. But it all amounts to the same thing, and means that we have been driven out of our house and home, bag and baggage, because a captain wanted that one set of quarters! Call it what one chooses, the experience was not pleasant and will be long remembered. Being turned out was bad enough in itself, but the manner in which it was done was humiliating in the extreme. We had been in the house only three weeks and had worked so hard during that time to make it at all comfortable. Findlay wanted to tear down the canvas partition in the dining room when we left the house, and I was sorry later on that I had not consented to his doing so.

One morning at ten o'clock I received a note from Faye, written at the guard house, saying that his set of quarters had been selected by a cavalry officer who had just arrived at the post, and that every article of ours must be out of the house that day by one o'clock! Also that, as he was officer of the guard, it would be impossible for him to assist me in the least, except to send some enlisted men to move the things. At first I was dazed and wholly incapable of comprehending the situation—it seemed so preposterous to expect anyone to move everything out of a house in three hours. But as soon as I recovered my senses I saw at once that not one second of the precious time must be wasted, and that the superintendence of the whole thing had fallen upon me.

So I gathered my forces, and the four men started to work in a way that showed they would do everything in their power to help me. All that was possible for us to do, however, was almost to throw things out in a side yard, for remember, please, we had only three short hours in which to move everything—and this without warning or preparation of any kind. All things, big and small, were out by one o'clock, and just in time, too, to avoid a collision with the colored soldiers of the incoming cavalry officer, who commenced taking furniture and boxes in the house at precisely that hour.

Of course there was no hotel or even restaurant for me to go to, and I was too proud and too indignant to beg shelter in the house of a friend—in fact, I felt as if I had no friend. So I sat down on a chair in the yard with the little dog by me, thinking, I remember, that the chair was our own property and no one had a right to object to my being there. And I also remember that the whole miserable affair brought to mind most vividly scenes of eviction that had been illustrated in the papers from time to time, when poor women had been evicted for nonpayment of rent!

Just as I had reached the very lowest depths of misery and woe, Mrs. Vincent appeared, and Faye almost immediately after. We three went to Mrs. Vincent's house for luncheon, and in fact I remained there until we came to this house. She had just heard of what had happened and hastened down to me. Captain Vincent said it was entirely the fault of the commanding officer for permitting such a disgraceful order to leave his office; that Captain Park's family could have remained one night longer in tents here, as they had been in camp every night on the road from Fort Sill.

There came a ludicrous turn to all this unpleasantness, for, by the ranking out of one junior second lieutenant, six or more captains and first lieutenants had to move. It was great fun the next day to see the moving up and down the officers' line of all sorts of household goods, for it showed that a poor second lieutenant was of some importance after all!

But I am getting on too fast. Faye, of course, was entitled to two rooms, some place in the post, but it seems that the only quarters he could take were those occupied by Lieutenant Cole, so Faye decided at once to go into tents himself, in preference to compelling Lieutenant Cole to do so. Now it so happened that the inspector general of the department was in the garrison, and as soon as he learned the condition of affairs, he ordered the post quartermaster to double two sets of quarters—that is, make four sets out of two—and designated the quartermaster's own house for one of the two. But Major Knox divided off two rooms that no one could possibly occupy, and in consequence has still all of his large house. But the other large set that was doubled was occupied by a senior captain, who, when his quarters were reduced in size, claimed a new choice, and so, turning another captain out, the ranking out went on down to a second lieutenant. But no one took our old house from Captain Park, much to my disappointment, and he still has it.

The house that we are in now is built of cedar logs, and was the commanding officer's house at one time. It has a long hall running through the center, and on the left side Major Hunt and his family have the four rooms, and we have the two on the right. Our kitchen is across the yard, and was a chicken house not so very long ago. It has no floor, of course, so we had loads of dirt dug out and all filled in again with clean white sand, and now, after the log walls have been scraped and whitened, and a number of new shelves put up, it is really quite nice. Our sleeping room has no canvas on the walls inside, and much of the chinking has fallen out, leaving big holes, and I never have a light in that room after dark, fearing that Indians might shoot me through those holes. They are skulking about the post all the time.

We have another cook now—a soldier of course—and one that is rather inexperienced. General Phillips ordered Findlay back to the company, saying he was much needed there, but he was company cook just one day when he was transferred to the general's own kitchen. Comment is unnecessary! But it is all for the best, I am sure, for Farrar is very fond of Hal, and sees how intelligent he is, just as I do. The little dog is chained to a kennel all the time now, and, like his mistress, is trying to become dignified.

Faye was made post adjutant this morning, which we consider rather complimentary, since the post commander is in the cavalry, and there are a number of cavalry lieutenants here. General Dickinson is a polished old gentleman, and his wife a very handsome woman who looks almost as young as her daughter. Miss Dickinson, the general's older daughter, is very

6

pretty and a fearless rider. In a few days we two are to commence our morning rides.

How very funny that I should have forgotten to tell you that I have a horse, at least I hope he will look like a horse when he has gained some flesh and lost much long hair. He is an Indian pony of very good size, and has a well-shaped head and slender little legs. He has a fox trot, which is wonderfully easy, and which he apparently can keep up indefinitely, and like all Indian horses can " run like a deer." So, altogether, he will do very well for this place, where rides are necessarily curtailed. I call him Cheyenne, because we bought him of Little Raven, a Cheyenne chief. I shall be so glad when I can ride again, as I have missed so much the rides and grand hunts at Fort Lyon.

Later: The mail is just in, and letters have come from Fort Lyon telling us of the death of Lieutenant Baldwin! It is dreadful—and seems impossible. They write that he became more and more despondent, until finally it was impossible to rouse him sufficiently to take an interest in his own life. Faye and I have lost a friend—a real, true friend. A brother could not have been kinder, more considerate than he was to both of us always. How terribly he must have grieved over the ruin of the horse he was so proud of, and loved so well!

CAMP SUPPLY, INDIAN TERRITORY,
September, 1872.

THE heat here is still intense, and it never rains, so everything is parched to a crisp. The river is very low and the water so full of alkali that we are obliged to boil every drop before it is used for drinking or cooking, and even then it is so distasteful that we flavor it with sugar of lemons so we can drink it at all. Fresh lemons are unknown here, of course. The ice has given out, but we manage to cool the water a little by keeping it in bottles and canteens down in the dug-out cellar.

Miss Dickinson and I continue our daily rides, but go out very early in the morning. We have an orderly now, as General Dickinson considers it unsafe for us to go without an escort, since we were chased by an Indian the other day. That morning the little son of General Phillips was with us, and as it was not quite as warm as usual, we decided to canter down the sunflower road a little way—a road that runs to the crossing of Wolf Creek through an immense field of wild sunflowers. These sunflowers grow to a tremendous height in this country, so tall that sometimes you cannot see over them even when on horseback. Just across the creek there is a village of Apache Indians, and as these Indians are known to be hostile, this particular road is considered rather unsafe.

But we rode on down a mile or more without seeing a thing, and had just turned our ponies' heads homeward when little Grote, who was back of us, called out that an Indian was coming. That was startling, but upon looking back we saw that he was a long distance away and coming leisurely, so we did not pay much attention to him.

But Grote was more watchful, and very soon screamed, " Mrs. Rae, Mrs. Rae, the Indian is coming fast—he's going to catch us!" And then, with-

out wasting time by looking back, we started our
ponies with a bound that put them at their best pace,
poor little Grote lashing his most unmercifully, and
crying every minute, " He'll catch us! He'll catch
us ! "

That the Indian was on a fleet pony and was gaining upon us was very evident, and what might have
happened had we not soon reached the sutler's store no
one can tell, but we did get there just as he caught
up with us, and as we drew in our panting horses that
hideous savage rode up in front of us and circled
twice around us, his pony going like a whirlwind;
and in order to keep his balance, the Indian leaned
far over on one side, his head close to the pony's
neck. He said " How " with a fiendish grin that
showed how thoroughly he was enjoying our frightened faces, and then turned his fast little beast back
to the sunflower road. Of course, as long as the road
to the post was clear we were in no very great danger,
as our ponies were fast, but if that savage could have
passed us and gotten us in between him and the
Apache village, we would have lost our horses, if not
our lives, for turning off through the sunflowers
would have been an impossibility.

The very next morning, I think it was, one of the
government mules wandered away, and two of the
drivers went in search of it, but not finding it in
the post, one of the men suggested that they should
go to the river where the post animals are watered.
It is a fork of the Canadian River, and is just over
a little sand hill, not one quarter of a mile back of
the quarters, but not in the direction of the sunflower road. The other man, however, said he would

not go—that it was not safe—and came back to
the corral, so the one who proposed going went on
alone.

Time passed and the man did not return, and
finally a detail was sent out to look him up. They
went directly to the river, and there they found him,
just on the other side of the hill—dead. He had been
shot by some fiendish Indian soon after leaving his
companion. The mule has never been found, and
is probably in a far-away Indian village, where he
brays in vain for the big rations of corn he used to
get at the government corral.

Last Monday, soon after luncheon, forty or fifty
Indians came rushing down the drive in front of the
officers' quarters, frightening some of us almost out
of our senses. Where they came from no one could
tell, for not one sentry had seen them until they were
near the post. They rode past the houses like mad
creatures, and on out to the company gardens, where
they made their ponies trample and destroy every
growing thing. Only a few vegetables will mature
in this soil and climate, but melons are often very good,
and this season the gardeners had taken much pains
with a crop of fine watermelons that were just beginning to ripen. But not one of these was spared—
every one was broken and crushed by the little hoofs
of the ponies, which seem to enjoy viciousness of this
kind as much as the Indians themselves.

A company of infantry was sent at once to the gardens, but as it was not quite possible for the men to
outrun the ponies, the mischief had been done before
they got there, and all they could do was to force
them back at the point of the bayonet. Cavalry was

"Forty or fifty Indians came rushing down the drive."

ordered out, also, to drive them away, but none of the troops were allowed to fire upon them, and that the Indians knew very well. It might have brought on an uprising!

It seems that the Indians were almost all young bucks out for a frolic, but quite ready, officers say, for any kind of devilment. They rode around the post three or four times at breakneck speed, each circle being larger, and taking them farther away. At last they all started for the hills and gradually disappeared—all but one, a sentinel, who could be seen until dark sitting his pony on the highest hill. I presume there were dozens of Indians on the sand hills around the post peeking over to see how the fun went on.

They seem to be watching the post every second of the day, ready to pounce upon any unprotected thing that ventures forth, be it man or beast. At almost any time two or three black dots can be seen on the top of the white sand hills, and one wonders how they can lie for hours in the hot, scorching sand with the sun beating down on their heads and backs. And all the time their tough little ponies will stand near them, down the hill, scarcely moving or making a sound. Some scouts declare that an Indian pony never whinnies or sneezes! But that seems absurd, although some of those little beasts show wonderful intelligence and appear to have been apt pupils in treachery.

CAMP SUPPLY, INDIAN TERRITORY,
October, 1872.

THIS place is becoming more dreadful each day, and every one of the awful things I feared might happen here seems to be coming to pass. Night before last the post was actually attacked by Indians! It was about one o'clock when the entire garrison was awakened by rifle shots and cries of " Indians! Indians!" There was pandemonium at once. The " long roll " was beaten on the infantry drums, and " boots and saddles " sounded by the cavalry bugles, and these are calls that startle all who hear them, and strike terror to the heart of every army woman. They mean that something is wrong—very wrong—and demand the immediate report for duty at their respective companies of every officer and man in the garrison.

Faye jumped into his uniform, and saying a hasty

good-by, ran to his company, as did all the other officers, and very soon we could hear the shouting of orders from every direction.

Our house is at the extreme end of the officers' line and very isolated, therefore Mrs. Hunt and I were left in a most deplorable condition, with three little children—one a mere baby—to take care of. We put them all in one bed and covered them as well as we could without a light, which we did not dare have, of course. Then we saw that all the doors and windows were fastened on both sides. We decided that it would be quite impossible for us to remain shut up inside the house, so we dressed our feet, put on long waterproof coats over our nightgowns as quickly and silently as possible, and then we sat down on the steps of the front door to await—we knew not what. I had firm hold of a revolver, and felt exceedingly grateful all the time that I had been taught so carefully how to use it, not that I had any hope of being able to do more with it than kill myself, if I fell in the hands of a fiendish Indian. I believe that Mrs. Hunt, however, was almost as much afraid of the pistol as she was of the Indians.

Ten minutes after the shots were fired there was perfect silence throughout the garrison, and we knew absolutely nothing of what was taking place around us. Not one word did we dare even whisper to each other, our only means of communication being through our hands. The night was intensely dark and the air was close—almost suffocating.

In this way we sat for two terrible hours, ever on the alert, ever listening for the stealthy tread of a moccasined foot at a corner of the house. And then, just before dawn, when we were almost exhausted by the great strain on our strength and nerves, our husbands came. They told us that a company of infantry had been quite near us all the time, and that a troop of cavalry had been constantly patrolling around the post. I cannot understand how such perfect silence was maintained by the troops, particularly the cavalry. Horses usually manage to sneeze at such times.

There is always a sentry at our corner of the garrison, and it was this sentinel who was attacked, and it is the general belief among the officers that the Indians came to this corner hoping to get the troops concentrated at the beat farthest from the stables, and thus give them a chance to steal some, if not all, of the cavalry horses. But Mr. Red Man's strategy is not quite equal to that of the Great Father's soldiers, or he would have known that troops would be sent at once to protect the horses.

There were a great many pony tracks to be seen in the sand the next morning, and there was a mounted sentinel on a hill a mile or so away. It was amusing to watch him through a powerful field glass, and we wished that he could know just how his every movement could be seen. He sat there on his pony for hours, both Indian and horse apparently perfectly motionless, but with his face always turned toward the post, ready to signal to his people the slightest movement of the troops.

Faye says that the colored troops were real soldiers that night, alert and plucky. I can readily believe that some of them can be alert, and possibly good soldiers, and that they can be good thieves too, for last Saturday night they stole from us the commis-

sary stores we had expected to last us one week—
everything, in fact, except coffee, sugar, and such
things that we keep in the kitchen, where it is dry.

The commissary is open Saturday mornings only,
at which time we are requested to purchase all supplies we will need from there for the following
week, and as we have no fresh vegetables whatever,
and no meat except beef, we are very dependent
upon the canned goods and other things in the commissary.

Last Saturday Mrs. Hunt and I sent over as usual,
and most of the supplies were put in a little dug-
out cellar in the yard that we use together—she
having one side, I the other. On Sunday morning
Farrar happened to be the first cook to go out for
things for breakfast, and he found that the door had
been broken open and the shelves as bare as Mother
Hubbard's. Everything had been carried off except a
few candles on Mrs. Hunt's side, and a few cakes of
laundry soap on mine! The candles they had no use
for, and the thieves were probably of a class that had
no use for soap, either.

Our breakfast that morning was rather light, but
as soon as word got abroad of our starving condition,
true army hospitality and generosity manifested itself.
We were invited out to luncheon, and to dinner, and
to breakfast the next morning. You can see how like
one big family a garrison can be, and how in times
of trouble we go to each other's assistance. Of course,
now and then we have disagreeable persons with us
—those who will give you only three hours to move
out of your house, or one who will order your cook
from you,

ALL that remained of Captain White was carried to the little cemetery yesterday, with all the military honors possible at such a far-away post. We have no chaplain, therefore one of the cavalry officers read the service for the dead at the house, just before the march to the cemetery. Almost all of the cavalry of the garrison was out, mounted, Captain White's own troop having the lead, of course, and the greater part of the infantry was out also, and there was a firing detail, with guns reversed.

The casket, covered with a large flag, was carried on a caisson, and his horse, led by an orderly, was covered with a large blanket of black cloth. Over this was the saddle, and on top of the saddle rested his helmet—the yellow horsehair plume and gold trimmings looking soiled by long service. His sabre was there, too, and strapped to the saddle on each side were his uniform boots, toes in stirrups—all reversed! This riderless horse, with its pall of black, yellow helmet, and footless boots, was the saddest sight imaginable.

I did not go to the cemetery, but we heard distinctly the firing of the three volleys over the grave and the sounding of taps on the bugles. The garrison flag had been drawn to half mast almost the moment of Captain White's death, but at the last sound of taps it was immediately pulled up to full mast, and soon the troops came back to their quarters, the field music playing lively airs.

This seemed so unnecessarily cruel, for Mrs. White

must have heard every note, and she is still so wretchedly ill. The tiny baby has been taken from the house by the motherly wife of an officer, and the other tots—four in all—are being cared for by others. We have all been taking turns in sitting up nights during the illness of husband and wife, and last night three of us were there, Captain Tillman and Faye in one room, and I with Mrs. White. It was a terrible night, probably the one that has exacted, or will exact, the greatest self-control, as it was the one before the burial.

In civil life a poor widow can often live right on in her old home, but in the Army, never! Mrs. White will have to give up the quarters just as soon as she and the little baby are strong enough to travel. She has been in a warm climate many years, and her friends are all in the North, so to-morrow a number of us are to commence making warm clothing for her and the children. She has absolutely nothing of the kind, and seems to be pitifully helpless and incapable of thinking for herself.

Soon after I got home this morning and was trying to get a little sleep, I heard screams and an awful commotion across the hall in one of Mrs. Hunt's rooms, and running over to see what was the matter, I found Mrs. Hunt standing upon a chair, and her cook running around like a madman, with a stick of wood in his hand, upsetting furniture and whacking things generally. I naturally thought of a mouse, and not being afraid of them, I went on in and closed the door. I doubt if Mrs. Hunt saw me, she was so intently watching the man, who kept on upsetting things. He stopped finally, and then held up on the wood a snake

—a dead rattlesnake! We measured it, and it was over two feet long.

You can see how the house is built by the photograph I sent you, that there are no chimneys, and that the stovepipes go straight up through the pole and sod roof. The children insist that the snake came down the pipe in the liveliest kind of a way, so it must have crawled up the logs to the roof, and finding the warmth of the pipe, got too close to the opening and slipped through. However that may be, he got into the room where the three little children were playing alone. Fortunately, the oldest recognized the danger at once, and ran screaming to her mother, the other two following. Mrs. Hunt was almost ill over the affair, and Major Hunt kept a man on top and around the old house hunting for snakes, until we began to fear it would be pulled down on our heads.

This country itself is bad enough, and the location of the post is most unfortunate, but to compel officers and men to live in these old huts of decaying, moldy wood, which are reeking with malaria and alive with bugs, and perhaps snakes, is wicked. Officers' families are not obliged to remain here, of course.

But at dreadful places like this is where the plucky army wife is most needed. Her very presence has often a refining and restraining influence over the entire garrison, from the commanding officer down to the last recruit. No one can as quickly grasp the possibilities of comfort in quarters like these, or as bravely busy herself to fix them up. She knows that the stay is indefinite, that it may be for six months, or possibly six years, but that matters not. It is her army home —Brass Button's home—and however discouraging its condition may be, for his sake she pluckily, and with wifely pride, performs miracles, always making the house comfortable and attractive.

FORT DODGE, KANSAS,
January, 1873.

OUR coming here was most unexpected and very unpleasant in every way. General Phillips and Major Barker quarreled over something, and Major Barker preferred charges against the general, who is his company commander, and now General Phillips is being tried here by general court martial. Faye and I were summoned as witnesses by Major Barker, just because we heard a few words that were said in front of our window late one night! The court has thoughtfully excused me from going into the court room, as I could only corroborate Faye's testimony. I am so relieved, for it would have been a terrible ordeal to have gone in that room where all those officers are sitting, in full-dress uniform, too, and General Phillips with them. I would have been too frightened to have remembered one thing, or to have known whether I was telling the truth or not.

General Dickinson and Ben Clark, his interpreter, came up in the ambulance with us, and the poor general is now quite ill, the result of an ice bath in the Arkansas River! When we started to come across on the ice here at the ford, the mule leaders broke through and fell down on the river bottom, and being mules, not only refused to get up, but insisted upon keeping their noses under the water. The wheelers broke through, too, but had the good sense to stand on their feet, but they gave the ambulance such a hard jerk that

the front wheels broke off more ice and went down to
the river bottom, also. By the time all this had occurred, I was the only one left inside, and found myself
very busy trying to keep myself from slipping down
under the front seat, where water had already come
in. General Dickinson and Faye were doing everything possible to assist the men.

Just how it was accomplished would make too long
a story to tell, but in a short time the leaders were
dragged out and on their feet, and the rear wheels of
the ambulance let down on the river bottom, and then
we were all pulled up on the ice again, and came on
to the post in safety. All but General Dickinson, who
undertook to hold out of the water the heads of the
two leaders who seemed determined to commit sui-
cide by keeping their noses down, the general forgetting for once that he was commanding officer. But
one of those government mules did not forget, and
with a sudden jerk of his big head he pulled the
general over and down from the ice into the water,
and in such a way that he was wedged tight in between the two animals. One would have expected
much objection on the part of the mules to the fishing
out of the general, but those two mules kept perfectly
still, apparently satisfied with the mischief that had
already been done. I can fancy that there is one mule
still chuckling over the fact of having gotten even
with a commanding officer! It is quite warm now,
and the ice has gone out of the river, so there will
be no trouble at the ford to-morrow, when we start
back.

There is one company of Faye's regiment stationed
here, and the officer in command of the post is major

of the Third, so we feel at home. We are staying with Lieutenant Harvey, who is making it very pleasant for us. Hal is with us, and is being petted by everybody, but most of all by the cavalry officers, some of whom have hunted with Magic, Hal's father.

Last evening, while a number of us were sitting on the veranda after dinner, a large turkey gobbler came stalking down the drive in front of the officers' quarters. Hal was squatted down, hound fashion, at the top of the steps, and of course saw the gobbler at once. He never moved, except to raise his ears a little, but I noticed that his eyes opened wider and wider, and could see that he was making an estimate of the speed of that turkey, and also making up his mind that it was his duty as a self-respecting hound to resent the airs that were being assumed by the queer thing with a red nose and only two legs. So as soon as the turkey passed, down he jumped after him, and over him and around him, until really the poor thing looked about one half his former size. Then Hal got back of the turkey and waited for it to run, which it proceeded to do without loss of time, and then a funny race was on! I could have cried, I was so afraid Hal would injure the turkey, but everyone else laughed and watched, as though it was the sporting event of the year, and they assured me that the dog would have to stop when he got to the very high gate at the end of the line. But they did not know that greyhound, for the gate gave him still another opportunity to show the thing that had wings to help its absurd legs along what a hound puppy could do. When they reached the gate the turkey went under, but the puppy went over, making a magnificent jump that landed him yards in advance of the turkey, thereby causing him the loss of the race, for before he could stop himself and turn, the gobbler had very wisely hidden himself in a back yard.

There was a shouting and clapping of hands all along the line because of the beautiful jump of so young a dog, but I must confess that all I thought of just then was gratitude that my dog had not made an untimely plucking of somebody's turkey, for in this country a turkey is something rare and valuable.

Hal came trotting back with his loftiest steps and tail high in the air, evidently much pleased with his part in the entertainment. He is very tall now, and ran by the ambulance all the way up, and has been following me on my rides for some time.

CIMARRON REDOUBT, KANSAS,
January, 1873.

WHEN Faye was ordered here I said at once that I would come, too, and so I came! We are at a mail station—that is, where the relay mules are kept and where the mail wagon and escort remain overnight on their weekly trips from Camp Supply to Fort Dodge. A non-commissioned officer and ten privates are here all the time.

The cause of Faye's being here is, the contractor is sending big trains of grain down to Camp Supply for the cavalry horses and other animals, and it was discovered that whisky was being smuggled to the Indians in the sacks of oats. So General Dickinson sent an officer to the redoubt to inspect each sack as it is carried past by the ox trains. Lieutenant Cole was the first officer to be ordered up, but the place did not

7

agree with him, and at the end of three weeks he appeared at the post on a mail wagon, a very sick man—very sick indeed! In less than half an hour Faye was ordered to relieve him, to finish Lieutenant Cole's tour in addition to his own detail of thirty days, which will give us a stay here of over five weeks.

As soon as I heard of the order I announced that I was coming, but it was necessary to obtain the commanding officer's permission first. This seemed rather hopeless for a time, the general declaring I would " die in such a hole," where I could have no comforts, but he did not say I should not come. Faye did not want to leave me alone at the post, but was afraid the life here would be too rough for me, so I decided the matter for myself and began to make preparations to come away, and that settled all discussion. We were obliged to start early the next morning, and there were only a few hours in which to get ready. Packing the mess chest and getting commissary stores occupied the most time, for after our clothing was put away the closing of the house was a farce, " *Peu de bien, peu de soin!* " Farrar was permitted to come, and we brought Hal and the horse, so the family is still together.

The redoubt is made of gunny sacks filled with sand, and is built on the principle of a permanent fortification in miniature, with bastions, flanks, curtains, and ditch, and has two pieces of artillery. The parapet is about ten feet high, upon the top of which a sentry walks all the time. This is technically correct, for Faye has just explained it all to me, so I could tell you about our castle on the plains. We have only two rooms for our own use, and these are partitioned off with vertical logs in one corner of the fortification, and our only roof is of canvas.

When we first got here the dirt floor was very much like the side of a mountain—so sloping that we had difficulty in sitting upon the chairs. Faye had these made level at once, and fresh, dry sand sprinkled everywhere.

We are right in the heart of the Indian country, almost on the line between Kansas and the Indian Territory, and are surrounded by any number of villages of hostile Indians. We are forty miles from Camp Supply and about the same distance from Fort Dodge. The weather is delightful—sunny and very warm.

I was prevented from finishing this the other day by the coming of a dozen or more Arapahoe Indians, but as the mail does not go north until to-morrow morning, I can tell you of the more than busy time we have had since then.

For two or three days the weather had been unseasonably warm—almost like summer—and one evening it was not only hot, but so sultry one wondered where all the air had gone. About midnight, however, a terrific wind came up, cold and piercing, and very soon snow began to fall, and then we knew that we were having a " Texas norther," a storm that is feared by all old frontiersmen. Of course we were perfectly safe from the wind, for only a cyclone could tear down these thick walls of sand, but the snow sifted in every place—between the logs of the inner wall, around the windows—and almost buried us. And the cold became intense.

In the morning the logs of that entire wall from top to bottom, were white inside with snow, and looked like a forest in the far North. The floor was covered with snow, and so was the foot of the bed! Our rooms were facing just right to catch the full force of the blizzard. The straightening out was exceedingly unpleasant, for a fire could not be started in either stove until after the snow had been swept out. But a few soldiers can work miracles at times, and this proved to be one of the times. I went over to the orderly room while they brushed and scraped everywhere and fixed us up nicely, and we were soon warm and dry.

The norther continued twenty-four hours, and the cold is still freezing. All the wood inside was soon consumed, and the men were compelled to go outside the redoubt for it, and to split it, too. The storm was so fierce and wholly blinding that it was necessary to fasten the end of a rope around the waist of each man as he went out, and tie the other end to the entrance gate to prevent him from losing his direction and wandering out on the plains. Even with this precaution it was impossible for a man to remain out longer than ten minutes, because of the terribly cold wind that at times was almost impossible to stand up against.

Faye says that he cannot understand why the place has never been made habitable, or why Lieutenant Cole did not have the wood brought inside, where it would be convenient in case of a storm. Some of the men are working at the wood still, and others are making their quarters a little more decent. Every tiny opening in our own log walls has been chinked with pieces of blanket or anything that could be found, and the entire dirt floor has been covered with clean grain sacks that are held down smooth and tight by little pegs of wood, and over this rough carpet we have three rugs we brought with us. At the small window are turkey-red curtains that make very good shades when let down at night. There are warm army blankets on the camp bed, and a folded red squaw blanket on the trunk. The stove is as bright and shining as the strong arm of a soldier could make it, and on it is a little brass teakettle singing merrily.

Altogether the little place looks clean and cheerful, quite unlike the "hole" we came to. Farrar has attended to his part in the kitchen also, and things look neat and orderly there. A wall tent has been pitched just outside our door that gives us a large storeroom and at the same time screens us from the men's quarters that are along one side of the sand-bag walls.

On the side farthest from us the mules and horses are stabled, but one would never know that an animal was near if those big-headed mules did not occasionally raise their voices in brays that sound like old squeaky pumps. When it is pleasant they are all picketed out.

At the first coming of the blizzard the sentry was ordered from the parapet, and is still off, and I am positive that unless one goes on soon at night I shall be wholly deaf, because I strain my ears the whole night through listening for Indians. The men are supposed to be ever ready for an attack, but if they require drums and cannon to awaken them in a garrison, how can they possibly hear the stealthy step of an Indian here? It is foolish to expect anything so unreasonable.

CIMARRON REDOUBT, KANSAS,
January, 1873.

FANCY our having given a dinner party at this sand-bag castle on the plains, miles and miles from a white man or woman! The number of guests was small, but their rank was immense, for we entertained Powder-Face, Chief of the Arapahoe Nation, and Wauk, his young squaw, mother of his little chief.

Two or three days ago Powder-Face came to make a formal call upon the " White Chief," and brought with him two other Indians—aides we would call them, I presume. A soldier offered to hold his horse, but he would not dismount, and sat his horse with grave dignity until Faye went out and in person invited him to come in and have a smoke. He is an Indian of striking personality—is rather tall, with square, broad shoulders, and the poise of his head tells one at once that he is not an ordinary savage.

We must have found favor with him, for as he was going away he announced that he would come again the next day and bring his squaw with him. Then Faye, in his hospitable way, invited them to a midday dinner! I was almost speechless from horror at the very thought of sitting at a table with an Indian, no matter how great a chief he might be. But I could say nothing, of course, and he rode away with the understanding that he was to return the following day. Faye assured me that it would be amusing to watch them, and be a break in the monotony here.

They appeared promptly, and I became interested

in Wauk at once, for she was a remarkable squaw.
Tall and slender, with rather a thin, girlish face, very
unlike the short, fat squaws one usually sees, and she
had the appearance of being rather tidy, too. I could
not tell if she was dressed specially for the occasion,
as I had never seen her before, but everything she had
on was beautifully embroidered with beads—mostly
white—and small teeth of animals. She wore a sort
of short skirt, high leggings, and of course moccasins,
and around her shoulders and falling far below her
waist was a queer-shaped garment—neither cape nor
shawl—dotted closely all over with tiny teeth, which
were fastened on at one end and left to dangle.

High up around her neck was a dog collar of fine
teeth that was really beautiful, and there were several
necklaces of different lengths hanging below it, one
of which was of polished elk teeth and very rare. The
skins of all her clothing had been tanned until they
were as soft as kid. Any number of bracelets were
on her arms, many of them made of tin, I think. Her
hair was parted and hung in loose ropes down each
shoulder in front. Her feet and hands were very
small, even for an Indian, and showed that life had
been kind to her. I am confident that she must have
been a princess by birth, she was so different from all
squaws I have seen. She could not speak one word
of English, but her lord, whom she seemed to adore,
could make himself understood very well by signs
and a word now and then.

Powder-Face wore a blanket, but underneath it was
a shirt of fine skins, the front of which was almost
covered with teeth, beads, and wampum. His hair
was roped on each side and hung in front, and the

scalp lock on top was made conspicuous by the usual long feather stuck through it.

The time came when dinner could no longer be put off, so we sat down. Our *ménu* in this place is necessarily limited, but a friend at Fort Dodge had added to our stores by sending us some fresh potatoes and some lettuce by the mail wagon just the day before, and both of these Powder-Face seemed to enjoy. In fact, he ate of everything, but Wauk was more particular—lettuce, potatoes, and ham she would not touch. Their table manners were not of the very best form, as might be expected, but they conducted themselves rather decently—far better than I had feared they would. All the time I was wondering what that squaw was thinking of things! Powder-Face was taken to Washington last year with chiefs of other nations to see the "Great Father," so he knew much of the white man's ways, but Wauk was a wild creature of the plains.

We kept them bountifully supplied with everything on the table, so our own portion of the dinner would remain unmolested, although neither Faye nor I had much appetite just then. When Farrar came in to remove the plates for dessert, and Powder-Face saw that the remaining food was about to disappear, he pushed Farrar back and commenced to attend to the table himself. He pulled one dish after another to him, and scraped each one clean, spreading all the butter on the bread, and piled up buffalo steak, ham, potatoes, peas—in fact, every crumb that had been left—making one disgusting mess, and then tapping it with his finger said, "Papoose! Papoose!" We had it all put in a paper and other things added, which made Wauk almost bob off her chair in her delight at having such a feast for her little chief. But the condition of my tablecloth made me want to bob up and down for other feelings than delight!

After dinner they all sat by the stove and smoked, and Powder-Face told funny things about his trip East that we could not always interpret, but which caused him and Wauk to laugh heartily. Wauk sat very close to him, with elbows on her knees, looking as though she would much prefer to be squatted down upon the floor.

The tepee odor became stifling, so in order to get as far from the Indians as possible, I went across the room and sat upon a small trunk by the window. I had not been there five minutes, however, before that wily chief, who had apparently not noticed my existence, got up from his chair, gathered his blanket around him, and with long strides came straight to me. Then with a grip of steel on my shoulder, he jerked me from the trunk and fairly slung me over against the wall, and turning to Faye with his head thrown back he said, "Whisk! Whisk!" at the same time pointing to the trunk.

The demand was imperious, and the unstudied poise of the powerfully built Indian, so full of savage dignity, was magnificent. As I calmly think of it now, the whole scene was grand. The rough room, with its low walls of sand-bags and logs, the Indian princess in her picturesque dress of skins and beads, the fair army officer in his uniform of blue, both looking in astonishment at the chief, whose square jaws and flashing eyes plainly told that he was accustomed to being obeyed, and expected to be obeyed then!

Faye says that I missed part of the scene; that, backed up against sand-bags and clinging to them on either side for support, stood a slender young woman with pigtail hanging down one shoulder, so terrified that her face, although brown from exposure to sun and wind, had become white and chalky. It is not surprising that my face turned white; the only wonder is that the pigtail did not turn white, too!

It was not right for Faye to give liquor to an Indian, but what else could be done under the circumstances? There happened to be a flask of brandy in the trunk, but fortunately there was only a small quantity that we had brought up for medicinal purposes, and it was precious, too, for we were far from a doctor. But Faye had to get it out for the chief, who had sat there smoking in such an innocent way, but who had all the time been studying out where there might be hidden some " whisk! " Wauk drank almost all of it, Powder-Face seeming to derive more pleasure in seeing her drink his portion than in drinking it himself. Consequently, when she went out to mount her horse her steps were a little unsteady, over which the chief laughed heartily.

It was with the greatest relief I saw them ride away. They certainly had furnished entertainment, but it was of a kind that would satisfy one for a long time. I was afraid they might come for dinner again the following day, but they did not.

Powder-Face thought that the pony Cheyenne was not a good enough horse for me, so the morning after he was here an Indian, called Dog, appeared with a very good animal, large and well gaited, that the chief had sent over, not as a present, but for a trade.

We let poor Cheyenne go back to the Indians, a quantity of sugar, coffee, and such things going with him, and now I have a strawberry-roan horse named Powder-Face.

Chief Powder-Face, who is really not old, is respected by everyone, and has been instrumental in causing the Arapahoe nation to cease hostilities toward white people. Some of the chiefs of lesser rank have much of the dignity of high-born savages, particularly Lone Wolf and his son Big Mouth, both of whom come to see us now and then. Lone Wolf is no longer a warrior, and of course no longer wears a scalp lock and strings of wampum and beads, and would like to have you believe that he has ever been the white man's friend, but I suspect that even now there might be brought forth an old war belt with hanging scalps that could tell of massacre, torture, and murder. Big Mouth is a war chief, and has the same grand physique as Powder-Face and a personality almost as striking. His hair is simply splendid, wonderfully heavy and long and very glossy. His scalp lock is most artistic, and undoubtedly kept in order by a squaw.

The picture of the two generations of chiefs is unique and rare. It shows in detail the everyday dress of the genuine blanket Indians as we see them here. Just how it was obtained I do not know, for Indians do not like a camera. We have daily visits from dozens of so-called friendly Indians, but I would not trust one of them. Many white people who have lived among Indians and know them well declare that an Indian is always an Indian; that, no matter how fine the veneering civilization may have given him, there ever lies dormant the traits of the savage, ready to spring forth without warning in acts of treachery and fiendish cruelty.

CIMARRON REDOUBT,
January, 1873.

IT was such a pleasant surprise yesterday when General Bourke drove up to the redoubt on his way to Camp Supply from dear old Fort Lyon. He has been ordered to relieve General Dickinson, and was taking down furniture, his dogs, and handsome team. Of course there was an escort, and ever so many wagons, some loaded with tents and camp outfits. We are rejoicing over the prospect of having an infantry officer in command when we return to the post. The general remained for luncheon and seemed to enjoy the broiled buffalo steak very much. He said that now there are very few buffalo in Colorado and Kansas, because of their wholesale slaughter by white men during the past year. These men kill them for the skins only, and General Bourke said that he saw hundreds of carcasses on the plains between Lyon and Dodge. They are boldly coming to the Indian Territory now, and cavalry has been sent out several times to drive them from the reservation.

If the Indians should attempt to protect their rights it would be called an uprising at once, so they have to lie around on the sand hills and watch their beloved buffalo gradually disappear, and all the time they know only too well that with them will go the skins that give them tepees and clothing, and the meat that furnishes almost all of their sustenance.

During the blizzard two weeks ago ten or twelve of these buffalo hunters were caught out in the storm, and being unable to find their own camps they wandered into Indian villages, each man about half dead from exposure to the cold and hunger. All were suffering more or less from frozen feet and hands. In every case the Indians fed and cared for them until the storm was over, and then they told them to go—and go fast and far, or it would not be well with them. Faye says that it was truly noble in the Indians to keep alive those men when they knew they had been stealing so much from them. But Faye can always see more good in Indians than I can. Even a savage could scarcely kill a man when he appeals to him for protection!

There is some kind of excitement here every day—some pleasant, some otherwise—usually otherwise. The mail escort and wagon are here two nights during the week, one on the way to Fort Dodge, the other on the return trip, so we hear the little bits of gossip from each garrison. The long trains of army wagons drawn by mules that carry stores to the post always camp near us one night, because of the water.

But the most exciting times are when the big ox trains come along that are taking oats and corn to the quartermaster for the cavalry horses and mules, for in these sacks of grain there is ever a possibility of liquor being found. The sergeant carefully punches the sacks from one end to the other with a long steel very much like a rifle rammer; but so far not a thing has been found, but this is undoubtedly because they know what to expect at this place now. Faye is always present at the inspection, and once I watched it a short distance away.

When there are camps outside I always feel a little

more protected from the Indians. I am kept awake hours every night by my uncontrollable fear of their getting on top of the parapet and cutting holes in the canvas over our very heads and getting into the room that way. A sentry is supposed to walk around the top every few minutes, but I have very little confidence in his protection. I really rely upon Hal more than the sentry to give warning, for that dog can hear the stealthy step of an Indian when a long distance from him. And I believe he can smell them, too.

We bought a beautiful buffalo-calf robe for a bed for him, and that night' I folded it down nicely and called him to it, thinking he would be delighted with so soft and warm a bed. But no! He went to it because I called him and patted it, but put one foot on it he would not. He gave a little growl, and putting his tail up, walked away with great dignity and a look of having been insulted.

Of course the skin smelled strong of the tepee and Indians. We sunned and aired it for days, and Farrar rubbed the fur with camphor and other things to destroy the Indian odor, and after much persuading and any amount of patience on our part, Hal finally condescended to use the robe. He now considers it the finest thing on earth, and keeps close watch of it at all times.

We have visits from Indians every day, and this variation from the monotony is not agreeable to me, but Faye goes out and has long powwows with them. They do not hesitate to ask for things, and the more you give the more you may.

The other morning Faye saw a buffalo calf not far from the redoubt, and decided to go for it, as we, also the men, were in need of fresh meat. So he started off on Powder-Face, taking only a revolver with him. I went outside to watch him ride off, and just as the calf disappeared over a little hill and he after it, an Indian rode down the bluff at the right, and about the same distance away as I thought Faye might be, and started in a canter straight across in the direction Faye had gone. Very soon he, also, was back of the little hill and out of sight.

I ran inside and called the sergeant, and was trying to explain the situation to him as briefly as possible when he, without waiting for me to finish, got his rifle and cartridge belt, and ordering a couple of men to follow, started off on a hard run in the direction I had designated. As soon as they reached the top of the hill they saw Faye, and saw also that the Indian was with him. The men went on over slowly, but stopped as soon as they got within rifle range of Faye, for of course the Indian would never have attempted mischief when he knew that the next instant he would be riddled with bullets. The Indian was facing the soldiers and saw them at once, but they were at Faye's back, so he did not know they were there until he turned to come home.

Faye says that the Indian was quite near before he saw him at all, as he had not been thinking of Indians in his race after the little buffalo. He came up and said "How!" of course, and then by signs asked to see Faye's revolver, which has an ivory handle with nickel barrel and trimmings, all of which the Indian saw at once, and decided to make his own without loss of time, and then by disarming Faye he would be master of things generally.

Faye pulled the pistol from its holster and held it out for the Indian to look at, but with a tight grip on the handle and finger on trigger, the muzzle pointed straight to his treacherous heart. This did not disturb the Indian in the least, for he grasped the barrel and with a twist of the wrist tried to jerk it down and out of Faye's hand. But this he failed to do, so, with a sarcastic laugh, he settled himself back on his pony to await a more favorable time when he could catch Faye off guard. He wanted that glistening pistol, and he probably wanted the fat pony also. And thus they sat facing each other for several minutes, the Indian apparently quite indifferent to pistols and all things, and Faye on the alert to protect himself against the first move of treachery.

It would have been most unsafe for Faye to have turned from the crafty savage, and just how long the heart-to-heart interview might have lasted or what would have happened no one can tell if the coming in sight of the soldiers with their long guns had not caused him to change his tactics. After a while he grunted " How! " again, and, assuming an air of great contempt for soldiers, guns, and shiny pistols, rode away and soon disappeared over the bluff. There was only the one Indian in sight, but, as the old sergeant said, " there might have been a dozen red devils just over the bluff! "

One never knows when the " red devils " are near, for they hide themselves back of a bunch of sage brush, and their ponies, whose hoofs are never shod, can get over the ground very swiftly and steal upon you almost as noiselessly as their owners. It is needless to say that we did not have fresh buffalo that day!

"He tried to jerk it out of Faye's hand."

And the buffalo calf ran on to the herd wholly unconscious of his narrow escape.

We expect to return to Camp Supply in a few days, and in many ways I shall be sorry to leave this place. It is terrible to be so isolated, when one thinks about it, especially if one should be ill. I shall miss Miss Dickinson in the garrison very much, and our daily rides together. General Dickinson and his family passed here last week on their way to his new station.

CAMP SUPPLY, INDIAN TERRITORY,
February, 1873.

UPON our return from the Cimarron we found a dear, clean house all ready for us to move into. It was a delightful surprise, and after the wretched huts we have been living in ever since we came to this post, the house with its white walls and board floors seems like fairyland. It is made of vertical logs of course, the same as the other quarters, but these have been freshly chinked, and covered on the inside with canvas. General Bourke ordered the quartermaster to fix the house for us, and I am glad that Major Knox was the one to receive the order, for I have not forgotten how disagreeable he was about the fixing up of our first house here. One can imagine how he must have fumed over the issuing of so much canvas, boards, and even the nails for the quarters of only a second lieutenant!

Many changes have been made during the few weeks General Bourke has been here, the most important having been the separating of the white troops from the colored when on guard duty. The officers and men of the colored cavalry have not liked this, naturally, but it was outrageous to put white and black in the same little guard room, and colored sergeants over white corporals and privates. It was good cause for desertion. But all that is at an end now. General Dickinson is no longer commanding officer, and best of all, the colored troops have been ordered to another department, and the two troops of white cavalry that are to relieve them are here now and in camp not far from the post, waiting for the barracks to be vacated.

We have felt very brave since the camp has been established, and two days ago several of us drove over to a Cheyenne village that is a mile or so up the creek. But soon after we got there we did not feel a bit brave, for we had not been out of the ambulance more than five minutes, when one of their criers came racing in on a very wet pony, and rode like mad in and out among the tepees, all the time screaming something at the top of his voice.

Instantly there was a jabbering by all of them and great commotion. Each Indian talked and there seemed to be no one to listen. Several tepees were taken down wonderfully quick, and a number of ponies were hurried in, saddled, and ridden away at race speed, a few squaws wailing as they watched them go, guns in their hands. Other squaws stood around looking at us, and showing intense hatred through their wicked eyes. It was soon discovered by all of us that the village was really not attractive, and four scared women came back to the garrison as fast as government mules could bring them! What was the cause of so much excitement we will probably never know—and of course we should not have gone there

"Saddled, and ridden away at race speed."

without an officer, and yet, what could one man have done against all those savages!

We were honored by a visit from a chief the other day. He was a Cheyenne from the village, presumably, and his name was White Horse. He must have been born a chief for he was young, very dignified, and very good-looking, too, for an Indian. Of course his face was painted in a hideous way, but his leggings and clothing generally were far more tidy than those of most Indians. His chest was literally covered with polished teeth of animals, beads, and wampum, arranged artistically in a sort of breastplate, and his scalp lock, which had evidently been plaited with much care, was ornamented with a very beautiful long feather.

Fortunately Faye was at home when he came, for he walked right in, unannounced, except the usual "How!" Faye gave him a chair, and this he placed in the middle of the room in a position so he could watch both doors, and then his rifle was laid carefully upon the floor at his right side. He could speak his name, but not another word of English, so, thinking to entertain him, Faye reached for a rifle that was standing in one corner of the room to show him, as it was of a recent make. Although the rifle was almost at the Indian's back the suspicious savage saw what Faye was doing, and like a flash he seized his own gun and laid it across his knees, all the time looking straight at Faye to see what he intended to do next. Not a muscle of his face moved, but his eyes were wonderful, brilliant, and piercing, and plainly said, "Go ahead, I'm ready!"

I saw the whole performance and was wondering if I had not better run for assistance, when Faye laughed, and motioned the Indian to put his rifle down again, at the same time pulling the trigger of his own to assure him that it was not loaded. This apparently satisfied him, but he did not put his gun back on the floor, but let it rest across his knees all the time he sat there. And that was for the longest time—and never once did he change his position, turn his head, or, as we could see, move an eyelid! But nevertheless he made one feel that it was not necessary for him to turn his head—that it was all eyes, that he could see up and down and across and could read one's very thoughts, too.

The Indian from whom we bought Powder-Face —his name is Dog, you will remember—has found us out, and like a dog comes every day for something to eat. He always walks right into the kitchen; if the door is closed he opens it. If he is not given things he stands around with the greatest patience, giving little grunts now and then, and watches Farrar until the poor soldier becomes worn out and in self-defense gives him something, knowing full well all the time that trouble is being stored up for the next day. The Indian never seems cross, but smiles at everything, which is most unusual in a savage.

With the white cavalry is a classmate of Faye's, Lieutenant Isham, and yesterday I went out to camp with him and rode his horse, a large, spirited animal. It was the horse's first experience with a side saddle, and at first he objected to the habit and jumped around and snorted quite a little, but he soon saw that I was really not a dangerous person and quieted down.

As Lieutenant Isham and I were cantering along at a nice brisk gait we met Faye, who was returning from the camp on Powder-Face, and it could be plainly seen that he disapproved of my mount. But he would not turn back with us, however, and we went on to camp without him. There is something very fascinating about a military camp—it is always so precise and trim—the little tents for the men pitched in long straight lines, each one looking as though it had been given especial attention, and with all things is the same military precision and neatness. It was afternoon stables and we rode around to the picket lines to watch the horses getting their grooming.

When I got home Faye was quick to tell me that I would certainly be killed if I continued to ride every untrained horse that came along! Not a very pleasant prospect for me; but I told him that I did not want to mortify him and myself, too, by refusing to mount horses that his own classmates, particularly those in the cavalry, asked me to ride, and that I knew very well he would much prefer to see me on a spirited animal than a " gentle ladies' horse " that any inexperienced rider could manage. So we decided that the horse, after all, was not a vicious beast, and I am to ride him again to-morrow.

Last evening we gave a delightful little dance in the hall in honor of the officers and their wives who are to go, and the officers who have come. We all wore our most becoming gowns, and anyone unacquainted with army life on the frontier would have been surprised to see what handsome dresses can be brought forth, even at this far-away post, when occasion demands. There are two very pretty girls from the East visiting in the garrison, and several of the wives of officers are young and attractive, and the mingling of the pretty faces and bright-colored dresses with the dark blue and gold of the uniforms made a beautiful scene. It is not in the least surprising that girls become so silly over brass buttons. Even the wives get silly over them sometimes!

CAMP SUPPLY, INDIAN TERRITORY,
April, 1873.

IN the last mail Faye heard from his application for transfer to another company, and the order will be issued as soon as the lieutenant in that company has been promoted, which will be in a few weeks. This will take us back to Fort Lyon with old friends, and Faye to a company whose captain is a gentleman. He was one of Faye's instructors at West Point.

I have a new horse—and a lively one, too—so lively that I have not ridden him yet. He was a present from Lieutenant Isham, and the way in which he happened to possess him makes a pretty little story. The troop had been sent out on a scout, and was on its way back to the post to be paid, when one evening this pony trotted into camp and at once tried to be friendly with the cavalry horses, but the poor thing was so frightfully hideous with its painted coat the horses would not permit him to come near them for some time. But the men caught him and brought him on to the stables, where there was trouble at once, for almost every man in the troop claimed ownership. So it was finally decided by the captain that as soon as the troop had been paid the horse should be raffled, that each man in that one troop could have the privilege of buying a chance at one dollar, and that the money should go in the troop fund. This arrangement delighted the men, as it promised something new in the way of a frolic.

In due time the paymaster arrived, the men were paid, and then in a few minutes there was brisk business going on over at the quarters of the troop! Every enlisted man in the troop—sergeants, corporals, and privates, eighty-four in all—bought a chance, thus making a fine sum for the fund. A private won the horse, of whom Lieutenant Isham immediately bought him and presented him to me.

He is about fifteen hands high and not in the least of a pony build, but is remarkably slender, with fine head and large intelligent eyes. Just what his color is we do not know, for he is stained in red-brown stripes all over his body, around his legs, and on his face, but we think he is a light gray. When he wandered to camp, a small bell was tied around his neck with a piece of red flannel, and this, with his having been so carefully stained, indicates almost conclusively that he was a pet. Some of the soldiers insist that he was a race pony, because he is not only very swift, but has been taught to take three tremendous jumps at the very beginning of his run, which gives him an immense advantage, but which his rider may sometimes fail to appreciate. These jumps are often taught the Indian race ponies. The horse is gentle with Faye and is certainly graceful, but he is hard to hold and inclined to bolt, so I will not try him until he becomes more civilized.

The Indians are very bold again. A few days ago

Lieutenant Golden was in to luncheon, and while we were at the table we saw several Kiowas rush across the creek and stampede five or six horses that belonged to our milkman, who has a ranch just outside the garrison. In a few minutes an orderly appeared with an order for Lieutenant Golden and ten men to go after them without delay, and bring the horses back.

Of course he started at once, and chased those Indians all the afternoon, and got so close to them once or twice that they saw the necessity of lightening the weight on their tired ponies, and threw off their old saddles and all sorts of things, even little bags of shot, but all the time they held on to their guns and managed to keep the stolen horses ahead of them. They had extra ponies, too, that they swung themselves over on when the ridden beasts began to lag a little. When night came on Lieutenant Golden was compelled to give up the chase, and had to return to the post without having recovered one of the stolen horses.

One never knows here what dreadful things may come up any moment. Everything was quiet and peaceful when we sat down to luncheon, yet in less than ten minutes we saw the rush of the Indians and the stampede of the milkman's horses right from our dining-room window. The horses were close to the post too. Splendid cavalry horses were sent after them, but it requires a very swift horse to overtake those tough little Indian ponies at any time, and the Kiowas probably were on their best ponies when they stampeded the horses, for they knew, undoubtedly, that cavalry would soon be after them.

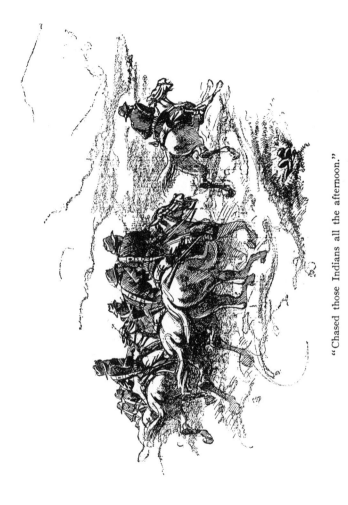

"Chased those Indians all the afternoon."

DODGE CITY, KANSAS,
June, 1873.

WE reached this place yesterday, expecting to take the cars this morning for Granada, but the servant who was to have come from Kansas City on that train will not be here until to-morrow. When the time came to say good-by, I was sorry to leave a number of the friends at Camp Supply, particularly Mrs. Hunt, with whom we stayed the last few days, while we were packing. Everyone was at the ambulance to see us off—except the Phillips family.

We were three days coming up, because of one or two delays the very first day. One of the wagons broke down soon after we left the post, and an hour or so was lost in repairing it, and at Buffalo Creek we were delayed a long time by an enormous herd of buffalo. It was a sight that probably we will never see again. The valley was almost black with the big animals, and there must have been hundreds and hundreds of them on either side of the road. They seemed very restless, and were constantly moving about instead of grazing upon the buffalo grass, which is unusually fine along that valley, and this made us suspect that they had been chased and hunted until the small bands had been driven together into one big herd. Possibly the hunters had done this themselves, so the slaughter could be the greater and the easier. It is remarkable that such grand-looking beasts should have so little sense as to invariably cross the road right in front of moving teams, and fairly challenge one to make targets of them. It was this crossing of large numbers that detained us so long yesterday.

When we got out about fifteen miles on the road, an Apache Indian appeared, and so suddenly that it seemed as if he must have sprung up from the ground. He was in full war dress—that is, no dress at all except the breech clout and moccasins—and his face and whole naked body were stained in many colors in the most hideous manner. In his scalp lock was fastened a number of eagle feathers, and of course he wore two or three necklaces of beads and wampum. There was nothing unusual about the pony he was riding, except that it was larger and in better condition than the average Indian horse, but the one he was leading—undoubtedly his war horse—was a most beautiful animal, one of the most beautiful I ever saw.

The Apache evidently appreciated the horse, for he had stained only his face, but this had been made quite as frightful as that of the Indian. The pony was of a bright cream color, slender, and with a perfect head and small ears, and one could see that he was quick and agile in every movement. He was well groomed, too. The long, heavy mane had been parted from ears to withers, and then twisted and roped on either side with strips of some red stuff that ended in long streamers, which were blown out in a most fantastic way when the pony was running. The long tail was roped only enough to fasten at the top a number of strips of the red that hung almost to the ground over the hair. Imagine all this savage hideousness rushing upon you—on a yellow horse with a mane of waving red! His very presence on an ordinary trotting pony was enough to freeze the blood in one's veins.

That he was a spy was plainly to be seen, and we

knew also that his band was probably not far away. He seemed in very good spirits, asked for " tobac," and rode along with us some distance—long enough to make a careful estimate of our value and our strength.

"Imagine all this savage hideousness rushing upon you!"

Finally he left us and disappeared over the hills. Then the little escort of ten men received orders from Faye to be on the alert, and hold themselves and their rifles ready for a sudden attack.

We rode on and on, hoping to reach the Cimarron Redoubt before dark, but that had to be given up

9

and camp was made at Snake Creek, ten miles the other side. Not one Indian had been seen on the road except the Apache, and this made us all the more uncomfortable. Snake Creek was where the two couriers were shot by Indians last summer, and that did not add to our feelings of security—at least not mine. We were in a little *coulée*, too, where it would have been an easy matter for Indians to have sneaked upon us. No one in the camp slept much that night, and most of the men were walking post to guard the animals. And those mules! I never heard mules, and horses also, sneeze and cough and make so much unnecessary noise as those animals made that night. And Hal acted like a crazy dog—barking and growling and rushing out of the tent every two minutes, terrifying me each time with the fear that he might have heard the stealthy step of a murderous savage.

Everyone lived through the night, however, but we were all glad to make an early start, so before daylight we were on the road. The old sergeant agreed with Faye in thinking that we were in a trap at the camp, and should move on early. We did not stop at the Redoubt, but I saw as we passed that the red curtains were still at the little window.

It seems that we are not much more safe in this place than we were in camp in an Indian country. The town is dreadful and has the reputation of being one of the very worst in the West since the railroad has been built. They say that gamblers and all sorts of "toughs" follow a new road. After breakfast this morning we started for a walk to give Hal a little run, but when we got to the office the hotel proprietor told us that the dog must be led, otherwise he would

undoubtedly be stolen right before our eyes. Faye
said: " No one would dare do such a thing; I would
have him arrested." But the man said there was no
one here who would make the arrest, as there certainly
would be two or more revolvers to argue with first,
and in any case the dog would be lost to us, for if the
thief saw that he could not hold him the dog would
undoubtedly be shot. Just imagine such a thing! So
Hal was led by his chain, but he looked so abused and
miserable, and I was so frightened and nervous, our
outing was short, and here we are shut up in our little
room.

We can see the car track from the window, and I
wonder how it will seem to go over in a car, the country that we came across in wagons only one year ago.
From Granada we will go to the post in an ambulance, a distance of forty or more miles. But a ride
of fifty miles over these plains has no terrors for me
now. The horses, furniture, and other things went
on in a box car this morning. It is very annoying to
be detained here so long, and I am a little worried
about that girl. The telegram says she was too sick
to start yesterday.

FORT LYON, COLORADO TERRITORY,
June, 1873.

IT has been impossible for me to write before, for I
have been more than busy, both day and night, ever
since we got here. The servant for whom we waited
at Dodge City, and who I had hoped would be a great
assistance to me in getting settled, came to us very
ill—almost too ill to be brought over from Granada.
But we could not leave her there with no one to take
care of her, and of course I could not remain with her,

so there was nothing else to be done—we had to bring her along. We had accepted Mrs. Wilder's invitation to stay with them a few days until we could get settled a little, but all that was changed when we got here, for we were obliged to come directly to our own house, unpack camp bedding and the mess chest, and do the best we could for ourselves and the sick girl.

The post surgeon told us as soon as he had examined the girl that she had tuberculosis in almost its last stage, and that she was threatened with double pneumonia! So you can imagine what I have been through in the way of nursing, for there was no one in the garrison who would come to assist me. The most unpleasant part of it all is, the girl is most ungrateful for all that is being done for her, and finds fault with many things. She has admitted to the doctor that she came to us for her health; that as there are only two in the family, she thought there would be so little for her to do she could ride horseback and be out of doors most of the time! What a nice arrangement it would have been—this fine lady sitting out on our lawn or riding one of our horses, and I in the kitchen preparing the dinner, and then at the end of the month humbly begging her to accept a little check for thirty dollars!

We have an excellent soldier cook, but the care of that miserable girl falls upon me, and the terrible experience we passed through at Dodge City has wholly unfitted me for anything of the kind. The second night we were there, about one o'clock, we were awakened by loud talking and sounds of people running; then shots were fired very near, and instantly there were screams of agony, " I'm shot! I'm shot! " from some person who was apparently coming across the street, and who fell directly underneath our window. We were in a little room on the second floor, and its one window was raised far up, which made it possible for us to hear the slightest sound or movement outside.

The shooting was kept up until after the man was dead, many of the bullets hitting the side of the hotel. It was simply maddening to have to stay in that room and be compelled to listen to the moans and death gurgle of that murdered man, and hear him cry, " Oh, my lassie, my poor lassie!" as he did over and over again, until he could no longer speak. It seemed as though every time he tried to say one word, there was the report of a pistol. After he was really dead we could hear the fiends running off, and then other people came and carried the body away.

The shooting altogether did not last longer than five or ten minutes, and at almost the first shot we could hear calls all over the wretched little town of " Vigilante! Vigilante! " and knew that the vigilantes were gathering, but before they could get together the murderous work had been finished. All the time there had been perfect silence throughout the hotel. The proprietor told us that he got up, but that it would have been certain death if he or anyone else had opened a door.

Hal was on the floor in a corner of our room, and began to growl after the very first scream, and I was terrified all the time for fear he would go to the open window and attract the attention of those murderers below, who would undoubtedly have commenced firing at the window and perhaps have killed all of us. But the moans of the dying man frightened the dog awfully, and he crawled under the bed, where he stayed during the rest of the horrible night. The cause of all the trouble seems to have been that a colored man undertook to carry in his wagon three or four men from Dodge City to Fort Dodge, a distance of five miles, but when he got out on the road a short distance he came to the conclusion, from their talk, that they were going to the post for evil purposes, and telling them that he would take them no farther, he turned his team around to come back home. On the way back the men must have threatened him, for when he got in town he drove to the house of some colored people who live on a corner across from the hotel and implored them to let him in, but they were afraid and refused to open the door, for by that time the men were shooting at him.

The poor man ran across the street, leaving a trail of blood that streamed from his wounds, and was brutally killed under our window. Early the next morning, when we crossed the street to go to the cars, the darky's mule was lying on the ground, dead, near the corner of the hotel, and stuck on one long ear was the murdered man's hat. Soon after we reached Granada a telegram was received giving an account of the affair, and saying also that in less than one half hour after the train had passed through, Dodge City was surrounded by troops of United States cavalry from Fort Dodge, that the entire town was searched for the murderers, but that not even a trace of one had been discovered.

When I got inside a car the morning after that awful, awful night, it was with a feeling that I was leaving behind me all such things and that by evening I would be back once more at our old army home and away from hostile Indians, and hostile desperadoes too. But when I saw that servant girl with the pale, emaciated face and flushed cheeks, so ill she could barely sit up, my heart went down like lead and Indians seemed small trials in comparison to what I saw ahead of me.

Well, she will go in a few days, and then I can give the house some attention. The new furniture and china are all here, but nothing has been done in the way of getting settled. The whole coming back has been cruelly disappointing, and I am so tired and nervous I am afraid of my own shadow. So after a while I think I will go East for a few weeks, which I know you will be glad to hear.

FORT LYON, COLORADO TERRITORY,
August, 1873.

WE have just come in from a drive to the Purgatoire with Colonel Knight behind his handsome horses. It makes me sad, always, to go over that familiar road and to scenes that are so closely associated with my learning to ride and shoot when we were here before. The small tree that was my target is dead but still standing, and on it are several little pieces of the white paper bull's eyes that Faye and Lieutenant Baldwin tacked on it for me.

We often see poor Tom. The post trader bought him after Lieutenant Baldwin's death, so the dear horse would always have good care and not be made to bring and carry for a cruel master. He wanders about as he chooses and is fat, but the coat that was once so silky and glossy is now dull and faded, and the horse looks spiritless and dejected. Poor Tom! The greyhound, Magic, still remembers their many, many hunts together when the horse would try to outrun the dog, and the hound often goes out to make him little visits, and the sight is pathetic. That big dog of the chaplain's is still here, and how the good man can conscientiously have him about, I cannot understand.

Colonel Knight has two large dogs also, but they are shut in the stable most of the time to guard his pair of valuable horses. The horses are not particularly fast or spirited, but they are very beautiful and perfectly matched in color and gait.

Ever since Hal has been old enough to run with a horse, he has always gone with me riding or driving. So the first time we drove with Colonel Knight I called Hal to go with us and he ran out of the house and over the fence with long joyful bounds, to be instantly pounced upon, and rolled over into the *acéquia* by the two big dogs of Colonel Knight's that I had not even heard of! Hal has splendid fighting blood and has never shown cowardice, but he is still a young dog and inexperienced, and no match for even one old fighter, and to have two notoriously savage, bloodthirsty beasts gnawing at him as though he was a bone was terrible. But Hal apparently never thought of running from them, and after the one howl of surprise gave his share of vicious growls and snaps. But the old dogs were protected by their heavy hair, while Hal's short coat and fine skin were easily torn.

We all rushed to his rescue, for it looked as though he would be torn in pieces, and when I saw a long cut in his tender skin I was frantic. But finally the

two black dogs were pulled off and Hal was dragged
out of the ditch and back to the house, holding back
and growling all the time, which showed plainly he
was not satisfied with the way the affair had ended.
The drive that day I did not enjoy!

Hal was not torn so deeply as to have unsightly
scars, for which I was thankful. From that day on,

"Hal . . . has always gone with me riding or driving."

however, he not only hated those dogs, but disliked
the man who cares for them, and seemed to consider
him responsible for their very existence. And it was
wonderful that he should recognize Cressy's step on
the ground as he passed at the side of our house. Several times when he would be stretched out on the
floor, to all appearances fast asleep, I have seen him

open his eyes wide and growl when the man and dogs were passing, although it was perfectly impossible for him to have seen them.

One morning about ten days ago when I was on the second floor, I heard an awful noise downstairs—whines, growls, and howls all so mingled together one would have thought there were a dozen dogs in the house. I ran down to see what could possibly be the matter, and found Hal at a window in the dining room that looked out on the back yard, every hair on his brindled back standing straight up and each white tooth showing. Looking out I saw that Turk, the more savage of the two black dogs, was in the yard and could not get out over the high board fence. Cressy was probably on guard that day, and sentry over the prisoners who had brought water. The dog must have followed him in and then managed to get left.

Hal looked up at me, and for one instant kept perfectly still, waiting to see what I would do. His big brown eyes were almost human in their beseeching, and plainly said, " You cannot have forgotten—you will surely let me out! " And let him out I did. I opened the doors leading to the yard, and almost pushing me over he rushed to the black dog with great leaps and the most blood-curdling growls, jumping straight over him, then around him, then over him again and again, and so like a whirlwind, the poor black beast was soon crazy, for snap as fast as he might, it was ever at the clear, beautiful air. Hal was always just out of reach.

After he had worried the dog all he wanted to Hal. proceeded to business. With a greyhound trick, he

swung himself around with great force and knocked
the big dog flat upon the ground, and holding him
down with his two paws he pulled out mouthful after
mouthful of long hair, throwing it out of his mouth
right and left. If the dog attempted to raise his big
head Hal was quick to give a wicked snap that made
the head fall down again. When I saw that Hal had
actually conquered the dog and had proved that he
was the splendid hound I had ever considered him to
be, I told West to go out at once and separate them.
But for the very first time West was slow—he went
like a snail. It seemed that one of the dogs had
snapped at his leg once, and I believe he would have
been delighted if Hal had gnawed the dog flesh
and bone. He pulled Hal in by his collar and opened
the gate for Turk, and soon things were quite once
more.

All that day Hal's eyes were like stars, and one
could almost see a grin on his mouth. He was ever
on the alert, and would frequently look out on the
yard, wag his tail and growl. The strangest thing
about it all is, that not once since that morning has he
paid the slightest attention to Cressy or the two dogs,
except to growl a little when they have happened to
meet. Turk must have told his companion about the
fight, for he, too, finds attractions in another direction when he sees Hal coming.

Some of our friends have found pleasure in teasing
me about my sporting taste, private arena, and so on,
but I do not mind so very much, since the fight
brought about peace, and proved that Hal has plenty
of pluck. Those two Knight dogs are looked upon as
savage wolves by every mother in the garrison, and

when it is known that they are out, mothers and nurses run to gather in their small people.

Hal has developed a taste for hunting that has been giving trouble lately, when he has run off with Magic and the other hounds. So now he is chained until after guard mounting, by which time the pack has gone. The signal officer of the department was here the other day when Faye and men from the company were out signaling, and after luncheon I told West to go out to him on Powder-Face and lead King, so he could ride the horse in, instead of coming in the wagon with the men. Late in the afternoon West came back and reported that he had been unable to find Faye, and then with much hesitation and choking he told me that he had lost Hal!

He said that as they had gone up a little hill, they had surprised a small band of antelope that were grazing rather near on the other side, and that the hound started after them like a streak, pulling one down before they had crossed the lowland, and then, not being satisfied, he had raced on again after the band that had disappeared over a hill farther on. That was the last he saw of him. West said that he wanted to bring the dead antelope to the post, but could not, as both horses objected to it.

My heart was almost broken over the loss of my dog, and I started for my own room to indulge in a good cry when, as I passed the front door that was open, I happened to look out, and there, squatted down on the walk to the gate was Hal! I ran out to pet him, but drew back in horror when I saw the condition he was in. His long nose and all of his white chest were covered with a thick coating of coarse an-

telope hair plastered in with dried blood. The dog
seemed too tired to move, and sat there with a listless,
far-away look that made me wish he could tell all
about his hunt, and if he had lost the second poor little
antelope. West almost danced from joy when he saw
him, and lost no time in giving him a bath and putting
him in his warm bed. Greyhounds are often great
martyrs to rheumatism, and Deacon, one of the pack,
will sometimes howl from pain after a hunt. And
the howl of a greyhound is far-reaching and something to be remembered.

Very soon now I will be with you! Faye has decided to close the house and live with the bachelors
while I am away. This will be much more pleasant
for him than staying here all alone.

FORT LYON, COLORADO TERRITORY,
October, 1873.

THE trip out was tiresome and seemed endless, but
nothing worth mentioning happened until I got
to Granada, where Faye met me with an ambulance
and escort wagon. It was after two o'clock in the
morning when the train reached the station, and as
it is the terminus of the road, every passenger left the
car. I waited a minute for Faye to come in, but as
he did not I went out also, feeling that something
was wrong.

Just as I stepped off the car, Mr. Davis, quartermaster's clerk, appeared and took my satchel, assuring
me that Faye was right there waiting for me. This
was so very unlike Faye's way of doing things, that at
once I suspected that the real truth was not being told.
But I went with him quickly through the little crowd,

and on up the platform, and then I saw Faye. He was standing at one corner of the building all alone, and I recognized him instantly by the long light-blue overcoat and big campaign hat with brim turned up.

And I saw also, standing on the corner of the platform in front of him, a soldier with rifle in hand, and on the end of it glistening in the moonlight was a long bayonet! I had lived with troops long enough to know that the bayonet would not be there unless the soldier was a sentry guarding somebody or something. I naturally turned toward Faye, but was held back by Mr. Davis, and that made me indignant, but Faye at once said quietly and in a voice just loud enough for me to hear, " Get in the ambulance and ask no questions! " And still he did not move from the corner. By this time I was terribly frightened and more and more puzzled. Drawn up close to the farther side of the platform was an ambulance, also an escort wagon, in which sat several soldiers, and handing my trunk checks to Mr. Davis, I got, into the ambulance, my teeth chattering as though I had a chill.

The very instant the trunks were loaded Faye and the sentry came, and after ordering the corporal to keep his wagon and escort close to us, and telling me to drop down in the bottom of the ambulance if I heard a shot, Faye got on the ambulance also, but in front with the driver. Leaning forward, I saw that one revolver was in his hand and the other on the seat by his side. In this way, and in perfect silence, we rode through the town and until we were well out on the open plain, when we stopped just long enough for Faye to get inside, and a soldier from the wagon to take his seat by the driver.

Then Faye told me of what had occurred to make necessary all these precautions. He had come over from Fort Lyon the day before, and had been with Major Carroll, the depot quartermaster, during the afternoon and evening. The men had established a little camp just at the edge of the miserable town where the mules could be guarded and cared for.

About nine o'clock Faye and Mr. Davis started out for a walk, but before they had gone far Faye remembered that he had left his pistols and cartridge belt on a desk in the quartermaster's office, and fearing they might be stolen they went back for them. He put the pistols on underneath his heavy overcoat, as the belt was quite too short to fasten outside.

Well, he and Mr. Davis walked along slowly in the bright moonlight past the many saloons and gambling places, never once thinking of danger, when suddenly from a dark passageway a voice said, "You are the man I want," and bang! went a pistol shot close to Faye's head—so close, in fact, that as he ducked his head down, when he saw the pistol pointed at him, the rammer slot struck his temple and cut a deep hole that at once bled profusely. Before Faye could get out one of his own pistols from underneath the long overcoat, another shot was fired, and then away skipped Mr. Davis, leaving Faye standing alone in the brilliant moonlight. As soon as Faye commenced to shoot, his would-be assassin came out from the dark doorway and went slowly along the walk, taking good care, however, to keep himself well in the shadow of the buildings.

They went on down the street shooting back and forth at each other, Faye wondering all the time why he could not hit the man. Once he got him in front of a restaurant window where there was a bright light back of him, and, taking careful aim, he thought the affair could be ended right there, but the ball whizzed past the man and went crashing through the window and along the tables, sending broken china right and left. Finally their pistols were empty, and Faye drew out a second, at the sight of which the man started to run and disappeared in the shadows.

As soon as the shooting ceased men came out from all sorts of places, and there was soon a little crowd around Faye, asking many questions, but he and Major Carroll went to a drug store, where his wounds could be dressed. For some time it was thought there must be a ball in the deep hole in his temple. When Faye had time to think he understood why he had done such poor shooting. He is an almost sure shot, but always holds his pistol in his left hand, and of course aims with his left eye. But that night his left eye was filled with blood the very first thing from the wound in his left temple, which forced him unconsciously to aim with his right eye, which accounts for the wild shots.

The soldiers heard of the affair in camp, and several came up on a run and stood guard at the drug store. A rumor soon got around that Oliver had gone off to gather some of his friends, and they would soon be at the store to finish the work. Very soon, however, a strange man came in, much excited, and said, " Lieutenant! Oliver's pals are getting ready to attack you at the depot as the train comes in," and out he went. The train was due at two o'clock A. M., and this caused Faye four hours of anxiety. He learned

"The little black shaved-tails pulled the ambulance."

that the man who shot at him was "Billy Oliver," a horse thief and desperado of the worst type, and that he was the leader of a band of horse thieves that was then in town. To be threatened by men like those was bad enough in itself, but Faye knew that I would arrive on that train. That was the cause of so much caution when the train came in. There were several rough-looking men at the station, but if they had intended mischief, the long infantry rifles in the hands of drilled soldiers probably persuaded them to attend to their own affairs. A man told the corporal, however, that Oliver's friends had decided not to kill Faye at the station, but had gone out on horseback to meet him on the road. This was certainly misery prolonged.

The mules were driven through the town at an ordinary gait, but when we got on the plain they were put at a run, and for miles we came at that pace. The little black shaved-tails pulled the ambulance, and I think that for once they had enough run. The moonlight was wonderfully bright, and for a long distance objects could be seen, and bunches of sage bush and Spanish bayonet took the forms of horsemen, and naturally I saw danger in every little thing we passed.

One thing occurred that night that deserves mentioning. Some one told the soldiers that Oliver was hidden in a certain house, and one of them, a private, started off without leave, and all alone for that house. When he got there the entire building was dark, not a light in it, except that of the moon which streamed in through two small windows. But the gritty soldier went boldly in and searched every little room and every little corner, even the cellar, but not a living thing was found. It may have been brave, but it was a dreadful thing for the trooper to do, for he so easily could have been murdered in the darkness, and Faye and the soldiers never have known what had become of him. Colonel Bissell declares that the man shall be made a corporal upon the first vacancy.

The man Oliver was in the jail at Las Animas last summer for stealing horses. The old jail was very shaky, and while it was being made more secure, he and another man—a wife murderer—were brought to the guardhouse at this post. They finally took them back, and Oliver promptly made his escape, and the sheriff had actually been afraid to re-arrest him. We have all begged Faye to get out a warrant for the man, but he says it would simply be a farce, that the sheriff would pay no attention to it. The whole left side of Faye's face is badly swollen and very painful, and the wound in his ankle compels him to use a cane. Just how the man managed to shoot Faye in the ankle no one seems to understand.

Granada must be a terrible place! The very afternoon Faye was there a Mexican was murdered in the main street, but not the slightest attention was paid to the shooting—everything went right on as though it was an everyday occurrence. The few respectable people are afraid even to try to keep order.

Dodge City used to be that way and there was a reign of terror in the town, until finally the twelve organized vigilantes became desperate and took affairs in their own hands. They notified six of the leading desperadoes that they must be out of the place by a certain day and hour. Four went, but two were defiant and remained. When the specified hour had passed, twelve double-barreled shotguns were loaded with buckshot, and in a body the vigilantes hunted these men down as they would mad dogs and riddled each one through and through with the big shot! It was an awful thing to do, but it seems to have been absolutely necessary and the only way of establishing law and order. Our friends at Fort Dodge tell us that the place is now quite decent, and that a man can safely walk in the streets without pistols and a belt full of cartridges.

FORT LYON, COLORADO TERRITORY,
October, 1873.

ONE naturally looks for all sorts of thrilling experiences when out on the frontier, but to have men and things mix themselves up in a maddening way in one's very own house, as has recently been done in mine, is something not usually counted upon. To begin with, Mrs. Rae is with us, and her coming was not only most unlooked for up to two days ago, but through a wretched mistake in a telegram she got here just twenty-four hours before we thought she would arrive. Ordinarily this would have been a delightful surprise, but, unfortunately, things had begun to " mix! "

Faye had suffered so much from the wound in his head that very little attention had been given the house since my return from the East, therefore it was not in the very best of order. It was closed during my two months' absence, as Faye had lived down with the bachelors. The very day that Mrs. Rae came the quartermaster had sent a man to repair one of the chimneys, and plaster and dirt had been left in my room, the one I had intended Mrs. Rae to occupy.

And then, to make matters just as bad as possible, there was a sand storm late in the afternoon that had, of course, sifted dust over all things.

But this was not all! My nerves had not recovered from the shock at Granada, and had given out entirely that day just before dinner, and had sent me to bed with an uncomfortable chill. Still, I was not disheartened. Before I went East many things had been put away, but West had unpacked and polished the silver several days before, and the glass was shining and the china closets in perfect order, all of which had been attended to with my own hands. Besides, the wife of one of the sergeants was to come the next morning to dust and clean the little house from top to bottom, so there was really nothing to worry about, as everything would be in order long before time for the stage to arrive that would bring Mrs. Rae.

But after the chill came a fever, and with the fever came dreams, most disturbing dreams, in which were sounds of crunching gravel, then far-away voices— voices that I seemed to have heard in another world. A door was opened, and then—oh! how can I ever tell you—in the hall came Faye's mother! By that time dreams had ceased, and it was cruel reality that had to be faced, and even now I wonder how I lived through the misery of that moment—the longing to throw myself out of the window, jump in the river, do anything, in fact, but face the mortification of having her see the awful condition of her son's house!

Her son's house—that was just it. I did not care at all for myself, my only thought was for Faye whose mother might find cause to *pity* him for the delinquencies of his wife! First impressions are indelible, and it would be difficult to convince Mrs. Rae ever that the house was not always dusty and untidy. How could she know that with pride I had ever seen that our house, however rough it might have been, was clean and cheerful. And of what use would it be to arrange things attractively now? She would be justified in supposing that it was only in its company dress.

I was weak and dizzy from fever and a sick heart, but I managed to get dressed and go down to do the best I could. West prepared a little supper, and we made things as comfortable as possible, considering the state of affairs. Mrs. Rae was most lovely about everything—said she understood it all. But that could not be, not until she had seen one of our sand storms, from the dust of which it is impossible to protect a thing. I have been wishing for a storm ever since, so Mrs. Rae could see that I was not responsible for the condition of things that night.

Now this was not all—far, far from it. On the way out in the cars, Mrs. Rae met the colonel of the regiment—a real colonel, who is called a colonel, too—who was also on his way to this post, and with him was Lieutenant Whittemore, a classmate of Faye's. Colonel Fitz-James was very courteous to Mrs. Rae, and when they reached Kit Carson he insisted upon her coming over with him in the ambulance that had been sent to meet him. This was very much more comfortable than riding in the old stage, so she gladly accepted, and to show her appreciation of the kindness, she invited the colonel, also Lieutenant Whittemore, to dine with us the following evening!

Yes, there is still more, for it so happens that Colonel

Fitz-James is known to be an epicure, to be fussy and finical about all things pertaining to the table, and what is worse takes no pains to disguise it, and in consequence is considered an undesirable dinner guest by the most experienced housekeepers in the regiment. All this I had often heard, and recalled every word during the long hours of that night as I was making plans for the coming day. The combination in its entirety could not have been more formidable. There was Faye's mother, a splendid housekeeper—her very first day in our house. His colonel and an abnormally sensitive palate—his very first meeting with each of us. His classmate, a young man of much wealth—a perfect stranger to me. A soldier cook, willing, and a very good waiter, but only a plain everyday cook; certainly not a maker of dainty dishes for a dinner party. And my own experiences in housekeeping had been limited to log huts in outlandish places.

Every little thing for that dinner had to be prepared in our own house. There was no obliging caterer around the corner where a salad, an ice, and other things could be hurriedly ordered; not even one little market to go to for fish, flesh, or fowl; only the sutler's store, where their greatest dainty is " cove " oysters! Fortunately there were some young grouse in the house which I had saved for Mrs. Rae and which were just right for the table, and those West could cook perfectly.

So with a head buzzing from quinine I went down in the morning, and with stubborn determination that the dinner should be a success, I proceeded to carry out the plans I had decided upon during the night.

The house was put in splendid order and the dinner prepared, and Colonel Knight was invited to join us. I attempted only the dishes that could be served well —nothing fancy or difficult—and the sergeant's wife remained to assist West in the kitchen. It all passed off pleasantly and most satisfactorily, and Colonel Fitz-James could not have been more agreeable, although he looked long and sharply at the soldier when he first appeared in the dining room. But he said not a word; perhaps he concluded it must be soldier or no dinner. I have been told several nice things he said about that distracting dinner before leaving the garrison. But it all matters little to me now, since it was not found necessary to take me to a lunatic asylum!

Mrs. Rae saw in a paper that Faye had been shot by a desperado, and was naturally much alarmed, so she sent a telegram to learn what had happened, and in reply Faye telegraphed for her to come out, and fearing that he must be very ill she left Boston that very night. But we understood that she would start the next day, and this misinterpretation caused my undoing—that and the sand storm.

That man Oliver has at last been arrested and is now in the jail at Las Animas, chained with another man—a murderer—to a post in the dark cellar. This is because he has so many times threatened the jailer. He says that some day he will get out, and then his first act will be to kill the keeper, and the next to kill Lieutenant Rae. He also declares that Faye kicked him when he was in the guardhouse at the post. Of course anyone with a knowledge of military discipline would know this assertion to be false, for if Faye had done such a thing as that, he might have been court-martialed.

The sheriff was actually afraid to make the arrest the first time he went over, because so many of Oliver's friends were in town, and so he came back without him, although he saw him several times. The second trip, however, Oliver was taken off guard and was handcuffed and out of the town before he had a chance to rally his friends to his assistance. He was brought to Las Animas during the night to avoid any possibility of a lynching. The residents of the little town are full of indignation that the man should have attempted to kill an officer of this garrison. He is a horse thief and desperado, and made his escape from their jail several months back, so altogether they consider that the country can very well do without him. I think so, too, and wish every hour in the day that the sheriff had been less cautious. Oliver cannot be tried until next May, when the general court meets, and I am greatly distressed over this fact, for the jail is old and most insecure, and he may get out at any time. The fear and dread of him is on my mind day and night.

FORT LYON, COLORADO TERRITORY,
December, 1873.

EVERYONE in the garrison seems to be more or less in a state of collapse! The *bal masqué* is over, the guests have departed, and all that is left to us now are the recollections of a delightful party that gave full return for our efforts to have it a success.

We did not dream that so many invitations would be accepted at far-away posts, that parties would come from Fort Leavenworth, Fort Riley, Fort Dodge, and

Fort Wallace, for a long ambulance ride was necessary from each place. But we knew of their coming in time to make preparations for all, so there was no confusion or embarrassment. Every house on the officers' line was filled to overflowing and scarcely a corner left vacant.

The new hospital was simply perfect for an elaborate entertainment. The large ward made a grand ballroom, the corridors were charming for promenading, and, yes, flirting, the dining room and kitchen perfect for the supper, and the office and other small rooms were a nice size for cloak rooms. Of course each one of these rooms, big and small, had to be furnished. In each dressing room was a toilet table fitted out with every little article that might possibly be needed during the evening, both before and after the removal of masks. All this necessitated much planning, an immense amount of work, and the stripping of our own houses. But there were a good many of us, and the soldiers were cheerful assistants. I was on the supper committee, which really dwindled down to a committee of one at the very last, for I was left alone to put the finishing touches to the tables and to attend to other things. The vain creatures seemed more interested in their own toilets, and went home to beautify themselves.

The commanding officer kept one eye, and the quartermaster about a dozen eyes upon us while we were decorating, to see that no injury was done to the new building. But that watchfulness was unnecessary, for the many high windows made the fastening of flags an easy matter, as we draped them from the casing of one window to the casing of the next, which covered much of the cold, white walls and gave an air of warmth and cheeriness to the rooms. Accoutrements were hung everywhere, every bit of brass shining as only an enlisted man can make it shine, and the long infantry rifles with fixed bayonets were "stacked" wherever they would not interfere with the dancing.

Much of the supper came from Kansas City—that is, the celery, fowls, and material for little cakes, ices, and so on—and the orchestra consisted of six musicians from the regimental band at Fort Riley. The floor of the ballroom was waxed perfectly, but it is hoped by some of us that much of the lightning will be taken from it before the hospital cots and attendants are moved in that ward.

Everybody was *en masque* and almost everyone wore fancy dress and some of the costumes were beautiful. The most striking figure in the rooms, perhaps, was Lieutenant Alden, who represented *Death!* He is very tall and very slender, and he had on a skin-tight suit of dark-brown drilling, painted from crown to toe with thick white paint to represent the skeleton of a human being; even the mask that covered the entire head was perfect as a skull. The illusion was a great success, but it made one shiver to see the awful thing walking about, the grinning skull towering over the heads of the tallest. And ever at its side was a red devil, also tall, and so thin one wondered what held the bones together. This red thing had a long tail. The devil was Lieutenant Perkins, of course.

Faye and Doctor Dent were dressed precisely alike, as sailors, the doctor even wearing a pair of Faye's shoes. They had been very sly about the twin arrangement, which was really splendid, for they are just about the same size and have hair very much the same color. But smart as they were, I recognized Faye at once. The idea of anyone thinking I would not know him!

We had queens and milkmaids and flower girls galore, and black starry nights and silvery days, and all sorts of things, many of them very elegant. My old yellow silk, the two black lace flounces you gave me, and a real Spanish mantilla that Mrs. Rae happened to have with her, made a handsome costume for me as a Spanish lady. I wore almost all the jewelry in the house; every piece of my own small amount and much of Mrs. Rae's, the nicest of all having been a pair of very large old-fashioned "hoop" earrings, set all around with brilliants. My comb was a home product, very showy, but better left to the imagination.

The dancing commenced at nine o'clock, and at twelve supper was served, when we unmasked, and after supper we danced again and kept on dancing until five o'clock! Even then a few of us would have been willing to begin all over, for when again could we have such a ballroom with perfect floor and such excellent music to dance by? But with the new day came a new light and all was changed, much like the change of a ballet with a new calcium light, only ours was not beautifying, but most trying to tired, painted faces; and seeing each other we decided that we could not get home too fast. In a few days the hospital will be turned over to the post-surgeon, and the beautiful ward will be filled with iron cots and sick soldiers, and instead of delicate perfumes, the odor of nauseous drugs will pervade every place.

I have been too busy to ride during the past week,

but am going out this afternoon with the chaplain's young daughter, who is a fearless rider, although only fourteen. King is very handsome now and his gait delightful, but he still requires most careful management. He ran away with me the other day, starting with those three tremendous strides, but we were out on a level and straight road, so nothing went wrong. All there was for me to do was to keep my seat. Lieutenant Perkins and Miss Campbell were a mile or more ahead of us, and after he had passed them he came down to a trot, evidently flattering himself that he had won a race, and that nothing further was expected of him.

He jumps the cavalry hurdles beautifully—goes over like a deer, Hal always following directly back of him. Whatever a horse does that dog wants to do also. Last spring, when we came up from Camp Supply, he actually tried to eat the corn that dropped from King's mouth as he was getting his supper one night in camp. He has scarcely noticed Powder-Face since the very day King was sent to me, but became devoted to the new horse at once. I wonder if he could have seen that the new horse was the faster of the two!

FORT LYON, COLORADO TERRITORY,
May, 1874.

THERE is such good news to send you to-day I can hardly write it fast enough. The Territorial Court has been in session, and yesterday that horse thief, Billy Oliver, was tried and sentenced to ten years' imprisonment in the penitentiary! The sheriff and a posse started for Cañon City this morning with him and another prisoner, and I hope that he will not make his escape on the way over. The sheriff told Faye confidentially the route he intended to take, which is not at all the one he is supposed to be going over, and threw out strong hints to the effect that if he wanted to put an end to the man's vicious career there would be no interference from him (the sheriff) or his posse. He even told Faye of a lonesome spot where it could be accomplished easily and safely!

This was a strange thing for a sheriff to do, even in this country of desperadoes, and shows what a fiend he considers Oliver to be. He said that the man was the leader of a gang of the lowest and boldest type of villains, and that even now it would be safer to have him out of the way. Sheriffs are afraid of these men, and do not like to be obliged to arrest them.

The day of the trial, and as Faye was about to go to the court room, a corporal came to the house and told him that he had just come from Las Animas, where he had heard from a reliable source that many of Oliver's friends were in the town, and that it was their intention to kill Faye as he came in the court room. He even described the man who was to do the dreadful work, and he told Faye that if he went over without an escort he would certainly be killed.

This was simply maddening, and I begged Faye to ask for a guard, but he would not, insisting that there was not the least danger, that even a desperado would not dare shoot an army officer in Las Animas in a public place, for he knew he would be hung the next moment. That was all very well, but it seemed to me that it would be better to guard against the murder itself rather than think of what would be done to the murderer. I knew that the corporal would never have come to the house if he had not heard much that was alarming.

So Faye went over without a guard, but did condescend to wear his revolvers. He says that the first thing he saw as he entered the court room were six big, brawny cavalrymen, each one a picked man, selected for bravery and determination. Of course each trooper was armed with large government revolvers and a belt full of cartridges. He also saw that they were sitting near, and where they could watch every move of a man who answered precisely to the corporal's description, and as he passed on up through the crowd he almost touched him. His hair was long and hung down on his shoulders about a face that was villainous, and he was " armed to the teeth." There were other tough-looking men seated near this man, each one armed also.

Colonel Bissell had heard of the threat to kill Faye, and ordered a corporal, the very man who searched so bravely through the dark house for Oliver at Granada, and five privates to the court, with instructions to shoot at once the first and every man who made the slightest move to harm Faye! Those men knew very well what the soldiers were there for, and I imagine that after one look at their weather-beaten faces, which told of many an Indian campaign, the villains decided that it would be better to keep quiet and let Oliver manage his own affairs.

A sergeant and one or two privates were summoned by Oliver to give testimony against Faye, but each one told the same story, and said most emphatically that Faye had not done more than speak to the man in the line of duty, and as any officer would have done. Directly after guard mounting, and as the new guard marches up to the guardhouse, the old guard is ordered out, also the prisoners, and the prisoners stand in the middle of the line with soldiers at each end, and every man, enlisted man and prisoner, is required to stand up straight and in line. It was at one of these times that Oliver claimed that Faye kicked him, when he was officer of the day. Faye and Major Tilford say that the man was slouching, and Faye told him to stand up and take his hands out of his pockets. A small thing to murder an officer for, but I imagine that any sort of discipline to a man of his character was most distasteful.

Of course Faye left the court room as soon as his testimony had been given. When the sentence was pronounced the judge requested all visitors to remain seated until after the prisoner had been removed, which showed that he was a little afraid of trouble, and knew the bitter feeling against the horse thief in the town. Several girls and young officers from the post were outside in an ambulance, and they commenced to cheer when told of the sentence, but the judge hurried a messenger out to them with a request that they make no demonstration whatever. He is a fearless and just judge, and it is a wonder that desperadoes have not killed him long ago.

Perhaps now I can have a little rest from the terrible fear that has been ever with me day and night during the whole winter, that Oliver would escape from the old jail and carry out his threat of double murder. He had made his escape once, and I feared that he might get out again. But that post and chain must have been very securely fixed down in that cellar.

11

FORT LYON, COLORADO TERRITORY,
June, 1874.

BY this time you have my letter telling you that the regiment has been ordered to the Department of the Gulf. Since then we have heard that it is to go directly to Holly Springs, Mississippi, for the summer, where a large camp is to be established. Just imagine what the suffering will be, to go from this dry climate to the humidity of the South, and from cool, thick-walled adobe buildings to hot, glary tents in the midst of summer heat! We will reach Holly Springs about the Fourth of July. Faye's allowance for baggage hardly carries more than trunks and a few chests of house linen and silver, so we are taking very few things with us. It is better to give them away than to pay for their transportation such a long distance.

Both horses have been sold and beautiful King has gone. The young man who bought him was a stranger here, and knew absolutely nothing about the horse except what some one in Las Animas had told him. He rode him around the yard only once, and then jumping down, pulled from his pocket a fat roll of bills, counted off the amount for horse, saddle, and bridle, and then, without saying one word more than a curt "good morning," he mounted the horse again and rode out of the yard and away. I saw the whole transaction from a window—saw it as well as hot, blinding tears would permit. Faye thinks the man might have been a fugitive and wanted a fast horse to get him out of the country. We learned not long ago, you know, that King had been an Indian race pony owned by a half-breed named Bent. He sent word from Camp Supply that I was welcome to the horse if I could ride him! The chaplain has bought Powder-Face, and I am to keep him as long as we are here. Hal will go with us, for I cannot give up that dog and horses, too.

Speaking of Hal reminds me of the awful thing that occurred here a few days ago. I have written often of the pack of beautiful greyhounds owned by the cavalry officers, and of the splendid record of Magic—Hal's father—as a hunter, and how the dog was loved by Lieutenant Baldwin next to his horse.

But unless the dogs were taken on frequent hunts, they would steal off on their own account and often be away a whole day, perhaps until after dark. The other day they went off this way, and in the afternoon, as Lieutenant Alden was riding along by the river, he came to a scene that made him positively ill. On the ground close to the water was the carcass of a calf, which had evidently been filled with poison for wolves, and near it on the bank lay Magic, Deacon, Dixie, and other hounds, all dead or dying! Blue has bad teeth and was still gnawing at the meat, and therefore had not been to the water, which causes almost instant death in cases of poisoning by wolf meat.

As soon as Lieutenant Alden saw that the other dogs were past doing for, he hurried on to the post with Blue, and with great difficulty saved her life. So Hal and his mother are sole survivors of the greyhounds that have been known at many of the frontier posts as fearless and tireless hunters, and plucky fighters when forced to fight. Greyhounds will rarely seek a fight, a trait that sometimes fools other dogs and brings them to their Waterloo. When Lieutenant

Alden told me of the death of the dogs, tears came in his eyes as he said, " I have shared my bed with old Magic many a time!" And how those dogs will be missed at the bachelor quarters! When we came here last summer, I was afraid that the old hounds would pounce upon Hal, but instead of that they were most friendly and seemed to know he was one of them— a wanderer returned.

ST. CHARLES HOTEL, NEW ORLEANS, LOUISIANA,
September, 1877.

LIFE in the Army is certainly full of surprises!
    At Pass Christian yesterday morning, Faye and I were sitting on the veranda reading the papers in an indifferent sort of way, when suddenly Faye jumped up and said, " The Third has been ordered to Montana Territory!" At first I could not believe him—it seemed so improbable that troops would be sent to such a cold climate at this season of the year, and besides, most of the regiment is at Pittsburg just now because of the great coal strike. But there in the *Picayune* was the little paragraph of half a dozen lines that was to affect our lives for years to come, and which had the immediate power to change our condition of indolent content, into one of the greatest activity and excitement!

Faye went at once to the telegraph office and by wire gave up the remainder of his leave, and also asked the regimental adjutant if transportation was being provided for officers' families. The distance is so great, and the Indians have been so hostile in Montana during the past two years, that we thought families possibly would not be permitted to go.

After luncheon we packed the trunks, carefully separating things so there would be no necessity for repacking if I could not go, and I can assure you that many an article was folded down damp with hot tears —the very uncertainty was so trying. In the evening we went around to say "good-by" to a few of the friends who have been so cordial and hospitable during the summer. Early this morning we came from Pass Christian, and soon after we got here telegrams came for Faye, one ordering him to proceed to Pittsburg and report for duty, and another saying that officers' families may accompany the regiment. This was glorious news to me. The fear and dread of having to be left behind had made me really ill—and what would have become of me if it had actually come to pass I cannot imagine. I can go—that is all sufficient for the present, and we expect to leave for Pittsburg this evening at nine o'clock.

The late start gives us a long day here with nothing to do. After a while, when it is not quite so hot outside, we are going out to take a farewell look at some of our old haunts. Our friends are all out of the city, and Jackson Barracks is too far away for such a warm day—besides, there is no one there now that we know.

It seems quite natural to be in this dear old hotel, where all during the past winter our "Army and Navy Club" cotillons were danced every two weeks. And they were such beautiful affairs, with two splendid military orchestras to furnish the music, one for the dancing and one to give choice selections in between the figures. We will carry with us to the snow and ice of the Rocky Mountains many, many delightful memories of New Orleans, where the French element gives a charm to everything. The Mardi-Gras parades, in which the regiment has each year taken such a prominent part—the courtly Rex balls—the balls of Comus—the delightful Creole balls in Grünewald Hall—the stately and exclusive balls of the Washington Artillery in their own splendid hall—the charming dancing receptions on the ironclad monitor *Canonicus,* also the war ship *Plymouth,* where we were almost afraid to step, things were so immaculate and shiny—and then our own pretty army fêtes at Jackson Barracks — regimental headquarters — each and all will be remembered, ever with the keenest pleasure.

But the event in the South that has made the deepest impression of all occurred at Vicksburg, where for three weeks we lived in the same house, *en famille* and intimately, with Jefferson Davis! I consider that to have been a really wonderful experience. You probably can recall a little of what I wrote you at the time—how we were boarding with his niece in her splendid home when he came to visit her.

I remember so well the day he arrived. He knew, of course, that an army officer was in the house, and Mrs. Porterfield had told us of his coming, so the meeting was not unexpected. Still, when we went down to dinner that night I was almost shivering from nervousness, although the air was excessively warm. I was so afraid of something unpleasant coming up, for although Mrs. Porterfield and her daughter were women of culture and refinement, they were also rebels to the very quick, and never failed at any time to remind one that their uncle was " President "

Davis! And then, as we went in the large dining room, Faye in his very bluest, shiniest uniform, looked as if he might be Uncle Sam himself.

But there was nothing to fear—nothing whatever. A tall, thin old man came forward with Mrs. Porterfield to meet us—a courtly gentleman of the old Southern school—who, apparently, had never heard of the Civil War, and who, if he noticed the blue uniform at all, did not take the slightest interest in what it represented. His composure was really disappointing! After greeting me with grave dignity, he turned to Faye and grasped his hand firmly and cordially, the whole expression of his face softening just a little. I have always thought that he was deeply moved by once again seeing the Federal Blue under such friendly circumstances, and that old memories came surging back, bringing with them the almost forgotten love and respect for the Academy—a love that every graduate takes to his grave, whether his life be one of honor or of disgrace.

One could very easily have become sentimental, and fancied that he was Old West Point, misled and broken in spirit, admitting in dignified silence his defeat and disgrace to Young West Point, who, with Uncle Sam's shoulder straps and brass buttons, could be generously oblivious to the misguidance and treason of the other. We wondered many times if Jefferson Davis regretted his life. He certainly could not have been satisfied with it.

There was more in that meeting than a stranger would have known of. In the splendid dining room where we sat, which was forty feet in length and floored with tiles of Italian marble, as was the entire large basement, it was impossible not to notice the unpainted casing of one side of a window, and also the two immense patches of common gray plaster on the beautifully frescoed walls, which covered holes made by a piece of shell that had crashed through the house during the siege of Vicksburg. The shell itself had exploded outside near the servants' quarters.

Then, again, every warm evening after dinner, during the time he was at the house, Jefferson Davis and Faye would sit out on the grand, marble porch and smoke and tell of little incidents that had occurred at West Point when each had been a cadet there. At some of these times they would almost touch what was left of a massive pillar at one end, that had also been shattered and cracked by pieces of shell from U. S. gunboats, one piece being still imbedded in the white marble.

For Jefferson Davis knew that Faye's father was an officer in the Navy, and that he had bravely and boldly done his very best toward the undoing of the Confederacy; and by his never-failing, polished courtesy to that father's son—even when sitting by pieces of shell and patched-up walls—the President of the Confederacy set an example of dignified self-restraint, that many a Southern man and woman—particularly woman—would do well to follow.

For in these days of reconstruction officers and their families are not always popular. But at Pass Christian this summer we have received the most hospitable, thoughtful attention, and never once by word or deed were we reminded that we were " Yank-Tanks," as was the case at Holly Springs the first year we were there. However, we did some fine reconstruction business for Uncle Sam right there with those pert Mississippi girls—two of whom were in a short time so thoroughly reconstructed that they joined his forces " for better or for worse!"

The social life during the three years we have been in the South has most of the time been charming, but the service for officers has often been most distasteful. Many times they have been called upon to escort and protect carpetbag politicians of a very low type of manhood—men who could never command one honest vote at their own homes in the North. Faye's company has been moved twenty-one times since we came from Colorado three years ago, and almost every time it was at the request of those unprincipled carpetbaggers. These moves did not always disturb us, however, as during most of the time Faye has been adjutant general of the District of Baton Rouge, and this kept us at Baton Rouge, but during the past winter we have been in New Orleans.

Several old Creole families whose acquaintance we made in the city last winter, have charming old-style Southern homes at Pass Christian, where we have ever been cordially welcomed. It was a common occurrence for me to chaperon their daughters to informal dances at the different cottages along the beach, and on moonlight sailing parties on Mr. Payne's beautiful yacht, and then, during the entire summer, from the time we first got there, I have been captain of one side of a croquet team, Mr. Payne having been captain of the other. The croquet part was, of course, the result of Major Borden's patient and exacting teaching at Baton Rouge.

Mentioning Baton Rouge reminds me of my dear

dog that was there almost a year with the hospital steward. He is now with the company at Mount Vernon Barracks, Alabama, and Faye has telegraphed the sergeant to see that he is taken to Pittsburg with the company.

We are going out now, first of all to Michaud's for some of his delicious *biscuit glacé!* Our city friends are all away still, so there will be nothing for us to do but wander around, *pour passer le temps* until we go to the station.

MONONGAHELA HOUSE,
PITTSBURG, PENNSYLVANIA,
September, 1877.

ONCE again we have our trunks packed for the long trip to Montana, and this time I think we will go, as the special train that is to take us is now at the station, and baggage of the regiment is being hurriedly loaded. Word came this morning that the regiment would start to-night, so it seems that at last General Sherman has gained his point. For three long weeks we have been kept here in suspense—packing and then unpacking—one day we were to go, the next we were not to go, while the commanding general and the division commander were playing "tug of war" with us.

The trip will be long and very expensive, and we go from a hot climate to a cold one at a season when the immediate purchase of warm clothing is imperative, and with all this unexpected expense we have been forced to pay big hotel bills for weeks, just because of a disagreement between two generals that should have been settled in one day. Money is very precious to the poor Army at present, too, for not one dollar has been paid to officers or enlisted men for over three months! How officers with large families can possibly manage this move I do not see—sell their pay accounts I expect, and then be court martialed for having done so.

Congress failed to pass the army appropriation bill before it adjourned, consequently no money can be paid to the Army until the next session! Yet the Army is expected to go along just the same, promptly pay Uncle Sam himself all commissary and quartermaster bills at the end of each month, and without one little grumble do his bidding, no matter what the extra expense may be. I wonder what the wise men of Congress, who were too weary to take up the bill before going to their comfortable homes—I wonder what they would do if the Army as a body would say, "We are tired, Uncle, dear, and are going home for the summer to rest. You will have to get along without us and manage the Indians and strikers the best way you can." This would be about as sensible as forcing the Army to be paupers for months, and then ordering regiments from East to West and South to North. Of course many families will be compelled to remain back, that might otherwise have gone.

We are taking out a young colored man we brought up with us from Holly Springs. He has been at the arsenal since we have been here, and Hal has been with him. It is over one year since the dog saw me, and I am almost afraid he will not know me to-night at the station. Before we left Pass Christian Faye telegraphed the sergeant to bring Hal with the company and purchase necessary food for him on the way up. So, when the company got here, bills were presented by several of the men, who claimed to have bought meat for the dog, the sum total of which was nine dollars for the two days! We were so pleased to know that Hal had been so well cared for. But the soldiers were welcome to the money and more with it, for we were so glad to have the dog with us again, safe and well.

We have quite a Rae family now—Faye and I —a darky, a greyhound, and one small gray squirrel! It will be a hard trip for Billie, but I have made for him a little ribbon collar and sewed securely to it a long tape which makes a fine " picket rope " that can be tied to various things in various places, and in this way he can be picketed and yet receive exercise and air.

We are to go almost straight north from the rail-road for a distance of over four hundred miles, and of course this will take several weeks under the most favorable conditions. But you must not mind our go-ing so far away—it will be no farther than the Indian Territory, and the climate of Montana must be very much better than it was at Camp Supply, and the houses must certainly be more comfortable, as the win-ters are so long and severe. I shall be so glad to have a home of my own again, and have a horse to ride also.

Faye has just come from the station and says that almost everything has been loaded, and that we are really to start to-night at eight o'clock. This is cheer-ing news, for I think that everyone is anxious to get to Montana, except the poor officers who cannot afford to take their families with them.

Corinne, Utah Territory,
September, 1877.

WE were almost one week coming out, but finally got here yesterday morning. Our train was a special, and having no schedule, we were often side-tracked for hours at a time, to make way for the regular trains. As soon as possible after we arrived, the tents were unpacked and put up, and it was amazing to see how soon there was order out of chaos. This morning the camp looks like a little white city—streets and all. There is great activity everywhere, as preparations have already commenced for the march north. Our camp " mess " has been started, and we will be very comfortable, I think, with a good soldier cook and Cagey to take care of the tents. I am making covers for the bed, trunk, and folding table, of dark-blue cretonne with white figures, which carries out the color scheme of the folding chairs and will give a little air of cheeriness to the tent, and of the same material I am making pockets that can be pinned on the side walls of the tent, in which various things can be tucked at night. These covers and big pockets will be folded and put in the roll of bedding every morning.

There are not enough ambulances to go around, so I had my choice between being crowded in with other people, or going in a big army wagon by myself, and having had one experience in crowding, I chose the wagon without hesitation. Faye is having the rear half padded with straw and canvas on the sides and bottom, and the high top will be of canvas drawn over " bows," in true emigrant fashion. Our tent will be folded to form a seat and placed in the back, upon which I can sit and look out through the round open-

ing and gossip with the mules that will be attached
to the wagon back of me. In the front half will be
packed all of our camp furniture and things, the knock-
down bed, mess-chest, two little stoves (one for cooking), the bedding which will be tightly rolled in canvas
and strapped, and so on. Cagey will sit by the driver.
There is not one spring in the wagon, but even without, I will be more comfortable than with Mrs. Hayden and three small children. They can have
the ambulance to themselves perhaps, and will have
all the room. I thought of Billie, too. He can be
picketed all the time in the wagon, but imagine the
little fellow's misery in an ambulance with three restless children for six or eight hours each day!

Hal is with us—in fact, I can hardly get away from
the poor dog, he is so afraid of being separated from
me again. When we got to the station at Pittsburg he
was there with Cagey, and it took only one quick
glance to see that he was a heart-broken, spirit-broken
dog. Not one spark was left of the fire that made
the old Hal try to pull me through an immense plate-
glass mirror, in a hotel at Jackson, Mississippi, to fight
his own reflection (the time the strange man offered
one hundred and fifty dollars for him), and certainly
he was not the hound that whipped the big bulldog at
Monroe, Louisiana, two years ago. He did not see me
as I came up back of him, and as he had not even heard
my voice for over one year, I was almost childishly
afraid to speak to him. But I finally said, " Hal, you
have not forgotten your old friend? " He turned instantly, but as I put my hand upon his head there
was no joyous bound or lifting of the ears and tail—
just a look of recognition, then a raising up full length

of the slender body on his back legs, and putting a
forefoot on each of my shoulders as far over as he
could reach, he gripped me tight, fairly digging his
toe nails into me, and with his head pressed close to
my neck he held on and on, giving little low whines
that were more like human sobs than the cry of a dog.
Of course I had my arms around him, and of course
I cried, too. It was so pitifully distressing, for it told
how keenly the poor dumb beast had suffered during
the year he had been away from us. People stared,
and soon there was a crowd about us with an abundance of curiosity. Cagey explained the situation,
and from then on to train time, Hal was patted and
petted and given dainties from lunch baskets.

He was in the car next to ours, coming out, and we
saw him often. Many times there were long runs
across the plains, when the only thing to be seen, far
or near, would be the huge tanks containing water for
the engines. At one of these places, while we were
getting water, Cagey happened to be asleep, and a
recruit, thinking that Hal was ill-treated by being
kept tied all the time, unfastened the chain from his
collar and led him from the car.

The first thing the dog saw was another dog, and
alas! a greyhound belonging to Ryan, an old soldier.
The next thing he saw was the dear, old, beautiful
plains, for which he had pined so long and wearily.
The two dogs had never seen each other before, but
hounds are clannish and never fail to recognize their
own kind, so with one or two jumps by way of introduction, the two were off and out of sight before anyone at the cars noticed what they were doing. I was
sitting by the window in our car and saw the dogs

go over the rolling hill, and saw also that a dozen or more soldiers were running after them. I told Faye what had happened, and he started out and over the hill on a hard run. Time passed, and we in the cars watched, but neither men nor dogs came back. Finally a long whistle was blown from the engine, and in a short time the train began to move very slowly. The officers and men came running back, but the dogs were not with them! My heart was almost broken; to leave my beautiful dog on the plains to starve to death was maddening. I wanted to be alone, so to the dressing room I went, and with face buried in a portière was sobbing my very breath away when Mrs. Pierce, wife of Major Pierce, came in and said so sweetly and sympathetically: "Don't cry, dear; Hal is following the car and the conductor is going to stop the train."

Giving her a hasty embrace, I ran back to the end of the last car, and sure enough, there was Hal, the old Hal, bounding along with tail high up and eyes sparkling, showing that the blood of his ancestors was still in his veins. The conductor did not stop the train, simply because the soldiers did not give him an opportunity. They turned the brakes and then held them, and if a train man had interfered there would have been a fight right then and there.

As soon as the train was stopped Faye and Ryan were the first to go for the dogs, but by that time the hounds thought the whole affair great fun and objected to being caught—at least Ryan's dog objected. The porter in our car caught Hal, but Ryan told him to let the dog go, that he would bring the two back together. This was shrewd in Ryan, for he reasoned that Major Carleton might wait for an officer's dog, but never for one that belonged to only an enlisted man; but really it was the other way, the enlisted men held the brakes. The dogs ran back almost a mile to the water tank, and the conductor backed the train down after them, and not until both dogs were caught and on board could steam budge it ahead.

The major was in temporary command of the regiment at that time. He is a very pompous man and always in fear that proper respect will not be shown his rank, and when we were being backed down he went through our car and said in a loud voice: " I am very sorry Mrs. Rae, that you should lose your fine greyhound, but this train cannot be detained any longer—it must move on!" I said nothing, for I saw the two big men in blue at the brake in front, and knew Major Carleton would never order them away, much as he might bluster and try to impress us with his importance, for he is really a tender-hearted man.

Poor Faye was utterly exhausted from running so long, and for some time Ryan was in a critical condition. It seems that he buried his wife quite recently, and has left his only child in New Orleans in a convent, and the greyhound, a pet of both wife and little girl, is all he has left to comfort him. Everyone is so glad that he got the dog. Hal was not unchained again, I assure you, until we got here, but poor Cagey almost killed himself at every stopping place running up and down with the dog to give him a little exercise.

It is really delightful to be in a tent once more, and I am anticipating much pleasure in camping through a strange country. A large wagon train of commissary stores will be with us, so we can easily add to

12

our supplies now and then. It is amazing to see the really jolly mood everyone seems to be in. The officers are singing and whistling, and we can often hear from the distance the boisterous laughter of the men. And the wives! there is an expression of happy content on the face of each one. We know, if the world does not, that the part we are to take on this march is most important. We will see that the tents are made comfortable and cheerful at every camp; that the little dinner after the weary march, the early breakfast, and the cold luncheon are each and all as dainty as camp cooking will permit. Yes, we are sometimes called "camp followers," but we do not mind—it probably originated with some envious old bachelor officer. We know all about the comfort and cheer that goes with us, and then—we have not been left behind!

RYAN'S JUNCTION, IDAHO TERRITORY,
October, 1877.

WE are snow-bound, and everyone seems to think that we will be compelled to remain here several days. It was bright and sunny when the camp was made yesterday, but before dark a terrible blizzard came up, and by midnight the snow was deep and the cold intense. As long as we remain inside the tents we are quite comfortable with the little conical sheet-iron stoves that can make a tent very warm. And the snow that had banked around the canvas keeps out the freezing wind. We have everything for our comfort, but such weather does not make life in camp at all attractive.

Faye just came in from Major Pierce's tent, where he says he saw a funny sight. They have a large hospital tent, on each side of which is a row of iron cots, and on the cots were five chubby little children— one a mere baby—kicking up their little pink feet in jolly defiance of their patient old mammy, who was trying to keep them covered up. The tent was warm and cozy, but outside, where the snow was so deep and the cold so penetrating, one could hardly have believed that these small people could have been made so warm and happy. But Mrs. Pierce is a wonderful mother! Major Pierce was opposed to bringing his family on this long march, to be exposed to all kinds of weather, but Mrs. Pierce had no idea of being left behind with two days of car and eight days of the worst kind of stage travel between her husband and herself; so, like a sensible woman, she took matters in her own hands, and when we reached Chicago, where she had been visiting, there at the station was the smiling Mrs. Pierce with babies, governess, nurses, and trunks, all splendidly prepared to come with us— and come they all did. After the major had scolded a little and eased his conscience, he smiled as much as the other members of the family.

The children with us seem to be standing the exposure wonderfully well. One or two were pale at first, but have become rosy and strong, although there is much that must be very trying to them and the mothers also. The tents are "struck" at six sharp in the morning, and that means that we have to be up at four and breakfast at five. That the bedding must be rolled, every little thing tucked away in trunks or bags, the mess chest packed, and the cooking stove and cooking utensils not only made ready to go safely in the wagon, but they must be carried out of the tents before six o'clock. At that time the soldiers come, and, when the bugle sounds, down go the tents, and if anything happens to be left inside, it has to be fished out from underneath the canvas or left there until the tent is folded. The days are so short now that all this has to be done in the darkness, by candle or lantern light, and how mothers can get their small people up and ready for the day by six o'clock, I cannot understand, for it is just all I can manage to get myself and the tent ready by that time.

We are on the banks of a small stream, and the tents are evidently pitched directly upon the roosting ground of wild geese, for during the snowstorm thousands of them came here long after dark, making the most dreadful uproar one ever heard, with the whirring of their big wings and constant " honk! honk! " of hundreds of voices. They circled around so low and the calls were so loud that it seemed sometimes as if they were inside the tents. They must have come home for shelter and become confused and blinded by the lights in the tents, and the loss of their ground. We must be going through a splendid country for game.

I was very ill for several days on the way up, the result of malaria—perhaps too many scuppernong grapes at Pass Christian, and jolting of the heavy army wagon that makes a small stone seem the size of a boulder. One morning I was unable to walk or even stand up, and Faye and Major Bryant carried me to the wagon on a buffalo robe. All of that day's march Faye walked by the side of my wagon, and that allowed him no rest whatever, for in order to make it as easy for me as possible, my wagon had been placed

at the extreme end of the long line. The troops march
fifty minutes and halt ten, and as we went much slower
than the men marched, we would about catch up with
the column at each rest, just when the bugle would be
blown to fall in line again, and then on the troops
and wagons would go, Faye was kept on a continuous tramp. I still think that he should have asked
permission to ride on the wagon, part of the day at
least, but he would not do so.

One evening when the camp was near a ranch, I
heard Doctor Gordon tell Faye outside the tent that I
must be left at the place in the morning, that I was
too ill to go farther! I said not a word about having
heard this, but I promised myself that I would go on.
The dread of being left with perfect strangers, of
whom I knew nothing, and where I could not possibly
have medical attendance, did not improve my condition, but fear gave me strength, and in the morning
when camp broke I assured Doctor Gordon that I was
better, very much better, and stuck to it with so much
persistence that at last he consented to my going on.
But during many hours of the march that morning
I was obliged to ride on my hands and knees! The
road was unusually rough and stony, and the jolting
I could not endure, sitting on the canvas or lying on
the padded bottom of the wagon.

It so happened that Faye was officer of the day
that day, and Colonel Fitz-James, knowing that he
was under a heavy strain with a sick wife in addition to
the long marches, sent him one of his horses to ride—
a very fine animal and one of a matched team. At the
first halt Faye missed Hal, and riding back to the
company saw he was not with the men, so he went on

to my wagon, but found that I was shut up tight, Cagey asleep, and the dog not with us. He did not speak to either of us, but kept on to the last wagon, where a laundress told him that she saw the dog going back down the road we had just come over.

The wagon master, a sergeant, had joined Faye, riding a mule, and the two rode on after the dog, expecting every minute to overtake him. But the recollection of the unhappy year at Baton Rouge with the hospital steward was still fresh in Hal's memory, and the fear of another separation from his friends drove him on and on, faster and faster, and kept him far ahead of the horses. When at last Faye found him, he was sitting by the smoking ashes of our camp stove, his long nose pointed straight up, giving the most blood-curdling howls of misery and woe possible for a greyhound to give, and this is saying much. The poor dog was wild with delight when he saw Faye, and of course there was no trouble in bringing him back; he was only too glad to have his old friend to follow. He must have missed Faye from the company in the morning, and then failing to find me in the shut-up wagon, had gone back to camp for us. This is all easily understood, but how did that hound find the exact spot where our tent had been, even the very ashes of our stove, on that large camp ground when he has no sense of smell?

I wondered all the day why I did not see Faye and when the stop for luncheon passed and he had not come I began to worry, as much as I could think of anything beyond my own suffering. Late in the afternoon we reached the camp for the night, and still Faye had not come and no one could tell me anything

about him. And I was very, very ill! Doctor Gordon
was most kind and attentive, but neither he nor other
friends could relieve the pain in my heart, for I felt
so positive that something was wrong.

Just as our tent had been pitched Faye rode up,
looking weary and worried, said a word or two to
me, and then rode away again. He soon returned,
however, and explained his long absence by telling
me briefly that he had gone back for the dog. But
he was quiet and *distrait*, and directly after dinner
he went out again. When he came back he told me
all about everything that had occurred.

Under any circumstances, it would have been a
dreadful thing for him to have been absent from the
command without permission, but when officer of the
day it was unpardonable, and to take the colonel's
horse with him made matters all the worse. And then
the wagon master was liable to have been called upon
at any time, if anything had happened, or the command had come to a dangerous ford. Faye told me
how they had gone back for the dog, and so on, and
said that when he first got in camp he rode immediately to the colonel's tent, turned the horse over to
an orderly, and reported his return to the colonel,
adding that if the horse was injured he would replace him. Then he came to his own tent, fully expecting an order to follow soon, placing him under
arrest.

But after dinner, as no order had come, he went
again to see the colonel and told him just how the unfortunate affair had come about, how he had felt that
if the dog was not found it might cost me my life, as
I was so devoted to the dog and so very ill at that

time. The colonel listened to the whole story, and then told Faye that he understood it all, that undoubtedly he would have done the same thing! I think it was grand in Colonel Fitz-James to have been so gentle and kind—not one word of reproach did he say to Faye. Perhaps memories of his own wife came to him. The colonel may have a sensitive palate that makes him unpopular with many, but there are two people in his regiment who know that he has a heart so tender and big that the palate will never be considered again by them. Of course the horse was not injured in the least.

We are on the stage road to Helena, and at this place there is a fork that leads to the northwest which the lieutenant colonel and four companies will take to go to Fort Missoula, Montana. The colonel, headquarters, and other companies are to be stationed at Helena during the winter. We expect to meet the stage going south about noon to-morrow, and you should have this in eight days. Billie squirrel has a fine time in the wagon and is very fat. He runs off with bits of my luncheon every day and hides them in different places in the canvas, to his own satisfaction at least. One of the mules back of us has become most friendly, and will take from my hand all sorts of things to eat.

Poor Hal had a fit the other day, something like vertigo, after having chased a rabbit. Doctor Gordon says that he has fatty degeneration of the heart, caused by having so little exercise in the South, but that he will probably get over it if allowed to run every day. But I do not like the very idea of the dog having anything the matter with his heart. It was so pathetic to have him stagger to the tent and drop at my feet, dumbly confident that I could give him relief.

CAMP NEAR HELENA, MONTANA TERRITORY,
November, 1877.

THE company has been ordered to Camp Baker, a small post nearly sixty miles farther on. We were turned off from the Helena road and the rest of the command at the base of the mountains, and are now about ten miles from Helena on our way to the new station, which, we are told, is a wretched little two-company post on the other side of the Big Belt range of mountains. I am awfully disappointed in not seeing something of Helena, and very, very sorry that we have to go so far from our friends and to such an isolated place, but it is the company's turn for detached service, so here we are.

The scenery was grand in many places along the latter part of the march, and it is grand here, also. We are in a beautiful broad valley with snow-capped mountains on each side. From all we hear we conclude there must be exceptionally good hunting and fishing about Camp Baker, and there is some consolation in that. The fishing was very good at several of our camps after we reached the mountains, and I can assure you that the speckled trout of the East and these mountain trout are not comparable, the latter are so far, far superior. The flesh is white and very firm, and sometimes they are so cold when brought out of the water one finds it uncomfortable to hold them. They are good fighters, too, and even small ones give splendid sport.

One night the camp was by a beautiful little stream

with high banks, and here and there bunches of
bushes and rocks—an ideal home for trout, so I started
out, hoping to catch something with a common willow
pole and ordinary hook, and grasshoppers for bait.
Faye tells everybody that I had only a bent pin for
a hook, but of course no one believes him.   Major
Stokes joined me and we soon found a deep pool just
at the edge of camp.   His fishing tackle was very
much like mine, so when we saw Captain Martin coming toward us with elegant jointed rod, shining new
reel, and a camp stool, we felt rather crestfallen.
Captain Martin passed on and seated himself com-
fortably on the bank just below us, but Major Stokes
and I went down the bank to the edge of the pool
where we were compelled to stand, of course.

The water was beautifully clear and as soon as
everybody and everything became quiet, we saw down
on the bottom one or two trout, then more appeared,
and still more, until there must have been a dozen or
so beautiful fish in between the stones, each one about
ten inches long.   But go near the hooks they would
not, neither would they rise to Captain Martin's most
tempting flies—for he, too, saw many trout, from
where he sat.   We stood there a long time, until
our patience was quite exhausted, trying to catch
some of those fish, sometimes letting the current take
the grasshoppers almost to their very noses, when
finally Major Stokes whispered, " There, Mrs. Rae
there, try to get that big fellow ! "   Now as we had
all been most unsuccessful with the little " fellows,"
I had no hope whatever of getting the big one, still
I tried, for he certainly was a beauty and looked very
large as he came slowly along, carefully avoiding the

stones.   Before I had moved my bait six inches, there
was a flash of white down there, and then with a little
jerk I hooked that fish—hooked him safely.

That was very, very nice, but the fish set up a terrible fight that would have given great sport with a
reel, but I did not have a reel, and the steep bank directly back of me only made matters worse.   I saw
that time must not be wasted, that I must not give
him a chance to slacken the line and perhaps shake
the hook off, so I faced about, and putting the pole
over my shoulder, proceeded to climb the bank of four
or five feet, dragging the flopping fish after me!   Captain Martin laughed heartily, but instead of laughing
at the funny sight, Major Stokes jumped to my assistance, and between us we landed the fish up on the
bank.   It was a lovely trout—by far the largest we
had seen, and Major Stokes insisted that we should
take him to the commissary scales, where he weighed
over three and one half pounds!

The jumping about of my big trout ruined the
fishing, of course, in that part of the stream for some
time, so, with a look of disgust for things generally,
Captain Martin folded his rod and camp stool and returned to his tent.   I had the trout served for our
dinner, and, having been so recently caught, it was
delicious.   These mountain trout are very delicate,
and if one wishes to enjoy their very finest flavor, they
should be cooked and served as soon as they are out
of the water.   If kept even a few hours this delicacy
is lost—a fact we have discovered for ourselves on
the march up.

The camp to-night is near the house of a German
family, and I am writing in their little prim sitting

room, and Billie squirrel is with me and very busy examining things generally. I came over to wait while the tents were being pitched, and was received with such cordial hospitality, and have found the little room so warm and comfortable that I have stayed on longer than I had intended. Soon after I came my kind hostess brought in a cup of most delicious coffee and a little pitcher of cream—real cream—something I had not tasted for six weeks, and she also brought a plate piled high with generous pieces of German cinnamon cake, at the same time telling me that I must eat every bit of it—that I looked " real peaked," and not strong enough to go tramping around with all those men! When I told her that it was through my own choice that I was " tramping," that I enjoyed it, she looked at me with genuine pity, and as though she had just discovered that I did not have good common sense.

We start on early in the morning, and it will take two or three days to cross the mountains. The little camp of one company looks lonesome after the large regimental camp we have been with so long. The air is really wonderful, so clear and crisp and exhilarating. It makes me long for a good horse, and horses we intend to have as soon as possible. We are anticipating so much pleasure in having a home once more, even if it is to be of logs and buried in snow, perhaps, during the winter. Hal is outside, and his beseeching whines have swelled to awful howls that remind me of neglected duties in the tent.

CAMP BAKER, MONTANA TERRITORY,
November, 1877.

IT was rather late in the afternoon yesterday when
we got to this post, because of a delay on the
mountains.   But this did not cause inconvenience to
anyone—there was a vacant set of quarters that Lieutenant Hayden took possession of at once for his family, and where with camp outfit they can be comfortable until the wagons are unloaded.   Faye and I are
staying with the commanding officer and his wife.
Colonel Gardner is lieutenant colonel of the —th Infantry, and has a most enviable reputation as a post
commander.   As an officer, we have not seen him yet,
but we do know that he can be a most charming host.
He has already informed Faye that he intends to
appoint him adjutant and quartermaster of the post.

We are in a little valley almost surrounded by
magnificent, heavily timbered mountains, and Colonel
Gardner says that at any time one can find deer, mountain sheep, and bear in these forests, adding that there
are also mountain lions and wild cats!   The scenery on
the road from Helena to Camp Baker was grand, but
the roads were dreadful, most of the time along the
sides of steep mountains that seemed to be one enormous pile of big boulders in some places and solid rock
in others.   These roads have been cut into the rock and
are scarcely wider than the wagon track, and often we
could look almost straight down seventy-five feet, or
even more, on one side, and straight up for hundreds
of feet on the other side.

And in the cañons many of the grades were so steep
that the wheels of the wagons had to be chained in
addition to the big brakes to prevent them from run-

ning sideways, and so off the grade. I rode down
one of these places, but it was the last as well as the
first. Every time the big wagon jolted over a stone
—and it was jolt over stones all the time—it seemed
as if it must topple over the side and roll to the
bottom; and then the way the driver talked to the
mules to keep them straight, and the creaking and
scraping of the wagons, was enough to frighten the
most courageous.

In Confederate Gulch we crossed a ferry that was
most marvelous. A heavy steel cable was stretched
across the river—the Missouri—and fastened securely
to each bank, and then a flat boat was chained at each
end to the cable, but so it could slide along when the
ferryman gripped the cable with a large hook, and
gave long, hard pulls. Faye says that the very swift
current of the stream assisted him much.

The river runs through a narrow, deep cañon where
the ferry is, and at the time we crossed everything
was in dark shadow, and the water looked black, and
fathoms deep, with its wonderful reflections. The
grandeur of these mountains is simply beyond imagination; they have to be seen to be appreciated, and
yet when seen, one can scarcely comprehend their im-
mensity. We are five hundred miles from a railroad,
with endless chains of these mountains between. All
supplies of every description are brought up that distance by long ox trains—dozens of wagons in a train,
and eight or ten pairs of oxen fastened to the one long
chain that pulls three or four heavily loaded wagons.
We passed many of these trains on the march up, and
my heart ached for the poor patient beasts.

We are to have one side of a large double house,

which will give us as many rooms as we will need
in this isolated place. Hal is in the house now, with
Cagey, and Billie is there also, and has the exclusive
run of one room. The little fellow stood the march
finely, and it is all owing to that terrible old wagon
that was such a comfort in some ways, but caused me
so much misery in others. These houses must be quite
warm; they are made of large logs placed horizontally, and the inner walls are plastered, which will
keep out the bitter cold during the winter. The smallest window has an outside storm window.

CAMP BAKER, MONTANA TERRITORY,
December, 1877.

THIS post is far over in the Belt Mountains and
quite cut off from the outside world, and there
are very few of us here, nevertheless the days pass
wonderfully fast, and they are pleasant days, also.
And then we have our own little excitements that are
of intense interest to us, even if they are never heard
of in the world across the snow and ice.

The Rae family was very much upset two days
ago by the bad behavior of my horse Bettie, when
she managed to throw Faye for the very first time
in his life! You know that both of our horses, although raised near this place, were really range animals, and were brought in and broken for us. The
black horse has never been very satisfactory, and
Faye has a battle with him almost every time he takes
him out, but Bettie had been lovely and behaved wonderfully well for so young a horse, and I have been
so pleased with her and her delightful gaits—a little
single foot and easy canter.

The other morning Faye was in a hurry to get out to a lumber camp and, as I did not care to go, he decided to ride my horse rather than waste time by arguing with the black as to which road they should go. Ben always thinks he knows more about such things than his rider. Well, Kelly led Bettie up from the corral and saddled and bridled her, and when Faye was ready to start I went out with him to give the horse a few lumps of sugar. She is a beautiful animal—a bright bay in color—with perfect head and dainty, expressive ears, and remarkably slender legs.

Faye immediately prepared to mount; in fact, bridle in hand, had his left foot in the stirrup and the right was over the horse, when up went Miss Bet's back, arched precisely like a mad cat's, and down in between her fore legs went her pretty nose, and high up in the air went everything—man and beast—the horse coming down on legs as rigid and unbending as bars of steel, and then—something happened to Faye! Nothing could have been more unexpected, and it was all over in a second.

Kelly caught the bridle reins in time to prevent the horse from running away, and Faye got up on his feet, and throwing back his best West Point shoulders, faced the excited horse, and for two long seconds he and Miss Bet looked each other square in the eye. Just what the horse thought no one knows, but Kelly and I remember what Faye *said!* All desire to laugh, however, was quickly crushed when I heard Kelly ordered to lead the horse to the sutler's store, and fit a Spanish bit to her mouth, and to take the saddle off and strap a blanket on tight with a surcingle, for I knew that a hard and dangerous fight between

man and horse was about to commence. Faye told
Cagey to chain Hal and then went in the house, soon
returning, however, without a blouse, and with moccasins on his feet and with leggings.

When Kelly returned he looked most unhappy, for
he loves horses and has been so proud of Bettie.
But Faye was not thinking of Kelly and proceeded
at once to mount, having as much fire in his eyes as
the horse had in hers, for she had already discovered
that the bit was not to her liking. As soon as she
felt Faye's weight, up went her back again, but
down she could not get her head, and the more she
pushed down, the harder the spoon of the bit pressed
against the roof of her mouth. This made her furious, and as wild as when first brought from the range.

She lunged and lunged—forward and sideways—
reared, and of course tried to run away, but with all
the vicious things her little brain could think of, she
could not get the bit from her mouth or Faye from
her back. So she started to rub him off—doing it
with thought and in the most scientific way. She first
went to the corner of our house, then tried the other
corner of that end, and so she went on, rubbing up
against every object she saw—house, tree, and fence
—even going up the steps at the post trader's. That
I thought very smart, for the bit was put in her mouth
there, and she might have hoped to find some kind
friend who would take it out.

It required almost two hours of the hardest kind
of riding to conquer the horse, and to teach her that
just as long as she held her head up and behaved herself generally, the bit would not hurt her. She finally
gave in, and is once more a tractable beast, and I have

13

ridden her twice, but with the Spanish bit. She is a nervous animal and will always be frisky. It has leaked out that the morning she bucked so viciously, a cat had been thrown upon her back at the corral by a playful soldier, just before she had been led up. Kelly did not like to tell this of a comrade. It was most fortunate that I had decided not to ride at that time, for a pitch over a horse's head with a skirt to catch on the pommel is a performance I am not seeking. And Bettie had been such a dear horse all the time, her single foot and run both so swift and easy. Kelly says, " Yer cawn't feel yerse'f on her, mum." Faye is quartermaster, adjutant, commissary, signal officer, and has other positions that I cannot remember just now, that compel him to be at his own office for an hour every morning before breakfast, in addition to the regular office hours during the day. The post commander is up and out at half past six every workday, and Sundays I am sure he is a most unhappy man. But Faye gets away for a hunt now and then, and the other day he started off, much to my regret, all alone and with only a rifle. I worry when he goes alone up in these dense forests, and when an officer goes with him I am so afraid of an accident, that one may shoot the other. It is impossible to take a wagon, or even ride a horse among the rocks and big boulders. There are panthers and wild cats and wolves and all sorts of fearful things up there. The coyotes often come down to the post at night, and their terrible, unearthly howls drive the dogs almost crazy—and some of the people, too.

I worried about Faye the other morning as usual, and thought of all the dreadful things that could so

easily happen. And then I tried to forget my anxiety
by taking a brisk ride on Bettie, but when I returned
I found that Faye had not come, so I worried all the
more. The hours passed and still he was away, and
I was becoming really alarmed. At last there was a
shout at a side door, and running out I found Faye
standing up very tall and with a broad smile on his
face, and on the ground at his feet was an immense
white-tail deer! He said that he had walked miles
on the mountain but had failed to find one living
thing, and had finally come down and was just starting to cross the valley on his way home, when he saw
the deer, which he fortunately killed with one shot at
very long range. He did not want to leave it to be
devoured by wolves while he came to the corral for
a wagon, so he dragged the heavy thing all the way
in. And that was why he was gone so long, for of
course he was obliged to rest every now and then.
I was immensely proud of the splendid deer, but it
did not convince me in the least that it was safe for
Faye to go up in that forest alone. Of course Faye
has shot other deer, and mountain sheep also, since
we have been here, but this was the first he had killed
when alone.

Of all the large game we have ever had—buffalo,
antelope, black-tail deer, white-tail deer—the mountain
sheep is the most delicious. The meat is very tender
and juicy and exceedingly rich in flavor. It is very
" gamey," of course, and is better after having been
frozen or hung for a few days. These wary animals
are most difficult to get, for they are seldom found except on the peaks of high mountains, where the many
big rocks screen them, so when one is brought in, it

is always with great pride and rejoicing. There are antelope in the lowlands about here, but none have been brought in since we came to the post. The ruffed grouse and the fule hens are plentiful, and of course nothing can be more delicious.

And the trout are perfect, too, but the manner in which we get them this frozen-up weather is not sportsmanlike. There is a fine trout stream just out-side the post which is frozen over now, but when we wish a few nice trout for dinner or breakfast, Cagey and I go down, and with a hatchet he will cut a hole in the ice through which I fish, and usually catch all we want in a few minutes. The fish seem to be hungry and rise quickly to almost any kind of bait except flies. They seem to know that this is not the fly season. The trout are not very large, about eight and ten inches long, but they are delicate in flavor and very delicious.

Cagey is not a wonderful cook, but he does very well, and I think that I would much prefer him to a Chinaman, judging from what I have seen of them here. Mrs. Conrad, wife of Captain Conrad, of the —th Infantry, had one who was an excellent servant in every way except in the manner of doing the laundry work. He persisted in putting the soiled linen in the boiler right from the basket, and no amount of talk on the part of Mrs. Conrad could induce him to do otherwise. Monday morning Mrs. Conrad went to the kitchen and told him once more that he must look the linen over, and rub it with plenty of water and soap be-fore boiling it. The heathen looked at her with a grin and said, " Allee light, you no likee my washee, you washee yousel'," and lifting the boiler from the stove he emptied its entire steaming contents out upon the floor! He then went to his own room, gathered up his few clothes and bedding, and started off. He knew full well that if he did not leave the reservation at once he would be put off after such a performance.

CAMP BAKER, MONTANA TERRITORY,
February, 1878.

HOME seems very cozy and attractive after the mountains of snow and ice we crossed and re-crossed on our little trip to Helena. The bitter cold of those cañons will long be remembered. But it was a delightful change from the monotonous life in this out-of-the-way garrison, even if we did almost freeze on the road, and it was more than pleasant to be with old friends again.

The ball at the hall Friday evening was most enjoyable, and it was simply enchanting to dance once more to the perfect music of the dear old orchestra. And the young people in Helena are showing their appreciation of the good music by dancing themselves positively thin this winter. The band leader brought from New Orleans the Creole music that was so popular there, and at the ball we danced *Les Variétés* four times; the last was at the request of Lieutenant Joyce, with whom I always danced it in the South. It is thoroughly French, bringing in the waltz, polka, schottische, mazurka, and redowa. Some of those Creole girls were the personification of grace in that dance.

We knew of the ball before leaving home, and went prepared for it, but had not heard one word about the *bal masqué* to be given by " The Army Social Club " at Mrs. Gordon's Tuesday evening. We did not have one thing with us to assist in the make-up of a fancy dress; nevertheless we decided to attend it. Faye said for me not to give him a thought, that he could manage his own costume. How I did envy his confidence in man and things, particularly things, for just then I felt far from equal to managing my own dress.

I had been told of some of the costumes that were to be worn by friends, and they were beautiful, and the more I heard of these things, the more determined I became that I would not appear in a domino! So Monday morning I started out for an idea, and this I found almost immediately in a little shop window. It was only a common pasteboard mask, but nevertheless it was a work of art. The face was fat and silly, and droll beyond description, and to look at the thing and not laugh was impossible. It had a heavy bang of fiery red hair. I bought it without delay, and was wondering where I could find something to go with it in that little town, when I met a friend—a friend indeed—who offered me some widths of silk that had been dyed a most hideous shade of green.

I gladly accepted the offer, particularly as this friend is in deep mourning and would not be at the ball to recognize me. Well, I made this really awful silk into a very full skirt that just covered my ankles, and near the bottom I put a broad band of orange-colored cambric—the stiff and shiny kind. Then I made a Mother Hubbard apron of white paper-cambric, also very stiff and shiny, putting a big full ruche of the cambric around neck, yoke, and bottom of sleeves. For my head I made a large cap of the white cambric with ruche all around, and fastened it on tight with wide strings that were tied in a large stiff bow under the chin. We drew my evening dress up underneath both skirt and apron and pinned it securely on my shoulders, and this made me stout and shapeless. Around this immense waist and over the apron was drawn a wide sash of bright pink, glossy cambric that was tied in a huge bow at the back. But by far the best of all, a real crown of glory, was a pigtail of red, red hair that hung down my back and showed conspicuously on the white apron. This was a loan by Mrs. Joyce, another friend in mourning, and who assisted me in dressing.

We wanted the benefit of the long mirror in the little parlor of the hotel, so we carried everything there and locked the door. And then the fun commenced! I am afraid that Mrs. Joyce's fingers must have been badly bruised by the dozens of pins she used, and how she laughed at me! But if I looked half as dreadful as my reflection in the mirror I must have been a sight to provoke laughter. We had been requested to give names to our characters, and Mrs. Joyce said I must be " A Country Girl," but it still seems to me that " An Idiot " would have been more appropriate.

I drove over with Major and Mrs. Carleton. The dressing rooms were crowded at Mrs. Gordon's, so it was an easy matter to slip away, give my long cloak and thick veil to a maid, and return to Mrs. Carleton before she had missed me, and it was most laughable to see the dear lady go in search for me, peering in everyone's face. But she did not find me, although we went down the stairs and in the drawing-room together, and neither did one person in those rooms recognize me during the evening. Lieutenant Joyce

said he knew to whom the hair belonged, but beyond
that it was all a mystery.

That evening will never be forgotten, for, as soon
as I saw that no one knew me, I became a child once
more, and the more the maskers laughed the more I
ran around. When I first appeared in the rooms there
was a general giggle and that was exhilarating, so
off I went. After a time Colonel Fitz-James adopted
me and tagged around after me every place; I simply could not get rid of the man. I knew him, of
course, and I also knew that he was mistaking me for
some one else, which made his attentions anything but
complimentary. I told him ever so many times that
he did not know me, but he always insisted that it
was impossible for him to be deceived, that he would
always know me, and so on. He was acting in a very
silly manner—quite too silly for a man of his years and
a colonel of a regiment, and he was keeping me from
some very nice dances, too, so I decided to lead him
a dance, and commenced a rare flirtation in cozy
corners and out-of-the-way places. I must admit,
though, that all the pleasure I derived from it was
when I heard the smothered giggles of those who saw
us. The colonel was in a domino and had not tried
to disguise himself.

We went in to supper together, and I managed to
be almost the last one to unmask, and all the time
Colonel Fitz-James, domino removed, was standing
in front of me, and looking down with a smile of se-
rene expectancy. The colonel of a regiment is a person of prominence, therefore many people in the room
were watching us, not one suspecting, however, who
I was. So when I did take off the mask there was

a shout: "Why, it is Mrs. Rae," and "Oh, look at Mrs. Rae," and several friends came up to us. Well, I wish you could have seen the colonel's face— the mingled surprise and almost horror that was expressed upon it. Of course the vain man had placed himself in a ridiculous position, chasing around and flirting with the wife of one of his very own officers —a second lieutenant at that! It came out later that he, and others also, had thought that I was a Helena girl whom the colonel admires very much. It was rather embarrassing, too, to be told that the girl was sitting directly opposite on the other side of the room, where she was watching us with two big, black eyes. And then farther down I saw Faye also looking at us—but then, a man never can see things from a woman's view point.

The heat and weight of the two dresses had been awful, and as soon as I could get away, I ran to a dressing room and removed the cambric. But the pins! There seemed to be thousands of them. Some of the costumes were beautiful and costly, also. Mrs. Manson, a lovely little woman of Helena, was "A Comet." Her short dress of blue silk was studded with gold stars, and to each shoulder was fastened a long, pointed train of yellow gauze sprinkled with diamond dust. An immense gold star with a diamond sunburst in the center was above her forehead, and around her neck was a diamond necklace. Mrs. Palmer, wife of Colonel Palmer, was "King of Hearts," the foundation a handsome red silk. Mrs. Spencer advertised the *New York Herald;* the whole dress, which was flounced to the waist, was made of the headings of that paper. Major Blair was recognized by no one as "An American citizen," in plain evening dress. I could not find Faye at all, and he was in a simple red domino, too.

I cannot begin to tell you of the many lovely costumes that seemed most wonderful to me, for you must remember that we were far up in the Rocky Mountains, five hundred miles from a railroad! I will send you a copy of the Helena paper that gives an account of the ball, in which you will read that " Mrs. Rae was inimitable—the best sustained character in the rooms." I have thought this over some, and I consider the compliment doubtful.

We remained one day longer in Helena than we had expected for the *bal masqué;* consequently we were obliged to start back the very next morning, directly after breakfast, and that was not pleasant, for we were very tired. The weather had been bitter cold, but during the night a chinook had blown up, and the air was warm and balmy as we came across the valley. When we reached the mountains, however, it was freezing again, and there was glassy ice every place, which made driving over the grades more dangerous than usual. In many places the ambulance wheels had to be " blocked," and the back and front wheels of one side chained together so they could not turn, in addition to the heavy brake, and then the driver would send the four sharp-shod mules down at a swinging trot that kept the ambulance straight, and did not give it time to slip around and roll us down to eternity.

There is one grade on this road that is notoriously dangerous, and dreaded by every driver around here because of the many accidents that have occurred there. It is cut in the side of a high mountain and

"Then the driver would send the four mules down at a swinging trot."

has three sharp turns back and forth, and the mountain is so steep, it is impossible to see from the upper grade all of the lower that leads down into the cañon called White's Gulch. This one mountain grade is a mile and a half long. But the really dangerous place is near the middle turn, where a warm spring trickles out of the rocks and in winter forms thick ice over the road; and if this ice cannot be broken up, neither man nor beast can walk over, as it is always thicker on the inner side.

I was so stiffened from the overheating and try-to-fool dancing at Mrs. Gordon's, it was with the greatest difficulty I could walk at all on the slippery hills, and was constantly falling down, much to the amusement of Faye and the driver. But ride down some of them I would not. At Cañon Ferry, where we remained over night, the ice in the Missouri was cracked, and there were ominous reports like pistol shots down in the cañon below. At first Faye thought it would be impossible to come over, but the driver said he could get everything across, if he could come at once. Faye walked over with me, and then went back to assist the driver with the mules that were still on the bank refusing to step upon the ice. But Faye led one leader, and the driver lashed and yelled at all of them, and in this way they crossed, each mule snorting at every step.

There were the most dreadful groans and creakings and loud reports during the entire night, and in the morning the river was clear, except for a few pieces of ice that were still floating down from above. The Missouri is narrow at Cañon Ferry, deep and very swift, and it is a dreadful place to cross at any time,

on the ice, or on the cable ferryboat. They catch a
queer fish there called the " ling." It has three sides,
is long and slender, and is perfectly blind. They gave
us some for supper and it was really delicious.

We found everything in fine order upon our return,
and it was very evident that Cagey had taken good
care of the house and Hal, but Billie grayback had
taken care of himself. He was given the run of my
room, but I had expected, of course, that he would
sleep in his own box, as usual. But no, the little rascal in some way discovered the warmth of the blankets on my bed, and in between these he had undoubtedly spent most of the time during our absence,
and there we found him after a long search, and there
he wants to stay all the time now, and if anyone happens to go near the bed they are greeted with the
fiercest kind of smothered growls.

The black horse has been sold, and Faye has
bought another, a sorrel, that seems to be a very satisfactory animal. He is not as handsome as Ben, nor as
fractious, either. Bettie is behaving very well, but is
still nervous, and keeps her forefeet down just long
enough to get herself over the ground. She is beautiful, and Kelly simply adores her and keeps her
bright-red coat like satin. Faye can seldom ride
with me because of his numerous duties, and not one
of the ladies rides here, so I have Kelly go, for one
never knows what one may come across on the roads
around here. They are so seldom traveled, and are
little more than trails.

CAMP BAKER, MONTANA TERRITORY,
March, 1878.

THE mail goes out in the morning, and in it a letter
must be sent to you, but it is hard—hard for me
to write—to have to tell you that my dear dog, my
beautiful greyhound, is dead—dead and buried! It
seems so cruel that he should have died now, so soon
after getting back to his old home, friends, and freedom. On Tuesday, Faye and Lieutenant Lomax went
out for a little hunt, letting Hal go with them, which
was unusual, and to which I objected, for Lieutenant
Lomax is a notoriously poor shot and hunter, and I
was afraid he might accidentally kill Hal—mistake
him for a wild animal. So, as they went down our
steps I said, " Please do not shoot my dog! " much
more in earnest than in jest, for I felt that he would
really be in danger, as it would be impossible to keep
him with them all the time.

As they went across the parade ground, rifles over
their shoulders, Hal jumped up on Faye and played
around him, expressing his delight at being allowed
to go on a hunt. He knew what a gun was made for
just as well as the oldest hunter. That was the last
I saw of my dog! Faye returned long before I had
expected him, and one quick glance at his troubled
face told me that something terrible had happened.
I saw that he was unhurt and apparently well, but—
where was Hal? With an awful pain in my heart I
asked, " Did Lieutenant Lomax shoot Hal? " After
a second's hesitation Faye said " No; but Hal is
dead! " It seemed too dreadful to be true, and at
first I could not believe it, for it had been only
such a short time since I had seen him bounding and

leaping, evidently in perfect health, and oh, so happy!

No one in the house even thought of dinner that night, and poor black Cagey sobbed and moaned so loud and long Faye was obliged to ask him to be quiet. For hours I could not listen to the particulars. Faye says that they had not gone out so very far when he saw a wild cat some distance away, and taking careful aim, he shot it, but the cat, instead of falling, started on a fast run. Hal was in another direction, but when he heard the report of the rifle and saw the cat running, he started after it with terrific speed and struck it just as the cat fell, and then the two rolled over and over together.

He got up and stood by Faye and Lieutenant Lomax while they examined the cat, and if there was anything wrong with him it was not noticed. But when they turned to come to the post, dragging the dead cat after them, Faye heard a peculiar sound, and looking back saw dear Hal on the ground in a fit much like vertigo. He talked to him and petted him, thinking he would soon be over it—and the plucky dog did get up and try to follow, but went down again and for the last time The swift run and excitement caused by encountering an animal wholly different from anything he had ever seen before was too great a strain upon the weak heart.

Before coming to the house Faye had ordered a detail out to bury him, with instructions to cover the grave with pieces of glass to keep the wolves away. The skin and head of the cat, which was really a lynx, are being prepared for a rug, but I do not see how I can have the thing in the house, although the black spots and stripes with the white make the fur very beautiful. The ball passed straight through the body.

The loneliness of the house is awful, and at night I imagine that I hear him outside whining to come in. Many a cold night have I been up two and three times to straighten his bed and cover him up. His bed was the skin of a young buffalo, and he knew just when it was smooth and nice, and then he would almost throw himself down, with a sigh of perfect content. If I did not cover him at once, he would get up and drop down again, and there he would stay hours at a time with the fur underneath and over him, with just his nose sticking out. He suffered keenly from the intense cold here because his hair was so short and fine. And then he was just from the South, too, where he was too warm most of the time.

It makes me utterly wretched to think of the long year he was away from us at Baton Rouge. But what could we have done? We could not have had him with us, in the very heart of New Orleans, for he had already been stolen from us at Jackson Barracks, a military post!

With him passed the very last of his blood, a breed of greyhounds that was known in Texas, Kansas, and Colorado as wonderful hunters, also remarkable for their pluck and beauty of form. Hal was a splendid hunter, and ever on the alert for game. Not one morsel of it would he eat, however, not even a piece of domestic fowl, which he seemed to look upon as game. Sheep he considered fine game, and would chase them every opportunity that presented itself. This was his

14

one bad trait, an expensive one sometimes, but it was the only one, and was overbalanced many times by his lovable qualities that made him a favorite with all. Every soldier in the company loved him and was proud of him, and would have shared his dinner with the dog any day if called upon to do so.

NATIONAL HOTEL, HELENA, MONTANA TERRITORY,
May, 1878.

TO hear that we are no longer at Camp Baker will be a surprise, but you must have become accustomed to surprises of this kind long ago. Regimental headquarters, the companies that have been quartered at the Helena fair grounds during the winter, and the two companies from Camp Baker, started from here this morning on a march to the Milk River country, where a new post is to be established on Beaver Creek. It is to be called Fort Assiniboine. The troops will probably be in camp until fall, when they will go to Fort Shaw.

We had been given no warning whatever of this move, and had less than two days in which to pack and crate everything. And I can assure you that in one way it was worse than being ranked out, for this time there was necessity for careful packing and crating, because of the rough mountain roads the wagons had to come over. But there were no accidents, and our furniture and boxes are safely put away here in a government storehouse.

At the time the order came, Faye was recorder for a board of survey that was being held at the post, and this, in addition to turning over quartermaster and other property, kept him hard at work night and

day, so the superintendence of all things pertaining
to the house and camp outfit fell to my lot. The soldiers were most willing and most incompetent, and
it kept me busy telling them what to do. The mess-
chest, and Faye's camp bedding are always in readiness for ordinary occasions, but for a camp of several
months in this climate, where it can be really hot one
day and freezing cold the next, it was necessary to
add many more things. Just how I managed to ac-
complish so much in so short a time I do not know,
but I do know that I was up and packing every precious minute the night before we came away, and the
night seemed very short too. But everything was
taken to the wagons in very good shape, and that
repaid me for much of the hard work and great
fatigue.

And I was tired—almost too tired to sit up, but at
eight o'clock I got in an ambulance and came nearly
forty miles that one day! Major Stokes and Captain
Martin had been on the board of survey, and as they
were starting on the return trip to Helena, I came
over with them, which not only got me here one day
in advance of the company, but saved Faye the trouble of providing for me in camp on the march from
Camp Baker. We left the post just as the troops were
starting out. Faye was riding Bettie and Cagey was
on Pete.

I brought Billie, of course, and at Cañon Ferry I
lost that squirrel! After supper I went directly to my
room to give him a little run and to rest a little myself,
but before opening his box I looked about for places
where he might escape, and seeing a big crack under
one of the doors, covered it with Faye's military

cape, thinking, as I did so, that it would be impossible for a squirrel to crawl through such a narrow place. Then I let him out. Instead of running around and shying at strange objects as he usually does, he ran straight to that cape, and after two or three pulls with his paws, flattened his little gray body, and like a flash he and the long bushy tail disappeared! I was *en déshabille,* but quickly slipped on a long coat and ran out after him.

Very near my door was one leading to the kitchen, and so I went on through, and the very first thing stumbled over a big cat! This made me more anxious than ever, but instead of catching the beast and shutting it up, I drove it away. In the kitchen, which was dining room also, sat the two officers and a disagreeable old man, and at the farther end was a woman washing dishes. I told them about Billie and begged them to keep very quiet while I searched for him. Then that old man laughed. That was quite too much for my overtaxed nerves, and I snapped out that I failed to see anything funny. But still he laughed, and said, " Perhaps you don't, but we do." I was too worried and unhappy to notice what he meant, and continued to look for Billie.

But the little fellow I could not find any place in the house or outside, where we looked with a lantern. When I returned to my room I discovered why the old man laughed, for truly I was a funny sight. I had thought my coat much longer than it really was— that is all I am willing to say about it. I was utterly worn out, and every bone in my body seemed to be rebelling about something, still I could not sleep, but listened constantly for Billie. I blamed myself so much for not having shut up the cat and fancied I heard the cat chasing him.

After a long, long time, it seemed hours, I heard a faint noise like a scratch on tin, and lighting a lamp quickly, I went to the kitchen and then listened. But not a sound was to be heard. At the farther end a bank had been cut out to make room for the kitchen, which gave it a dirt wall almost to the low ceiling, and all across this wall were many rows of shelves where tins of all sorts and cooking utensils were kept, and just above the top shelf was a hole where the cat could go out on the bank. I put the lamp back of me on the table and kept very still and looked all along the shelves, but saw nothing of Billie. Finally, I heard the little scratch again, and looking closely at some large tins where I thought the sound had come from, I saw the little squirrel. He was sitting up in between two of the pans that were almost his own color, with his head turned one side, and "hands on his heart," watching me inquisitively with one black eye.

He was there and apparently unharmed, but to catch him was another matter. I approached him in the most cautious manner, talking and cooing to him all the time, and at last I caught him, and the little fellow was so glad to be with friends once more, he curled himself in my hands, and put two little wet paws around a thumb and held on tight. It was raining, and he was soaking wet, so he must have been out of doors. It would have been heartbreaking to have been obliged to come away without finding that little grayback, and perhaps never know what became of him. I know where my dear dog is, and that is bad enough. We heard just before leaving the post that men of the company had put up a board at Hal's grave with his name cut in it. We knew that they loved him and were proud of him, but never dreamed that any one of them would show so much sentiment. Faye has taken the horses with him and Cagey also.

The young men of Helena gave the officers an informal dance last night. At first it promised to be a jolly affair, but finally, as the evening wore on, the army people became more and more quiet, and at the last it was distressing to see the sad faces that made dancing seem a farce. They are going to an Indian country, and the separation may be long. I expect to remain here for the present, but shall make every effort to get to Benton after a while, where I will be nearly one hundred and fifty miles nearer Faye. The wife of the adjutant and her two little children are in this house, and other families of officers are scattered all over the little town.

COSMOPOLITAN HOTEL, HELENA, MONTANA TERRITORY,
August, 1878.

YOU will see that at last I decided to move over to this hotel. I made a great mistake in not coming before and getting away from the cross old housekeeper at the International, who could not be induced by entreaties, fees, or threats, to get the creepy, crawly things out of my room. How I wish that every one of them would march over to her some fine night and keep her awake as they have kept me. It made me so unhappy to leave Mrs. Hull there with a sick child, but she would not come with me, although she must know it would be better for her and the boy

to be here, where everything is kept so clean and attractive. There are six wives of officers in the house,
among them the wife of General Bourke, who is in
command of the regiment. She invited me to sit at
her table, and I find it very pleasant there. She is a
bride and almost a stranger to us.

The weather has been playing all sorts of pranks
upon us lately, and we hardly know whether we are in
the far North or far South. For two weeks it was
very warm, positively hot in this gulch, but yesterday
we received a cooling off in the form of a brisk snowstorm that lasted nearly two hours. Mount Helena
was white during the rest of the day, and even now
long streaks of snow can be seen up and down the
peak. But a snowstorm in August looked very tame
after the awful cloud-burst that came upon us without warning a few days before, and seemed determined to wash the whole town down to the Missouri
River.

It was about eleven o'clock, and four of us had gone
to the shops to look at some pretty things that had
just been brought over from a boat at Fort Benton by
ox train. Mrs. Pierce and Mrs. Hull had stopped at a
grocery next door, expecting to join Mrs. Joyce and
me in a few minutes. But before they could
make a few purchases, a few large drops of rain began to splash down, and there was a fierce flash of
lightning and deafening thunder, then came the del-
uge! Oceans of water seemed to be coming down,
and before we realized what was happening, things
in the street and things back of the store were being
rushed to the valley below.

All along the gulch runs a little stream that comes

from the cañon above the town. The stream is tiny and the bed is narrow. On either side of it are stores with basements opening out on these banks. Well, in an alarmingly short time that innocent-looking little creek had become a roaring, foaming black river, carrying tables, chairs, washstands, little bridges—in fact everything it could tear up—along with it to the valley. Many of these pieces of furniture lodged against the carriage bridge that was just below the store where we were, making a dangerous dam, so a man with a stout rope around his waist went in the water to throw them out on the bank, but he was tossed about like a cork, and could do nothing. Just as they were about to pull him in the bridge gave way, and it was with the greatest difficulty he was kept from being swept down with the floating furniture. He was dragged back to our basement in an almost unconscious condition, and with many cuts and bruises.

The water was soon in the basements of the stores, where it did much damage. The store we were in is owned by a young man—one of the beaux of the town—and I think the poor man came near losing his mind. He rushed around pulling his hair one second, and wringing his hands the next, and seemed perfectly incapable of giving one order, or assisting his clerks in bringing the dripping goods from the basement. Very unlike the complacent, diamond-pin young man we had danced with at the balls!

The cloud-burst on Mount Helena had caused many breaks in the enormous ditches that run around the mountain and carry water to the mines on the other side. No one can have the faintest conception of how

terrible a cloud-burst is until they have been in one.
It is like standing under an immense waterfall.   At
the very beginning we noticed the wagon of a coun-
tryman across the street with one horse hitched to it.
The horse was tied so the water from an eaves trough
poured directly upon his back, and not liking that,
he stepped forward, which brought the powerful
stream straight to the wagon.

Unfortunately for the owner, the wagon had been
piled high with all sorts of packages, both large and
small, and all in paper or paper bags.   One by one
these were swept out, and as the volume of water increased in force and the paper became wet and easily
torn, their contents went in every direction.   Down in
the bottom was a large bag of beans, and when the
pipe water reached this, there was a white spray resembling a geyser.   Not one thing was left in that
wagon—even sacks of potatoes and grain were washed
out!   It is a wonder that the poor horse took it all
as patiently as he did.

During all this time we had not even heard from
our friends next door; after a while, however, we got
together, but it was impossible to return to the hotel
for a long time, because of the great depth of water
in the street.   Mrs. Pierce, whose house is on the
opposite side of the ravine, could not get to her home
until just before dark, after a temporary bridge had
been built across the still high stream.   Not one bridge
was left across the creek, and they say that nothing
has been left at Chinatown—that it was washed clean.
Perhaps there is nothing to be regretted in this, however, except that any amount of dirt has been piled up
right in the heart of Helena.   The millionaire resi-

dents seem to think that the great altitude and dry atmosphere will prevent any ill effects of decaying débris.

We went to the assay building the other day to see a brick of gold taken from the furnace. The mold was run out on its little track soon after we got there, and I never dreamed of what "white heat" really means, until I saw the oven of that awful furnace. We had to stand far across the room while the door was open, and even then the hot air that shot out seemed blasting. The men at the furnace were protected, of course. The brick mold was in another mold that after a while was put in cold water, so we had to wait for first the large and then the small to be opened before we saw the beautiful yellow brick that was still very hot, but we were assured that it was then too hard to be in danger of injury. It was of the largest size, and shaped precisely like an ordinary building brick, and its value was great. It was to be shipped on the stage the next morning on its way to the treasury in Washington.

It is wonderful that so few of those gold bricks are stolen from the stage. The driver is their only protector, and the stage route is through miles and miles of wild forests, and in between huge boulders where a "hold-up" could be so easily accomplished.

CAMP ON MARIAS RIVER, MONTANA TERRITORY,
September, 1878.

AN old proverb tells us that "All things come to him who waits," but I never had faith in this, for I have patiently waited many times for things that never found me. But this time, after I had waited and waited the tiresome summer through, ever hoping to come to Fort Benton, and when I was about discouraged, " things come," and here I am in camp with Faye, and ever so much more comfortable than I would have been at the little old hotel at Benton.

There are only two companies here now—all the others having gone with regimental headquarters to Fort Shaw—otherwise I could not be here, for I could not have come to a large camp. Our tents are at the extreme end of the line in a grove of small trees, and next to ours is the doctor's, so we are quite cut off from the rest of the camp. Cagey is here, and Faye has a very good soldier cook, so the little mess, including the doctor, is simply fine. I am famished all the time, for everything tastes so delicious after the dreadful hotel fare. The two horses are here, and I brought my saddle over, and this morning Faye and I had a delightful ride out on the plain. But how I did miss my dear dog! He was always so happy when with us and the horses, and his joyous bounds and little runs after one thing and another added much to the pleasure of our rides.

Fort Benton is ten miles from camp, and Faye met me there with an ambulance. I was glad enough to get away from that old stage. It was one of the jerky, bob-back-and-forth kind that pitches you off the seat every five minutes. The first two or three times you bump heads with the passenger sitting opposite, you can smile and apologize with some grace, but after a while your hat will not stay in place and your head becomes sensitive, and finally you discover that the passenger is the most disagreeable person you ever saw, and that the man sitting beside you is inconsiderate and selfish, and really occupying two thirds of the seat.

We came a distance of one hundred and forty miles, getting fresh horses every twenty miles or so. The morning we left Helena was glorious, and I was half ashamed because I felt so happy at coming from the town, where so many of my friends were in sorrow, but tried to console myself with the fact that I had been ordered away by Doctor Gordon. There were many cases of typhoid fever, and the rheumatic fever that has made Mrs. Sargent so ill has developed into typhoid, and there is very little hope for her recovery.

The driver would not consent to my sitting on top with him, so I had to ride inside with three men. They were not rough-looking at all, and their clothes looked clean and rather new, but gave one the impression that they had been made for other people. Their pale faces told that they were " tenderfeet," and one could see there was a sad lacking of brains all around.

The road comes across a valley the first ten or twelve miles, and then runs into a magnificent cañon that is sixteen miles long, called Prickly-Pear Cañon. As I wrote some time ago, everything is brought up to this country by enormous ox trains, some coming from the railroad at Corinne, and some that come from Fort Benton during the Summer, having been brought up by boat on the Missouri River. In the cañons these trains are things to be dreaded. The roads are very narrow and the grades often long and steep, with immense boulders above and below.

We met one of those trains soon after we entered the cañon, and at the top of a grade where the road was scarcely wider than the stage itself and seemed

to be cut into a wall of solid rock. Just how we were
to pass those huge wagons I did not see. But the
driver stopped his horses and two of the men got out,
the third stopping on the step and holding on to the
stage so it was impossible for me to get out, unless
I went out the other door and stood on the edge of an
awful precipice. The driver looked back, and not
seeing me, bawled out, "Where is the lady?" "Get
the lady out!" The man on the step jumped down
then, but the driver did not put his reins down, or
move from his seat until he had seen me safely on the
ground and had directed me where to stand.

In the meantime some of the train men had come
up, and, as soon as the stage driver was ready, they
proceeded to lift the stage—trunks and all—over and
on some rocks and tree tops, and then the four horses
were led around in between other rocks, where it
seemed impossible for them to stand one second.
There were three teams to come up, each consisting
of about eight yoke of oxen and three or four wagons.
It made me almost ill to see the poor patient oxen
straining and pulling up the grade those huge wagons
so heavily loaded. The crunching and groaning of
the wagons, rattling of the enormous cable chains, and
the creaking of the heavy yokes of the oxen were
awful sounds, but above all came the yells of the
drivers, and the sharp, pistol-like reports of the long
whips that they mercilessly cracked over the backs of
the poor beasts. It was most distressing.

After the wagons had all passed, men came back
and set the stage on the road in the same indifferent
way and with very few words. Each man seemed to
know just what to do, as though he had been train-

ing for years for the moving of that particular stage. The horses had not stirred and had paid no attention to the yelling and cracking of whips. While coming through the cañons we must have met six or seven of those trains, every one of which necessitated the setting in mid-air of the stage coach. It was the same performance always, each man knowing just what to do, and doing it, too, without loss of time. Not once did the driver put down the reins until he saw that "the lady" was safely out and it was ever with the same sing-song, "balance to the right," voice that he asked about me—except once, when he seemed to think more emphasis was needed, when he made the cañon ring by yelling, "Why in hell don't you get the lady out!" But the lady always got herself out. Rough as he was, I felt intuitively that I had a protector. We stopped at Rock Creek for dinner, and there he saw that I had the best of everything, and it was the same at Spitzler's, where we had supper.

We got fresh horses at The Leavings, and when I saw a strange driver on the seat my heart sank, fearing that from there on I might not have the same protection. We were at a large ranch—sort of an inn—and just beyond was Frozen Hill. The hill was given that name because a number of years ago a terrible blizzard struck some companies of infantry while on it, and before they could get to the valley below, or to a place of shelter, one half of the men were more or less frozen—some losing legs, some arms. They had been marching in thin clothing that was more or less damp from perspiration, as the day had been excessively hot. These blizzards are so fierce and wholly blinding, it is unsafe to move a step if caught out in one on the plains, and the troops probably lost their bearings as soon as the storm struck them.

It was almost dark when we got in the stage to go on, and I thought it rather queer that the driver should have asked us to go to the corral, instead of his driving around to the ranch for us. Very soon we were seated, but we did not start, and there seemed to be something wrong, judging by the way the stage was being jerked, and one could feel, too, that the brake was on. One by one those men got out, and just as the last one stepped down on one side the heads of two cream-colored horses appeared at the open door on the other side, their big troubled eyes looking straight at me.

During my life on the frontier I have seen enough of native horses to know that when a pair of excited mustang leaders try to get inside a stage, it is time for one to get out, so I got out! One of those men passengers instantly called to me, " You stay in there! " I asked, " Why? " " Because it is perfectly safe," said a second man. I was very indignant at being spoken to in this way and turned my back to them. The driver got the leaders in position, and then looking around, said to me that when the balky wheelers once started they would run up the hill " like the devil," and I would surely be left unless I was inside the stage.

I knew that he was telling the truth, and if he had been the first man to tell me to get in the coach I would have done so at once, but it so happened that he was the fourth, and by that time I was beginning to feel abused. It was bad enough to have to obey just one man, when at home, and then to have four strange men—three of them idiots, too—suddenly take upon themselves to order me around was not to be endured. I had started on the trip with the expectation of taking care of myself, and still felt competent to do so. Perhaps I was very tired, and perhaps I was very cross. At all events I told the driver I would not get in—that if I was left I would go back to the ranch. So I stayed outside, taking great care, however, to stand close to the stage door.

The instant I heard the loosening of the brake I jumped up on the step, and catching a firm hold each side of the door, was about to step in when one of those men passengers grabbed my arm and tried to jerk me back, so he could get in ahead of me! It was a dreadful thing for anyone to do, for if my hands and arms had not been unusually strong from riding hard-mouthed horses, I would undoubtedly have been thrown underneath the big wheels and horribly crushed, for the four horses were going at a terrific gait, and the jerky was swaying like a live thing. As it was, anger and indignation gave me extra strength and I scrambled inside with nothing more serious happening than a bruised head. But that man! He pushed in back of me and, not knowing the nice little ways of jerkies, was pitched forward to the floor with an awful thud. But after a second or so he pulled himself up on his seat, which was opposite mine, and there we two sat in silence and in darkness. I noticed the next morning that there was a big bruise on one side of his face, at the sight of which I rejoiced very much.

It was some distance this side of the hill when the

driver stopped his horses and waited for the two men who had been left. They seemed much exhausted when they came up, but found sufficient breath to abuse the driver for having left them; but he at once roared out, " Get in, I tell you, or I'll leave you sure enough ! " That settled matters, and we started on again. Very soon those men fell asleep and rolled off their seats to the floor, where they snored and had bad dreams. I was jammed in a corner without mercy, and of course did not sleep one second during the long wretched night. Twice we stopped for fresh horses, and at both places I walked about a little to rest my cramped feet and limbs. At breakfast the next morning I asked the driver to let me ride on top with him, which he consented to, and from there on to Benton I had peace and fresh air—the glorious air of Montana.

Yesterday—the day after I got here—I was positively ill from the awful shaking up, mental as well as physical, I received on that stage ride. We reached Benton at eleven. Faye was at the hotel with an ambulance when the stage drove up, and it was amusing to look at the faces of those men when they saw Faye in his uniform, and the government outfit. We started for camp at once, and left them standing on the hotel porch watching us as we drove down the street. It is a pity that such men cannot be compelled to serve at least one enlistment in the Army, and be drilled into something that resembles a real man. But perhaps recruiting officers would not accept them.

15

FORT SHAW, MONTANA TERRITORY,
October, 1878.

MY stay at the little town of Sun River Crossing was short, for when I arrived there the other day in the stage from Benton, I found a note awaiting me from Mrs. Bourke, saying that I must come right on to Fort Shaw, so I got back in the stage and came to the post, a distance of five miles, where General Bourke was on the lookout for me. He is in command of the regiment as well as the post, as Colonel Fitz-James is still in Europe. Of course regimental headquarters and the band are here, which makes the garrison seem very lively to me. The band is out at guard mounting every pleasant morning, and each Friday evening there is a fine concert in the hall by the orchestra, after which we have a little dance. The sun shines every day, but the air is cool and crisp and one feels that ice and snow are not very far off.

The order for the two companies on the Marias to return to the Milk River country was most unexpected. That old villain Sitting Bull, chief of the Sioux Indians, made an official complaint to the " Great Father " that the half-breeds were on land that belonged to his people, and were killing buffalo that were theirs also. So the companies have been sent up to arrest the half-breeds and conduct them to Fort Belknap, and to break up their villages and burn their cabins. The officers disliked the prospect of doing all this very much, for there must be many women and little children among them. Just how long it will take no one can tell, but probably three or four weeks.

And while Faye is away I am staying with General

and Mrs. Bourke. I cannot have a house until he comes, for quarters cannot be assigned to an officer until he has reported for duty at a post. There are two companies of the old garrison here still, and this has caused much doubling up among the lieutenants— that is, assigning one set of quarters to two officers— but it has been arranged so we can be by ourselves. Four rooms at one end of the hospital have been cut off from the hospital proper by a heavy partition that has been put up at the end of the long corridor, and these rooms are now being calcimined and painted. They were originally intended for the contract surgeon. We will have our own little porch and entrance hall and a nice yard back of the kitchen. It will all be so much more private and comfortable in every way than it could possibly have been in quarters with another family.

It is delightful to be in a nicely furnished, well-regulated house once more. The buildings are all made of adobe, and the officers' quarters have low, broad porches in front, and remind me a little of the houses at Fort Lyon, only of course these are larger and have more rooms. There are nice front yards, and on either side of the officers' walk is a row of beautiful cottonwood trees that form a complete arch. They are watered by an *acéquia* that brings water from Sun River several miles above the post. The post is built along the banks of that river but I do not see from what it derived its name, for the water is muddy all the time. The country about here is rather rolling, but there are two large buttes— one called Square Butte that is really grand, and the other is Crown Butte. The drives up and down the river are lovely, and I think that Bettie and I will soon have many pleasant mornings together on these roads. After the slow dignified drives I am taking almost every day, I wonder how her skittish, affected ways will seem to me!

I am so glad to be with the regiment again—that is, with old friends, although seeing them in a garrison up in the Rocky Mountains is very different from the life in a large city in the far South! Four companies are still at Fort Missoula, where the major of the regiment is in command. Our commanding officer and his wife were there also during the winter, therefore those of us who were at Helena and Camp Baker, feel that we must entertain them in some way. Consequently, now that everyone is settled, the dining and wining has begun. Almost every day there is a dinner or card party given in their honor, and several very delightful luncheons have been given. And then the members of the old garrison, according to army etiquette, have to entertain those that have just come, so altogether we are very gay. The dinners are usually quite elegant, formal affairs, beautifully served with dainty china and handsome silver. The officers appear at these in full-dress uniform, and that adds much to the brilliancy of things, but not much to the comfort of the officers, I imagine.

Everyone is happy in the fall, after the return of the companies from their hard and often dangerous summer campaign, and settles down for the winter. It is then that we feel we can feast and dance, and it is then, too, that garrison life at a frontier post becomes so delightful. We are all very fond of dancing, so I think that Faye and I will give a cotillon later on.

In fact, it is about all we can do while living in those four rooms.

We have Episcopal service each alternate Sunday, when the Rev. Mr. Clark comes from Helena, a distance of eighty-five miles, to hold one service for the garrison here and one at the very small village of Sun River. And once more Major Pierce and I are in the same choir. Doctor Gordon plays the organ, and beautifully, too. For some time he was organist in a church at Washington, and of course knows the service perfectly. Our star, however, is a sergeant! He came to this country with an opera troupe, but an attack of diphtheria ruined his voice for the stage, so he enlisted! His voice (barytone) is still of exquisite quality, and just the right volume for our hall.

FORT SHAW, MONTANA TERRITORY,
January, 1879.

THERE has been so much going on in the garrison, and so much for me to attend to in getting the house settled, I have not had time to write more than the note I sent about dear little Billie. I miss him dreadfully, for, small as he was, he was always doing something cunning, always getting into mischief. He died the day we moved to this house, and it hurts even now when I think of how I was kept from caring for him the last day of his short life. And he wanted to be with me, too, for when I put him in his box he would cling to my fingers and try to get back to me. It is such a pity that we ever cracked his nuts. His lower teeth had grown to perfect little tusks that had bored a hole in the roof of his mouth. As soon as that was discovered, we had them cut off, but it was too late—the little grayback would not eat.

We are almost settled now, and Sam, our Chinese cook, is doing splendidly. At first there was trouble, and I had some difficulty in convincing him that I was mistress of my own house and not at all afraid of him. Cagey has gone back to Holly Springs. He had become utterly worthless during the summer camp, where he had almost nothing to do.

Our little entertainment for the benefit of the mission here was a wonderful success. Every seat was occupied, every corner packed, and we were afraid that the old theater might collapse. We made eighty dollars, clear of all expenses. The tableaux were first, so the small people could be sent home early. Then came our pantomime. Sergeant Thompson sang the words and the orchestra played a soft accompaniment that made the whole thing most effective. Major Pierce was a splendid Villikins, and as Dinah I received enough applause to satisfy anyone, but the curtain remained down, motionless and unresponsive, just because I happened to be the wife of the stage manager!

The prison scene and *Miserere* from Il Trovatore were beautiful. Sergeant Mann instructed each one of the singers, and the result was far beyond our expectations. Of course the fine orchestra of twenty pieces was a great addition and support. Our duet was not sung, because I was seized with an attack of stage fright at the last rehearsal, so Sergeant Mann sang an exquisite solo in place of the duet, which was ever so much nicer. I was with Mrs. Joyce in one scene of her pantomime, " John Smith," which was

far and away the best part of the entertainment. Mrs.
Joyce was charming, and showed us what a really fine
actress she is. The enlisted men went to laugh, and
they kept up a good-natured clapping and laughing
from first to last.

It was surprising that so many of the Sun River
and ranch people came, for the night was terrible,
even for Montana, and the roads must have been im-
passable in places. Even here in the post there were
great drifts of snow, and the path to the theater was
cut through banks higher than our heads. It had been
mild and pleasant for weeks, and only two nights
before the entertainment we had gone to the hall for
rehearsal with fewer wraps than usual. We had been
there about an hour, I think, when the corporal of the
guard came in to report to the officer of the day, that
a fierce blizzard was making it impossible for sentries
to walk post. His own appearance told better than
words what the storm was. He had on a long buffalo
coat, muskrat cap and gauntlets, and the fur from his
head down, also heavy overshoes, were filled with
snow, and at each end of his mustache were icicles
hanging. He made a fine, soldierly picture as he
brought his rifle to his side and saluted. The officer
of the day hurried out, and after a time returned, he
also smothered in furs and snow. He said the storm
was terrific and he did not see how many of us could
possibly get to our homes.

But of course we could not remain in the hall until
the blizzard had ceased, so after rehearsing a little
more, we wrapped ourselves up as well as we could
and started for our homes. The wind was blowing
at hurricane speed, I am sure, and the heavy fall of

snow was being carried almost horizontally, and how each frozen flake did sting! Those of us who lived in the garrison could not go very far astray, as the fences were on one side and banks of snow on the other, but the light snow had already drifted in between and made walking very slow and difficult. We all got to our different homes finally, with no greater mishap than a few slightly frozen ears and noses. Snow had banked up on the floor inside of our front door so high that for a few minutes Faye and I thought that we could not get in the house.

Major Pierce undertook to see Mrs. Elmer safely to her home at the sutler's store, and in order to get there they were obliged to cross a wide space in between the officers' line and the store. Nothing could be seen ten feet from them when they left the last fence, but they tried to get their bearings by the line of the fence, and closing their eyes, dashed ahead into the cloud of blinding, stinging snow. Major Pierce had expected to go straight to a side door of the store, but the awful strength of the wind and snow pushed them over, and they struck a corner of the fence farthest away—in fact, they would have missed the fence also if Mrs. Elmer's fur cape had not caught on one of the pickets, and gone out on the plains to certain death. Bright lights had been placed in the store windows, but not one had they seen. These storms kill so many range cattle, but the most destructive of all is a freeze after a chinook, that covers the ground with ice so it is impossible for them to get to the grass. At such times the poor animals suffer cruelly. We often hear them lowing, sometimes for days, and can easily imagine that we see the starving beasts wandering on and on, ever in search of an uncovered bit of grass. The lowing of hundreds of cattle on a cold winter night is the most horrible sound one can imagine.

Cold as it is, I ride Bettie almost every day, but only on the high ground where the snow has been blown off. We are a funny sight sometimes when we come in—Bettie's head, neck, and chest white with her frozen breath, icicles two or three inches long hanging from each side of her chin, and my fur collar and cap white also. I wear a sealskin cap with broad ear tabs, long sealskin gauntlets that keep my hands and arms warm, and high leggings and moccasins of beaver, but with the fur inside, which makes them much warmer. A tight chamois skin waist underneath my cadet-cloth habit and a broad fur collar completes a riding costume that keeps me warm without being bungling. I found a sealskin coat too warm and heavy.

No one will ride now and they do not know what fine exercise they are missing. And I am sure that Bettie is glad to get her blood warm once during the twenty-four hours. Friends kindly tell me that some day I will be found frozen out on the plains, and that the frisky Bettie will kill me, and so on. I ride too fast to feel the cold, and Bettie I enjoy—all but the airs she assumes inside the post. Our house is near the center of the officers' line, and no matter which way I go or what I do, that little beast can never be made to walk one step until we get out on the road, but insists upon going sideways, tossing her head, and giving little rears. It looks so affected and makes me feel very foolish, particularly since Mrs.

Conger said to me the other day : " Why do you make your horse dance that way—he might throw you." I then asked her if she would not kindly ride Bettie a few times and teach her to keep her feet down. But she said it was too cold to go out!

We have much more room in this house than we had in the hospital, and are more comfortable every way. Almost every day or evening there is some sort of an entertainment—german, dinner, luncheon, or card party. I am so glad that we gave the first cotillon that had ever been given in the regiment, for it was something new on the frontier ; therefore everyone enjoyed it. Just now the garrison seems to have gone cotillon crazy, and not being satisfied with a number of private ones, a german club has been organized that gives dances in the hall every two weeks. So far Faye has been the leader of each one. With all this pleasure, the soldiers are not being neglected. Every morning there are drills and a funny kind of target practice inside the quarters, and of course there are inspections and other things.

FORT ELLIS, MONTANA TERRITORY,
January, 1879.

IT is still cold, stinging cold, and we are beginning to think that there was much truth in what we were told on our way over last fall—that Fort Ellis is the very coldest place in the whole territory. For two days the temperature was fifty below, and I can assure you that things hummed! The logs of our house made loud reports like pistol shots, and there was frost on the walls of every room that were not near roaring fires. No one ventures forth such weather unless compelled to do so, and then, of course, every precaution is taken to guard against freezing. In this altitude one will freeze before feeling the cold, as I know from experience, having at the present time two fiery red ears of enormous size. They are fiery in feeling, too, as well as in color.

The atmosphere looks like frozen mist, and is wonderful, and almost at any time between sunrise and sunset a " sun dog " can be seen with its scintillating rainbow tints, that are brilliant yet exquisitely delicate in coloring. Our houses are really very warm —the thick logs are plastered inside and papered, every window has a storm sash and every room a double floor, and our big stoves can burn immense logs. But notwithstanding all this, our greatest trial is to keep things to eat. Everything freezes solid, and so far we have not found one edible that is improved by freezing. It must be awfully discouraging to a cook to find on a biting cold morning, that there is not one thing in the house that can be prepared for breakfast until it has passed through the thawing process; that even the water in the barrels has become solid, round pieces of ice! All along the roof of one side of our house are immense icicles that almost touch the snow on the ground. These are a reminder of the last chinook!

But only last week it was quite pleasant—not real summery, but warm enough for one to go about in safety. Faye came down from the saw-mill one of those days to see the commanding officer about something and to get the mail. When he was about to start back, in fact, was telling me good-by, I happened to say that I wished I could go, too. Faye said: "You could not stand the exposure, but you might wear my little fur coat." Suggesting the coat was a give-in that I at once took advantage of, and in precisely twenty minutes Charlie, our Chinese cook, had been told what to do, a few articles of clothing wrapped and strapped, and I on Bettie's back ready for the wilds. An old soldier on a big corral horse was our only escort, and to his saddle were fastened our various bags and bundles.

Far up a narrow valley that lies in between two mountain ranges, the government has a saw-mill that is worked by twenty or more soldiers under the supervision of an officer, where lumber can be cut when needed for the post. One of these ranges is very high, and Mount Bridger, first of the range and nearest Fort Ellis, along whose base we had to go, has snow on its top most of the year. Often when wind is not noticeable at the post, we can see the light snow being blown with terrific force from the peak of this mountain for hundreds of yards in a perfectly horizontal line, when it will spread out and fall in a magnificent spray another two or three hundred feet.

The mill is sixteen miles from Fort Ellis, and the snow was very deep—so deep in places that the horses had difficulty in getting their feet forward, and as we got farther up, the valley narrowed into a ravine where the snow was even deeper. There was no road or even trail to be seen; the bark on trees had been cut to mark the way, but far astray we could not have gone unless we had deliberately ridden up the side of a mountain. The only thing that resembled a house along the sixteen miles was a deserted cabin about half way up, and which only accentuated the awful loneliness.

Bettie had been standing in the stable for several days, and that, with the biting cold air in the valley, made her entirely too frisky, and she was very nervous, too, over the deep snow that held her feet down. We went Indian file—I always in the middle—as there were little grades and falling-off places all along that were hidden by the snow, and I was cautioned constantly by Faye and Bryant to keep my horse in line. The snow is very fine and dry in this altitude, and never packs as it does in a more moist atmosphere.

When we had ridden about one half the distance up we came to a little hill, at the bottom of which was known to be a bridge that crossed the deep-cut banks of one of those mountain streams that are dry eleven months of the year and raging torrents the twelfth, when the snow melts. It so happened that Faye did not get on this bridge just right, so down in the light snow he and Pete went, and all that we could see of them were Faye's head and shoulders and the head of the horse with the awful bulging eyes! Poor Pete was terribly frightened, and floundered about until he nearly buried himself in snow as he tried to find something solid upon which to put his feet.

I was just back of Faye when he went down, but the next instant I had retreated to the top of the hill, and had to use all the strength in my arms to avoid being brought back to the post. When Bettie saw Pete go down, she whirled like a flash and with two or three bounds was on top of the hill again. She was awfully frightened and stood close to Bryant's horse, trembling all over. Poor Bryant did not know what to do or which one to assist, so I told him to go down and get the lieutenant up on the bank and I would follow. Just how Faye got out of his difficulty I did not see, for I was too busy attending to my own affairs. Bettie acted as though she was be-witched, and go down to the bridge she would not. Finally, when I was about tired out, Faye said we must not waste more time there and that I had better ride Pete.

So I dismounted and the saddles were changed, and then there was more trouble. Pete had never been ridden by a woman before, and thinking, perhaps, that his sudden one-sidedness was a part of the bridge per-formance, at once protested by jumps and lunges, but he soon quieted down and we started on again. Bettie danced a little with Faye, but that was all. She evi-dently remembered her lost battle with him at Camp Baker.

It was almost dark when we reached the saw-mill, and as soon as it became known that I was with the " lieutenant " every man sprang up from some place underneath the snow to look at me, and two or three ran over to assist Bryant with our things. It was awfully nice to know that I was a person of im-portance, even if it was out in a camp in the moun-tains where probably a woman had never been before. The little log cabin built for officers had only the one long room, with large, comfortable bunk, two tables, chairs, a " settle " of pine boards, and near one end of the room was a box stove large enough to heat two rooms of that size. By the time my stiffened body could get inside, the stove had been filled to the top

"There was no road or even trail to be seen."

with pine wood that roared and crackled in a most cheerful and inviting manner.

But the snow out there! I do not consider it advisable to tell the exact truth, so I will simply say that it was higher than the cabin, but that for some reason it had left an open space of about three feet all around the logs, and that gave us air and light through windows which had been thoughtfully placed unusually high. The long stable, built against a bank, where the horses and mules were kept, was entirely buried underneath the snow, and you would never have dreamed that there was anything whatever there unless you had seen the path that had been shoveled down to the door. The cabin the men lived in, I did not see at all. We were in a ravine where the pine forest was magnificent, but one could see that the trees were shortened many feet by the great depth of snow.

Our meals were brought to us by Bryant from the soldiers' mess, and as the cook was only a pick-up, they were often a mess indeed, but every effort was made to have them nice. The day after we got there the cook evidently made up his mind that some recognition should be shown of the honor of my presence in the woods, so he made a big fat pie for my dinner. It was really fat, for the crust must have been mostly of lard, and the poor man had taken much pains with the decorations of twisted rings and little balls that were on the top. It really looked very nice as Bryant set it down on the table in front of me, with an air that the most dignified of butlers might have envied, and said, " Compliments of the cook, ma'am! " Of course I was, and am still, delighted with the attention from the cook, but for some reason I was

16

suspicious of that pie, it was so very high up, so I continued to talk about it admiringly until after Bryant had gone from the cabin, and then I tried to cut it! The filling—and there was an abundance—was composed entirely of big, hard raisins that still had their seeds in. The knife could not cut them, so they rolled over on the table and on the floor, much like marbles. I scooped out a good-sized piece as well as I could, gathered up the runaway raisins, and then—put it in the stove.

And this I did at every dinner while I was there, almost trembling each time for fear Bryant would come in and discover how the pie was being disposed of. It lasted long, for I could not cut off a piece for Faye, as Bryant had given us to understand in the beginning that the *chef d'œuvre* was for me only.

Nothing pleases me more than to have the enlisted men pay me some little attention, and when the day after the pie a beautiful little gray squirrel was brought to me in a nice airy box, I was quite overcome. He is very much like Billie in size and color, which seems remarkable, since Billie was from the far South and this little fellow from the far North. I wanted to take him out of the box at once, but the soldier said he would bite, and having great respect for the teeth of a squirrel, I let him stay in his prison while we were out there.

The first time I let him out after we got home he was frantic, and jumped on the mantel, tables, and chairs, scattering things right and left. Finally he started to run up a lace window curtain back of the sewing machine. On top of the machine was a plate

of warm cookies that Charlie had just brought to me,
and getting a sniff of those the squirrel stopped instantly, hesitated just a second, and then over he
jumped, took a cookie with his paws and afterwards
held it with his teeth until he had settled himself com-
fortably, when he again took it in his paws and proceeded to eat with the greatest relish. After he had
eaten all he very well could, he hid the rest back of
the curtain in quite an at-home way. There was nothing at all wonderful in all this, except that the squirrel
was just from the piney woods where warm sugar
cakes are unknown, so how did he know they were
good to eat?

I was at the saw-mill four days, and then we all
came in together and on bob sleds. There were four
mules for each sleigh, so not much attention was paid
to the great depth of snow. Both horses knew when
we got to the bridge and gave Bryant trouble. Every
bit of the trail out had been obliterated by drifting
snow, and I still wonder how these animals recognized
the precise spot when the snow was level in every
place.

We found the house in excellent order, and consider
our new Chinaman a treasure. A few days before
Faye went to the mill I made some Boston brown
bread. I always make that myself, as I fancy I can
make it very good, but for some reason I was late in
getting it on to steam that day, so when I went to the
kitchen to put it in the oven I found a much-abused
Chinaman. When he saw what I was about to do he
became very angry and his eyes looked green. He
said, " You no put him in l'oven." I said, " Yes,
Charlie, I have to for one hour." He said, " You no

care workman, you sploil my dee-nee, you get some other boy."

Now Charlie was an excellent servant and I did not care to lose him, but to take that bread out was not to be considered. I would no longer have been mistress of my own house, so I told him quietly, " Very well," and closed the oven door with great deliberation. The dinner was a little better than usual, and I wondered all the time what the outcome would be. I knew that he was simply piqued because I had not let him make the bread. After his work was all done he came in and said, with a smile that was almost a grin, " I go now—I send 'nother boy," and go he did. But the " other boy " came in time to give us a delicious breakfast, and everything went on just the same as when old Charlie was here. He is in Bozeman and comes to see us often.

This Charlie takes good care of my chickens that are my pride and delight. There are twenty, and every one is snow white; some have heavy round topknots. I found them at different ranches. It is so cold here that chicken roosts have to be covered with strips of blanket and made flat and broad, so the feathers will cover the chickens' feet, otherwise they will be frozen. It is a treat to have fresh eggs, and without having to pay a dollar and a half per dozen for them. That is the price we have paid for eggs almost ever since we came to the Territory.

FORT ELLIS, MONTANA TERRITORY,
June, 1880.

EVERYTHING is packed and on the wagons—
that is, all but the camp outfit which we will use
on the trip over—and in the morning we will start on
our way back to Fort Shaw. With the furniture
that belongs to the quarters and the camp things, we
were so comfortable in our own house we decided
that there was no necessity to go to Mrs. Adams's,
except for dinner and breakfast, although both General and Mrs. Adams have been most hospitable and
kind.

The way these two moves have come about seems
very funny to me. Faye was ordered over here to
command C Company when it was left without an
officer, because he was senior second lieutenant in the
regiment and entitled to it. The captain of this company has been East on recruiting service, and has just
been relieved by Colonel Knight, captain of Faye's
company at Shaw; as that company is now without
an officer, the senior second lieutenant has to return and command his own company. This recognition of a little rank has been expensive to us, and disagreeable too. The lieutenants are constantly being
moved about, often details that apparently do not
amount to much but which take much of their small
salary.

The Chinaman is going with us, for which I am
most thankful, and at his request we have decided to
take the white chickens. Open boxes have been made
specially for them that fit on the rear ends of the
wagons, and we think they will be very comfortable—
but we will certainly look like emigrants when on the

road. The two squirrels will go also. The men of the company have sent me three squirrels during the winter. The dearest one of all had been injured and lived only a few days. The flying squirrel is the least interesting and seems stupid. It will lie around and sleep during the entire day, but at dark will manage to get on some high perch and flop down on your shoulder or head when you least expect it and least desire it, too. The little uncanny thing cannot fly, really, but the webs enable it to take tremendous leaps. I expect that it looks absurd for us to be taking across the country a small menagerie, but the squirrels were presents, and of course had to go, and the chickens are beautiful, and give us quantities of eggs. Besides, if we had left the chickens, Charlie might not have gone, for he feeds them and watches over them as if they were his very own, and looks very cross if the striker gives them even a little corn.

Night before last an unusually pleasant dancing party was given by Captain McAndrews, when Faye and I were guests of honor. It was such a surprise to us, and so kind in Captain McAndrews to give it, for he is a bachelor. Supper was served in his own quarters, but dancing was in the vacant set adjoining. The rooms were beautifully decorated with flags, and the fragrant cedar and spruce. Mrs. Adams, wife of the commanding officer, superintended all of the arrangements and also assisted in receiving. The supper was simply delicious—as all army suppers are—and I fancy that she and other ladies of the garrison were responsible for the perfect salads and cakes.

The orchestra was from Bozeman, so the music **was**

very good. Quite a party of young people also, many
of them friends of ours, came up from Bozeman,
which not only swelled the number of guests, but gave
life to the dance, for in a small garrison like this the
number of partners is limited. The country about
here is beautiful now; the snow is melting on the
mountains, and there is such a lovely green every
place, I almost wish that we might have remained
until fall, for along the valleys and through the cañons
there are grand trails for horseback riding, while
Fort Shaw has nothing of the kind.

Fort Shaw, Montana Territory,
July, 1880.

WE are with the commanding officer and his wife
for a few days while our house is being settled. Every room has just been painted and tinted and
looks so clean and bright. The Chinaman, squirrels,
and chickens are there now, and are already very
much at home, and Charlie is delighted that the
chickens are so much admired.

The first part of the trip over was simply awful!
The morning was beautiful when we left Ellis—warm
and sunny—and everybody came to see us off. We
started in fine spirits, and all went well for ten or
twelve miles, when we got to the head waters of the
Missouri, where the three small rivers, Gallatin, Jefferson, and Madison join and make the one big river.
The drive through the forest right there is usually
delightful, and although we knew that the water was
high in the Gallatin by Fort Ellis, we were wholly un-
prepared for the scene that confronted us when we
reached the valley. Not one inch of ground could

be seen—nothing but the trees surrounded by yellow, muddy water that showed quite a current.

The regular stage road has been made higher than the ground because of these July freshets, when the snow is melting on the mountains, but it was impossible to keep on it, as its many turns could not be seen, and it would not have helped much either, as the water was deep. The ambulance was in the lead, of course, so we were in all the excitement of exploring unseen ground. The driver would urge the mules, and if the leaders did not go down, very good—we would go on, perhaps a few yards. If they did go down enough to show that it was dangerous that way, he would turn them in another direction and try there. Sometimes it was necessary almost to turn around in order to keep upon the higher ground. In this way mules and drivers worked until four o'clock in the afternoon, the dirty water often coming up over the floor of the ambulance, and many times it looked as if we could not go on one step farther without being upset in the mud and water.

But at four we reached an island, where there was a small house and a stable for the stage relay horses, and not far beyond was another island where Faye decided to camp for the night. It was the only thing he could have done. He insisted upon my staying at the house, but I finally convinced him that the proper place for me was in camp, and I went on with him. The island was very small, and the highest point above water could not have been over two feet. Of course everything had to be upon it—horses, mules, wagons, drivers, Faye and I, and the two small squirrels, and the chickens also. In addition to our

own traveling menagerie there were native inhabitants
of that island—millions and millions of mosquitoes,
each one with a sharp appetite and sharp sting. We
thought that we had learned all about vicious mosquitoes while in the South, but the Southern mosquitoes are slow and caressing in comparison to those
Montana things.

It was very warm, and the Chinaman felt sorry for
the chickens shut up in the boxes, where fierce quarrels seemed to be going on all the time. So after he
had fed them we talked it over, and decided to let
them out, as they could not possibly get away from
us across the big body of water. There were twenty
large chickens in one big box, and twenty-seven small
ones that had been brought in a long box by themselves. Well, Charlie and one of the men got the
boxes down and opened them. At once the four or
five mother hens clucked and scratched and kept on
clucking until the little chicks were let out, when
every one of them ran to its own mother, and each
hen strutted off with her own brood. That is the absolute truth, but is not all. When night came the
chickens went back to their boxes to roost—all but
the small ones. Those were left outside with their
mothers, and just before daylight Charlie raised a
great commotion when he put them up for the day's
trip.

When we were about ready to start in the morning,
a man came over from the house and told Faye that
he would pilot us through the rest of the water, that
it was very dangerous in places, where the road had
been built up, and if a narrow route was not carefully
followed, a team would go down a bank of four or

five feet. He had with him just the skeleton of a
wagon—the four wheels with two or three long boards
on top, drawn by two horses. So we went down in
the dirty water again, that seemed to get deeper and
deeper as we splashed on.

Now and then I could catch a glimpse of our pilot
standing up on the boards very much like a circus
rider, for the wagon wheels were twisting around
over the roots of trees and stones, in a way that required careful balancing on his part. We got along
very well until about noon, when a soldier came
splashing up on a mule and told Faye that one of
the wagons had turned over! That was dreadful
news and made me most anxious about the trunks and
chests, and the poor chickens, too, all of which might
be down under the water.

They got the ambulance under some trees, unfastened the mules and led them away, leaving me alone,
without even the driver. The soldier had thoughtfully led up Pete for Faye to ride back, and the
mules were needed to assist in pulling the wagon up.
Fortunately the wagon was caught by a tree and did
not go entirely over, and it so happened, too, that it
was the one loaded more with furniture than anything
else, so not much damage was done.

Our pilot had left us some time before, to hurry on
and get any passengers that might come in the stage
that runs daily between Helena and Bozeman. As
soon as I began to look around a little after I was left
alone in the ambulance, I discovered that not so very
far ahead was an opening in the trees and bushes, and
that a bit of beautiful dry land could be seen. I was
looking at it with longing eyes when suddenly some-

thing came down the bank and on into the water, and
not being particularly brave, I thought of the unprotected position I was in. But the terrible monster
turned out to be our pilot, and as he came nearer, I
saw that he had something on the wagon—whether
men or women or mere bags of stuff I could not tell.

But in time he got near enough for me to see that
two men were with him—most miserable, scared tourists—both standing up on the seesawing boards, the
first with arms around the pilot's neck, and the second
with his arms around him. They were dressed very
much alike, each one having on his head an immaculate white straw hat, and over his coat a long—very
long—linen duster, and they both had on gloves!
Their trousers were pulled up as high as they could
get them, giving a fine display of white hose and low
shoes. The last one was having additional woe, for
one leg of his trousers was slipping down, and of
course it was impossible for him to pull it up and
keep his balance. Every turn of the wheels the thick
yellow water was being spattered on them, and I can
imagine the condition they were in by the time they
reached the little inn on the island. The pilot thought
they were funny, too, for when he passed he grinned
and jerked his head back to call my attention to them.
He called to know what had happened to me, and I
told him that I was a derelict, and he would ascertain the cause farther on.

After a while—it seemed hours to me—Faye and
the wagons came up, and in time we got out of the
awful mess and on dry land. It was the Fourth of
July, and we all wished for a gun or something that
would make a loud noise wherewith we could cele-

brate—not so much the day as our rejoicing at getting
out of the wilderness. The men were in a deplorable
condition, wet and tired, for no one had been able
to sleep the night before because of the vicious mosquitoes and the stamping of the poor animals. So,
when Faye saw one of the drivers go to a spring for
water, and was told that it was a large, fine spring,
he decided to camp right there and rest before going
farther.

But rest we could not, for the mosquitoes were
there also, and almost as bad as they had been on the
island, and the tents inside were covered with them
as soon as they were pitched. If there is a person who
thinks that a mosquito has no brain, and is incapable
of looking ahead, that person will soon learn his mistake if ever he comes to the Missouri River, Montana!
The heat was fierce, too, and made it impossible for
us to remain in the tents, so we were obliged, after
all, to sit out under·the trees until the air had cooled
at night sufficiently to chill the mosquitoes.

The chickens were let out at every camp, and each
time, without fail, they flew up to their boxes on the
wagons. Charlie would put in little temporary roosts,
that made them more comfortable, and before daylight every morning he would gather up the little ones
and the mothers and put them in the crates for the
day. He is willing and faithful, but has queer ideas
about some things. Just as I was getting in the ambulance the second morning on the trip, I heard a
crunching sound and then another, and looking back,
I saw the Chinaman on top of the mess chest with
head bent over and elbows sticking out, jumping up
and down with all his strength.

I ran over and told him not to do so, for I saw at once what was the matter. But he said, " He velly blig —he no go downee—me flixee him," and up and down he went again, harder than ever. After a lengthy argument he got down, and I showed him once more how to put the things in so the top would shut tight. There were a good many pieces of broken china, and these Charlie pitched over in the water with a grin that plainly said, " You see—me flixee you ! " Of course the soldiers saw it all and laughed heartily, which made Charlie very angry, and gave him a fine opportunity to express himself in Chinese. The rest of the trip was pleasant, and some of the camps were delightful, but I am afraid that I no longer possess beautiful white chickens—my China- man seems to be the owner of all, big and small.

FORT SHAW, MONTANA TERRITORY,
August, 1880.

THE company has been ordered to " proceed with- out delay " to Fort Maginnis, a post that is just being established, and to assist another company in building temporary log quarters. The other company will go from Fort Missoula, and has to remain at the new post during the winter, but Faye's company will return here in November. We were all ready to go to the Yellowstone Park next week with Gen- eral and Mrs. Bourke, but this order from Department Headquarters upsets everything. The company was designated there, and go it must, although Faye has been at Fort Shaw only six weeks. He has command, of course, as Colonel Knight is East on recruiting serv- ice, and the first lieutenant is abroad.

General and Mrs. Bourke could not understand at first why I would not go with them to the park, just the same, but I understood perfectly, and said at once that I would go to Maginnis with Faye. For, to go in one direction where there is only a weekly mail, and Faye to go in another direction where there is no mail at all, and through an Indian country, was not to be considered one second. I was half afraid that the commanding officer might forbid my going with Faye, as he could have done, but he did not, and when he saw that I could not be persuaded to change my mind, an ambulance was ordered to go with the command, so I can have a shelter when it storms, for I shall ride Bettie on the trip.

The distance over is one hundred and fifty miles right across mountains and valleys, and there will be only a faint trail to guide us, and I am anticipating great delight in such a long horseback ride through a wild country. We will have everything for our comfort, too. Faye will be in command, and that means much, and a young contract surgeon, who has been recently appointed, will go with us, and our Chinese cook will go also. I have always wanted to take a trip of this kind, and know that it will be like one long picnic, only much nicer. I never cared for real picnics —they always have so much headache with them. We have very little to do for the march as our camp outfit is in unusually fine condition. After Charlie's " flixee " so much mess-chest china, Faye had made to order a complete set for four people of white agate ware with blue bands. We have two sets of plates, vegetable dishes, cups and saucers, egg cups, soup plates, and a number of small pieces. The plates and

dishes, also platters, can be folded together, and consequently require very little room, and it is a great
comfort to know that these things are unbreakable,
and that we will not be left without plates for the
table when we get in the wilds, and the ware being
white looks very nice, not in the least like tin. It
came yesterday, just in time.

The two squirrels I carried to the woods and turned
loose. I could not take them, and I would not leave
them to be neglected perhaps. The " Tiger " was still
a tiger, and as wild and fierce as when he came from
the saw-mill, and was undoubtedly an old squirrel not
to be taught new tricks. The flying thing was wholly
lacking in sense. I scattered pounds of nuts all about
and hope that the two little animals will not suffer.
The Chinaman insisted upon our taking those chickens! He goes out every now and then and gives them
big pans of food and talks to them in Chinese with a
voice and expression that makes one almost want to
weep, because the chickens have to be left behind.

We are to start on the eighteenth, and on the nine-
teenth we had expected to give a dinner—a very nice
one, too. I am awfully sorry that we could not have
given it before going away, for there are so many
things to do here during the winter. The doctor has
had no experience whatever in camp life, and we are
wondering how he will like it. He looks like a man
who would much prefer a nice little rocking-chair in
a nice little room.

CAMP NEAR JUNOT'S, IN THE JUDITH BASIN,
August, 1880.

THIS will be left at a little trading store as we pass to-morrow morning, with the hope that it will soon be taken on to Benton and posted.

So far, the trip has been delightful, and every bit as nice as I had anticipated. The day we left the post was more than hot—it was simply scorching; and my whole face on the right side, ear and all, was blistered before we got to the ferry. Just now I am going through a process of peeling which is not beautifying, and is most painful.

Before we had come two miles it was discovered that a " washer " was lacking on one of the wheels of a wagon, and a man was sent back on a mule to get one. This caused a delay and made Faye cross, for it really was inexcusable in the wagon master to send a wagon out on a trip like this in that condition. The doctor did not start with the command, but rode up while we were waiting for the man with the washer. The soldiers were lounging on the ground near the wagons, talking and laughing; but when they saw the doctor coming, there was perfect silence over there, and I watched and listened, curious to see what effect the funny sight would have upon them. First one sat up, then another, and some stood up, then some one of them giggled, and that was quite enough to start everyone of them to laughing. They were too far away for the laughing and snickering to be disrespectful, or even to be noticed much, but I knew why they laughed, for I laughed too.

The doctor did not present a military appearance. He is the very smallest man I ever saw, and he was on

a government horse that is known by its great height—
sixteen hands and two inches, I believe—and the little
man's stirrups were about half way down the horse's
sides, and his knees almost on the horse's back. All
three of us are wearing officers' white cork helmets,
but the doctor's is not a success, being ever so much
too large for his small head, consequently it had tilted
back and found a resting place on his shoulders, covering his ears and the upper part of his already hot
face. For a whip he carried a little switch not much
longer than his gauntlets, and which would have puzzled the big horse, if struck by it. With it all the
little man could not ride, and as his government saddle was evidently intended for a big person, he seemed
uncertain as to which was the proper place to sit—
the pommel, the middle, or the curved back. All during that first day's march the soldiers watched him.
I knew this, although we were at the head of the
column—for every time he would start his horse up
a little I could hear smothered laughter back of us.

It was late when we finally got across the Missouri
on the funny ferryboat, so we camped for the night
on this side near the ferryman's house. It was the
doctor's first experience in camp, and of course he
did not know how to make himself comfortable. He
suffered from the heat, and became still warmer by
rushing up and down fanning himself and fighting
mosquitoes. Then after dinner he had his horse saddled, a soldier helped him to mount, and he rode back
and forth bobbing all sorts of ways, until Faye could
stand it no longer and told him to show some mercy
to the beast that had carried him all day, and would
have to do the same for days to come.

17

Most of the camps have been in beautiful places—
always by some clear stream where often there was
good trout fishing. In one or two of these we found
grayling, a very gamey fish, that many epicures consider more delicate than the trout. We have a fine
way of keeping fish for the following day. As soon
as possible after they have been caught we pack them
in long, wet grass and put them in a cool spot, and in
this way they will keep remarkably fresh.

We have had an abundance of game, too—all kinds
of grouse and prairie chicken, and the men killed one
antelope. The Chinaman thought that Faye shot
quite too many birds, and began to look cross when
they were brought in, which annoyed me exceedingly,
and I was determined to stop it. So one evening, after
Faye had taken some young chicken to the cook tent,
I said to the doctor, " Come with me," and going over
to the tent I picked up the birds and went to some
trees near by, and handing the doctor one, asked him
to help me pick them, at the same time commencing
to pull the feathers out of one myself. The poor doctor looked as though he was wishing he had made a
specialty of dementia, and stood like a goose, looking
at the chicken. Charlie soon became very restless—
went inside the tent, and then came out, humming all
the time. Finally he gave in, and coming over to us,
fairly snatched the birds from me and said, " Me
flixee him," and carried the whole bunch back of his
tent where we could not see him. Since that evening
Charlie has been the most delighted one in camp when
Faye has brought birds in.

All the way we have had only a faint trail to follow, and often even that could not be seen after we

had crossed a stream. At such places Faye, the doctor, and I would spread out and search for it. As Bettie and I were always put in the middle, we were usually the finders. One day we came up a hill that was so steep that twelve mules had to be hitched to each wagon in order to get it up. Another day we went down a hill where the trail was so sidling, that the men had to fasten big ropes to the upper side of each wagon to hold it right side up as it was drawn down. Another day we made only a few miles because of the deep-cut banks of a narrow little stream that wound around and across a valley, and which we had to cross eight times. At every crossing the banks had to be sloped off and the bed built up before the wagons could be drawn over. Watching all this has been most entertaining and the whole trip is making a man of the doctor.

To-night we are in camp in the Judith Basin and by the Judith River—a beautiful stream, and by far the largest we have seen on the march. And just across the river from us is a stockade, very high and very large, with heavy board gate that was closed as we came past. We can see the roof of the cabin inside, and a stovepipe sticking up through it. Faye says that he has just heard that the place is a nest of horse thieves of the boldest and most daring type, and that one of them is coming to see him this evening! He was told all this by the Frenchman, Junot, who has a little trading store a mile or so from here.

Faye and the doctor rode over there as soon as the tents had been pitched, to ascertain if the company from Missoula had passed. Our trail and the one from the Bitter Root valley fork there. The company passed several days ago, so we will go on in the morning; otherwise we would have been obliged to wait for it.

I had to stay here all alone as Faye would not consent to my going with him. He gave me one of his big pistols, and I had my own small one, and these I put on a table in the tent, after they had gone, and then fastened the tent flaps tight and sat down to await events. But the tent soon became stifling, and it occurred to me that it was foolish to shut myself up so I could not see whatever might come until it was right upon me, so putting my pistol in my pocket and hiding the other, I opened the tent and went out. The first thing I saw was a fishing pole with line and fly, and that I took, and the next was the first sergeant watching me. I knew then that Faye had told him to take care of me.

I went over to tell him that I was going for a fish, and then on down to the beautiful river, whose waters are green and very much the color of the Niagara River. I cast the fly over on the water, and instantly a large fish came up, took the fly, and went down again so easily and gracefully that he scarcely made a ripple on the water until he felt the pull of the line. That was when I forgot everything connected with camp—Faye, horse thieves, and Indians! I had no reel, of course, and getting the big fish out of the water was a problem, for I was standing on a rather high and steep bank. It jumped and jerked in a way that made me afraid I might be pulled down instead of my pulling the fish up, so I began to draw him in, and then up, hand over hand, not daring to breathe while he was suspended in the air. It called for every

"The trail was so sidling that the men had to fasten big ropes to the upper side of each wagon."

bit of my strength, as the shiny thing was so heavy. But I got him; and his length was just twice the width of my handkerchief—a splendid salmon trout. I laid it back of a rock in the shade, and went on down the stream, casting my one fly, and very soon I caught another trout of precisely the same size as the first, and which I landed the same way, too. I put it by the rock with the other.

I kept on down the river, whipping it with my lucky fly every few steps, but I caught no more fish, neither did I get a rise, but I did not mind that, for I had the two beauties, and I was having a grand time too. I had caught both large fish without assistance and with a common willow pole. All that serenity was upset, however, when I heard my name called with such a roar that I came near jumping over the bank to save myself from whatever was after me, but the "What are you doing so far from camp?" came just in time to stop me.

It was Faye, of course, and he was cross because I had gone so far alone, and had, in a way, disregarded his instructions—had done as I pleased after he had left me alone. I wanted to go to Junot's, therefore was not one bit sorry that I had frightened him, and said not a word to his sputtering about the danger from Indians and horse thieves as we started back to camp. After we had gone a little distance up I said, " I left something by that rock." I tried to lift the big fish to show him, but they were too heavy, and I had to hold up one at a time as I said, " This is Mr. Indian and this Mr. Horse Thief!" Faye was almost speechless over my having caught two such large trout, and started to camp with them at such a pace I had to run, almost, to keep up. He thought of something of great importance to say to the first sergeant, simply because he wanted to show them to the company. Some beautiful trout have been brought in by the enlisted men who went up the river, and I am so glad, for now they will have such a nice supper.

The horse thieves undoubtedly knew this country well, when they selected this valley for their hiding place. They have an abundance of delicious fish the year round at their very door, and there is any amount of game near, both furred and feathered, and splendid vegetables they can certainly raise, for they have just sent Faye a large grain sack overflowing with tender, sweet corn, new beets, turnips, cabbage, and potatoes. These will be a grand treat to us, as our own vegetables gave out several days ago. But just think of accepting these things from a band of desperadoes and horse thieves! Their garden must be inside the immense stockade, for there is nothing of the kind to be seen outside. They probably keep themselves in readiness for a long siege by sheriff and posse that may come down upon them at any time without warning. And all the time they know that if ever caught stealing horses, their trial will last just as long as it will take to drag them to a tree that has a good strong branch.

Charlie says that he is a mason and reads every evening in a book that is of his own printing. It is really wonderful. Every evening after dinner he sits out in front of his tent with a large silk handkerchief over his head, and perhaps another with which to fight the ever-present mosquitoes, and reads until dark. He is the only literary person in the command and we are quite proud of him. He is a great comfort to Faye and me, for his cooking is delicious. The doctor has a camp appetite now and is not as finicky as when we started on the trip.

FORT MAGINNIS, MONTANA TERRITORY,
September, 1880.

IT is almost one week since we got here, but I have not written before as no mail has been sent out. I hope that the letter left with Junot has been received, also the two or three notes that were given to horsemen we met on their way to Fort Benton.

At first, Faye did not tell me all that he knew about those horse thieves in the Judith Basin, but it finally came out that the trader, Junot, had told him a most blood-curdling tale of events to come. He had declared most positively that the desperadoes were planning to attack the command, the very next morning while crossing the Judith Mountains, with a hope, of course, of getting the animals. He also told Faye that one of them would be in camp that evening to ask permission to go with him to Maginnis. Faye said the whole story was absurd, particularly the attack, as those horse thieves would never dare attack government troops. Besides, he had over fifty good men with him, and probably there were only ten or twelve horse thieves. So not much attention was paid to what the old Frenchman had said.

But after dinner, when we were sitting outside and Faye and the doctor were smoking, a man came around the corner of the tent with long, swinging strides, and was in our midst before we had dreamed of anyone being near. He spoke to Faye courteously, and declining a chair, dropped down full length on the ground, with elbows in the grass and chin on the palms of his hands. His feet were near the tent and his face out, which placed him in a fine position to observe everything in the camp without anyone seeing that he was doing so, especially as his eyes were screened by a soft, broad-brimmed hat. It was impossible to see their color, of course.

He was young—not over twenty-eight or thirty—and handsome, with a face that was almost girlish in its fairness. His hair was neatly cut, and so was his light mustache, and his smooth face showed that he had recently shaved. He was tall and lithe, and from his chin to his toes was dressed in fine buckskin—shirt, trousers, leggings, and moccasins—and around his neck was tied a blue cotton handkerchief, new and clean. That the man could be a horse thief, an out-law, seemed most incredible.

He talked very well, too, of the country and the game, and we were enjoying the change in our usual after-dinner camp conversation, when suddenly up he jumped, and turning around looked straight at Faye, and then like a bomb came the request to be allowed to go with him to Fort Maginnis! He raised the brim of his hat, and there seemed to be a look of defiance in his steel-blue eyes. But Faye had been expecting this, and knowing that he was more than a match for the villain, he got up from his camp stool leisurely, and with great composure told the man: " Certainly, I will be very glad to have some one along who knows the trail so well." To be told that he knew the trail must have been disconcerting to the man, but not one word did he say in reference to it.

After he had gone, Faye went over to the company, where he remained some time, and I learned later that he had been giving the first sergeant careful instructions for the next day. I could not sleep that night because of horrible dreams—dreams of long, yellow snakes with fiery eyes crawling through green grass. I have thought so many times since of how perfectly maddening it must have been to those horse thieves to have twenty-two nice fat mules and three horses brought almost within the shadow of their very own stockade, and yet have it so impossible to gather them in!

At the appointed time the buckskin-man appeared the following morning on a beautiful chestnut horse with fancy bridle and Mexican saddle, and with him came a friend, his "pal" he told Faye, who was much older and was a sullen, villainous-looking man. Both were armed with rifles and pistols, but there was nothing remarkable in that; in this country it is a necessity. We started off very much as usual, except that Faye kept rather close to the "pal," which left Bettie and me alone most of the time, just a little at one side. I noticed that directly back of the horse thieves walked a soldier, armed with rifle and pistol, and Faye told me that night that he was one of the best sharpshooters in the Army, and that he was back of those men with orders to shoot them down like dogs if they made one treacherous move. The buckskin man was one of the most graceful riders I ever saw, and evidently loved his fine mount, as I saw him stroke his neck several times—and the man himself was certainly handsome.

Faye had told me that I must not question anything he might tell me to do, so after we had crossed the valley and gone up the mountains a little distance he called to me in a voice unnecessarily loud, that I must be tired riding so far, and had better get in the ambulance for a while. I immediately dismounted, and giving the bridle rein to a soldier, I waited for the ambulance to come up. As I got in, I felt that perhaps I was doing the first act in an awful tragedy. The horsemen and wagons had stopped during the minute or two I was getting in, but I saw soldiers moving about, and just as soon as I was seated I looked out to see what was going on.

A splendid old sergeant was going to the front with four soldiers, whom I knew were men to be trusted, each one with rifle, bayonet, and belt full of cartridges, and then I saw that some of the plans for that day's trip had not been told to me. The men were placed in front of everyone, four abreast, and Faye at once told the thieves that under no conditions must one ever get in front of the advance guard. How they must have hated it all—four drilled soldiers in front of them and a sharpshooter back of them, and all the time treated by Faye as honored guests!

There were four men at the rear of the wagons, and the posting of these rear and advance guards, and placing men on either side of the wagons, had been done without one order from Faye, so my dismounting must have been the signal for the sergeant to carry out the orders Faye had given him the night before.

Not by one turn of the head did those outlaws show that they noticed those changes.

In that way we crossed the range. We met a dozen or more men of the very roughest type, each one heavily armed. They were in parties of two and three, and Faye thinks that a signal was passed between one of them and the " pal." But there was no attack as had been predicted! What might have taken place, however, if Faye had not been prepared, no one can tell. Certainly part of Junot's story had been carried out—the horse thief came to the tent and came with us to Maginnis, and it was not because he wanted the protection of the troops. Faye insists that an attack was never thought of, but as he was responsible for government property, including the animals, he had to make preparation to protect them. Of course those men wanted only the animals. We passed many places on the divide that were ideal for an ambush—bluffs, huge boulders, and precipices—everything perfect for a successful hold up.

The men came on to the post with us, and were in camp two nights with the soldiers. The second day from the Judith, we stopped for luncheon near a small stream where there were a great many choke-cherry bushes, and " Buckskin Joe "[1] —that was his name—

---

[1] About six years after this occurrence, there was a graphic account in the Western papers of the horrible death of "Buckskin Joe," who was known as one of the most daring and slippery horse thieves in the Territory. After evading arrest many times, he was finally hunted down by a sheriff's posse, when his fiendish fighting excited the admiration of those who were killing him. A bullet broke one of his legs, and he went down, but he kept on shooting—and so fast that no one dared approach him. And when the forearm of his pistol hand was shattered, he grasped the pistol with the other hand

brought large bunches of the cherries to me. His manner showed refinement, and I saw that his wonderful eyes could be tender as well as steely. Perhaps he had sisters at the old home, and perhaps, too, I was the first woman he had seen in months to remind him of them. I shall always believe that he is from good people some place East, that his " dare-devil " nature got him into some kind of trouble there, and that he came to this wild country to hide from justice. The very morning after we got here, not long after our breakfast, he appeared at our tent with a fine young deer slung across the back of his horse, which he presented to us. He had just killed it. It was most acceptable, as there was no fresh meat in camp. He and his " pal " stayed around that day and night, and then quietly disappeared. Not one of the soldiers, even, saw them go.

It was pleasant to meet our old friends here. Colonel Palmer is in command, and I was particularly glad to see them. After Mrs. Palmer had embraced me she held me off a little and said: " What have you been doing to your face? my, but you are ugly!" The skin on the blistered side has peeled off in little strips, leaving the new skin very white in between the parched brown of the old, so I expect I do resemble a zebra or an Indian with his war paint on. The post, which is only a camp as yet, is located at the upper end of a beautiful valley, and back of us is a cañon and moun-

---

and continued to shoot, even when he could not sit up, but had to hold himself up by the elbow of his broken arm. He was finally killed, fairly riddled with bullets. He knew, of course, all the time what his fate would be if taken alive, and he chose the cold lead instead of the end of a rope.

"The death of 'Buckskin Joe.'"

tains are on both sides. Far down the valley is a large Indian village, and we can distinctly see the tepees, and often hear the "tom-toms" when the Indians dance. There are other Indian camps near, and it is not safe to go far from the tents without an escort. It seems to be a wonderful country for game—deer, grouse, and prairie chicken. Twice we have seen deer come down from the mountains and drink from the stream just below the post. Bettie and I have scared up chicken every time we have taken little runs around the camp, and Faye has shot large bags of them. They are not as great a treat to us as to our friends, for we had so many on the way over.

We have two wall tents, one for sitting room and one for bedroom, and in front a "fly" has been stretched. Our folding camp furniture makes the tents very comfortable. Back of these is the mess, or dining tent, and back of that is the cook tent. Charlie has a small range now, which keeps him squeaking or half singing all the time. One morning, before we got this stove from the quartermaster, breakfast was late, very late. The wind was blowing a gale, and after waiting and waiting, we concluded that Charlie must be having trouble with the little sheet-iron camp stove. So Faye went back to see what was the matter. He returned laughing, and said he had found a most unhappy Chinaman; that Charlie was holding the stove down with a piece of wood with one hand, and with the other was trying to keep the breakfast on the stove.

You know the stovepipe goes up through a piece of tin fastened in the roof of the tent, which is slanting, and when the canvas catches the wind and flops up

18

and down and every other way, the stovepipe naturally
has to go with it. The wind was just right that morning to flop everything—canvas, pipe, stove, and breakfast, too—particularly the delicate Saratoga chips
Charlie had prepared for us, and which, Faye said,
were being blown about like yellow rose leaves. The
poor little heathen was distracted, but when he saw
Faye he instantly became a general and said at once,
" You hole-ee him—me takee bleckfus." So Faye having a desire for breakfast, held down the stove while
Charlie got things together. The Saratoga chips were
delicate and crisp and looked nice, too, but neither
the doctor nor I asked Faye if they were some of the
" rose leaves " or just plain potatoes from a dish!

Charlie is splendid and most resourceful. Very
near our tent is a small stream of cold, clear water,
and on one side of this he has made a little cave of
stones through which the water runs, and in this he
keeps the butter, milk, and desserts that require a cool
place. He is pottering around about something all
the time. There is just one poor cow in the whole
camp, so we cannot get much milk—only one pint each
day—but we consider ourselves very fortunate in getting any at all. I brought over fourteen dozen eggs,
packed in boxes with salt. We are to start back the
first of November, so after we got here I worked out
a little problem in mathematics, and found that the
eggs would last by using only two each day. But
Charlie does better than this; he will manage to get
along without eggs for a day or two, and will then
surprise us with a fine omelet or custard. But he
keeps an exact account and never exceeds his allowance.

The doctor is still with us, and shows no inclination to join the officers' mess that has just been started. He seems to think that he is one of the family, and would be greatly surprised, and hurt probably, if he should discover that we would rather be alone.

FORT MAGINNIS, MONTANA TERRITORY,
September, 1880.

THERE is a large village of Cree Indians in the valley below, and for several days they were a great nuisance in the garrison. One bright morning it was discovered that a long line of them had left their tepees and were coming in this direction. They were riding single file, of course, and were chanting and beating "tom-toms" in a way to make one's blood feel frozen. I was out on one of the little hills at the time, riding Bettie, and happened to be about the first to see them. I started for the post at once at a fast gait and told Faye and Colonel Palmer about them, but as soon as it was seen that they were actually coming to the post, I rode out again about as fast as I had come in, and went to a bit of high ground where I could command a view of the camp, and at the same time be screened by bushes and rocks. And there I remained until those savages were well on their way back to their own village.

Then I went in, and was laughed at by everyone, and assured by some that I had missed a wonderful sight. The Crees are Canadian Indians and are here for a hunt, by permission of both governments. They and the Sioux are very hostile to each other; therefore when four or five Sioux swooped down upon them a few days ago and drove off twenty of their ponies, the Crees were frantic. It was an insult not to be put up with, so some of their best young warriors were sent after them. They recaptured the ponies and killed one Sioux.

Now an Indian is shrewd and wily! The Sioux had been a thief, therefore the Crees cut off his right hand, fastened it to a long pole with the fingers pointing up, and with much fuss and feathers—particularly feathers—brought it to the "White Chief," to show him that the good, brave Crees had killed one of the white man's enemies! The leading Indian carried the pole with the hand, and almost everyone of those that followed carried something also—pieces of flags, or old tin pans or buckets, upon which they beat with sticks, making horrible noises. Each Indian was chanting in a sing-song, mournful way. They were dressed most fancifully; some with red coats, probably discarded by the Canadian police, and Faye said that almost everyone had on quantities of beads and feathers.

Bringing the hand of a dead Sioux was only an Indian's way of begging for something to eat, and this Colonel Palmer understood, so great tin cups of hot coffee and boxes of hard-tack were served to them. Then they danced and danced, and to me it looked as though they intended to dance the rest of their lives right on that one spot. But when they saw that any amount of furious dancing would not boil more coffee, they stopped, and finally started back to their village.

Faye tells me that as he was going to his tent from the dancing, he noticed an Indian who seemed to be unusually well clad, his moccasins and leggings were embroidered with beads and he was wrapped in a

bright-red blanket, head as well as body. As he
passed him a voice said in the purest English, " Lieutenant, can you give me a sear spring for my rifle? "
The only human being near was that Indian, wrapped
closely in a blanket, with only his eyes showing, precisely as one would expect to see a hostile dressed.
Faye said that it gave him the queerest kind of a
sensation, as though the voice had come from another
world. He asked the Indian where he had learned
such good English and technical knowledge of guns,
and he said at the Carlisle school. He said also that
he was a Piegan and on a visit to some Cree friends.
This was one of the many proofs that we have had,
that no matter how good an education the Indian may
receive, he will return to his blanket and out-of-the-
pot way of living just as soon as he returns to his
people. It would be foolish to expect anything different.

But those Cree Indians! The coffee had been good,
very good, and they wanted more, so the very next
morning they brought to Colonel Palmer an old dried
scalp lock, scalp of " White Chief's enemy," with the
same ceremony as they had brought the hand. Then
they sat around his tent and watched him, giving
little grunts now and then until in desperation he
ordered coffee for them, after which they danced.
The men gave them bits of tobacco too. Well, they
kept this performance up three or four days, each day
bringing something to Colonel Palmer to make him
think they had killed a Sioux. This became very tiresome; besides, the soldiers were being robbed of coffee,
so Colonel Palmer shut himself in his tent and refused
to see them one day, and an orderly told them to go

away and make no noise. They finally left the post, looking very mournful, the men said. I told Colonel Palmer that he might better have gone out on the hills as I did; that it was ever so much nicer than being shut up in a tent.

Bettie is learning to rear higher and higher, and I ride Pete now. The last time I rode her she went up so straight that I slipped back in my saddle, and some of the enlisted men ran out to my assistance. I let her have her own way and came back to the tent, and jumping down, declared to Faye that I would never ride her again. She is very cute in her badness, and having once discovered that I didn't like a rearing horse, she has proceeded to rear whenever she wanted her own way. I have enjoyed riding her because she is so graceful and dainty, but I have been told so many times that the horse was dangerous and would throw me, that perhaps I have become a little nervous about her.

A detail of soldiers goes up in the mountains twice every day for poles with which to make the roofs of the log quarters. They go along a trail on the other side of the creek, and on this side is a narrow deer path that runs around the rocky side of a small mountain. Ever since I have been here I have wanted to go back of the mountain by that path. So, when I happened to be out on Pete yesterday afternoon at the time the men started, I at once decided to take advantage of their protection and ride around the little mountain.

About half a mile up, there were quantities of bushes eight and ten feet high down in the creek bed, and the narrow trail that Pete was on was about on a level with the tops of the bushes. At my left the hill was very steep and covered with stones. I was having a delightful time, feeling perfectly safe with so many soldiers within call. But suddenly things changed. Down in those bushes there was a loud crashing and snapping, and then straight up into the air jumped a splendid deer! His head and most of his neck were above the bushes, and for just one instant he looked at us with big inquisitive eyes before he went down again.

When the deer went up Pete went up, too, on the steep hill, and as I was on his back I had to go with him. The horse was badly frightened, snorted, and raised his tail high, and when I tried to get him down on the trail, the higher up he went on the rolling stones. I could almost touch the side of the mountain with my whip in places, it was so steep. It was a most dangerous position to be in, and just what elevation I might have been carried to eventually I do not know, had not the deer stopped his crashing through the bushes and bounded up on the opposite bank, directly in front of the first team of mules, and then on he streaked it across a plateau and far up a mountain side, his short white tail showing distinctly as he ran. With the deer, Pete seemed to think that the Evil One had gone, too, and consented to return to the trail and to cross the stream over to the wagons.

The corporal had stopped the wagons until he saw that I was safely down, and I asked him why he had not killed the deer—we are always in need of game— and he said that he had not seen him until he was in front of the mules, and that it was impossible then, as the deer did not wait for them to get the rifles out of their cases on the bottom of the wagons.   That evening at the whist table I told Colonel Palmer about the deer and Pete, and saw at once that I had probably gotten the poor corporal in trouble.   Colonel Palmer was very angry that the men should even think of going several miles from the post, in an Indian country, with their rifles cased and strapped so they would have been practically useless in case of an attack.

Faye says that the men were not thinking of Indians, but simply trying to keep their rifles from being marred and scratched, for if they did get so they would be " jumped " at the first inspection.   Colonel Palmer gave most positive orders for the soldiers to hold their rifles in their hands on their way to and from the mountains, which perhaps is for the best. But I am afraid they will blame me for such orders having been issued.

FORT MAGINNIS, MONTANA TERRITORY,
October, 1880.

IT is not surprising that politicians got a military post established here, so this wonderful country could be opened and settled, for the country itself is not only beautiful, but it has an amount of game every place that is almost beyond belief.   Deer are frequently seen to come down from the mountains to the creek for water, and prairie chicken would come to our very tents, I fancy, if left to follow their inclinations.

Faye is officer of the day every third day, but the other two days there is not much for him to do, as the company is now working on the new quarters under the supervision of the quartermaster.   So we often go off on little hunts, usually for chicken, but sometimes we go up on one of the mountains, where there are quantities of ruffed grouse. These are delicious, with meat as tender and white as young chicken, and they are so pretty, too, when they spread the ruffs around their necks and make fans of their short tail feathers.

Yesterday we went out for birds for both tables— the officers' mess and our own. The other officers are not hunters, and Faye is the possessor of the only shot-gun in the garrison, therefore it has been a great pleasure to us to bring in game for all. Faye rides Bettie now altogether, so I was on Pete yesterday. We had quite a number of chickens, but thought we would like to get two or three more; therefore, when we saw a small covey fly over by some bushes, and that one bird went beyond and dropped on the other side, Faye told me to go on a little, and watch that bird if it rose again when he shot at the others. It is our habit usually for me to hold Faye's horse when he dismounts to hunt, but that time he was some distance away, and had slipped his hand through the bridle rein and was leading Bettie that way. Both horses are perfectly broken to firearms, and do not in the least mind a gun. I have often seen Bettie prick up her ears and watch the smoke come from the barrel with the greatest interest.

Everything went on very well until I got where I might expect to see the chicken, and then I presume I gave more thought to the bird than to the ground the horse was on. At all events, it suddenly occurred to me that the grass about us was very tall, and look-ing down closely I discovered that Pete was in an alkali bog and slowly going down. I at once tried to get him back to the ground we had just left, but in his frantic efforts to get his feet out of the sticky mud, he got farther to one side and slipped down into an alkali hole of nasty black water and slime. That I knew to be exceedingly dangerous, and I urged the horse by voice and whip to get him out before he sank down too deep, but with all his efforts he could do nothing, and was going down very fast and groaning in his terror.

Seeing that I must have assistance without delay, I called to Faye to come at once, and sat very still until he got to us, fearing that if I changed my position the horse might fall over. Faye came running, and finding a tuft of grass and solid ground to stand upon, pulled Pete by the bridle and encouraged him until the poor beast finally struggled out, his legs and stomach covered with the black slime up to the flaps of my saddle, so one can see what danger we were in. There was no way of relieving the horse of my weight, as it was impossible for me to jump and not get stuck in the mud myself. This is the only alkali hole we have discovered here. It is screened by bunches of tall grass, and I expect that many a time I have ridden within a few feet of it when alone, and if my horse had happened to slip down on any one of these times, we probably would have been sucked from the face of the earth, and not one person to come to our assistance or to know what had happened to us.

When Faye heard my call of distress, he threw the bridle back on Bettie, and slipping the shotgun through the sling on the saddle, hurried over to me, not giving Bettie much thought. The horse has always shown the greatest disinclination to leaving Pete, but having her own free will that time, she did the unexpected and trotted to a herd of mules not far off, and as she went down a little hill the precious shotgun slipped out of the sling to the ground, and the stock broke! The gun is perfectly useless, and the loss of it is great to us and our friends. To be in this splendid game country without a shotgun is deplorable; still, to have been buried in a hole of black water and muck would have been worse.

Later. Such an awful wind storm burst upon us

"Pete was in an alkali bog and slowly going down."

while I was writing two days ago, I was obliged to stop. The day was cold and our tents were closed tight to keep the heat in, so we knew nothing of the storm until it struck us, and with such fierceness it seemed as if the tents must go down. Instantly there was commotion in camp—some of the men tightening guy ropes, and others running after blankets and pieces of clothing that had been out for an airing, but every man laughed and made fun of whatever he was doing. Soldiers are always so cheerful under such difficulties, and I dearly love to hear them laugh, and yell, too, over in their tents.

The snow fell thick and fast, and the wind came through the cañon back of us with the velocity of a hurricane. As night came on it seemed to increase, and the tents began to show the strain and one or two had gone down, so the officers' families were moved into the unfinished log quarters for the night. Colonel Palmer sent for me to go over also, and Major Bagley came twice for me, saying our tents would certainly fall, and that it would be better to go then, than in the middle of the night. But I had more faith in those tents, for they were new and pitched remarkably well. Soon after we got here, long poles had been put up on stakes all along each side of, and close to, the tents, and to these the guy ropes of both tents and " fly " covers had been securely fastened, all of which had prevented much flopping of canvas. Dirt had been banked all around the base of the tents, so with a very little fire we could be warm and fairly comfortable.

The wind seemed to get worse every minute, and once in a while there would be a loud " boom " when a big Sibley tent would be ripped open, and then would come yells from the men as they scrambled after their belongings. After it became dark it seemed dismal, but Faye would not go in a building, and I would not leave him alone to hold the stove down. This was our only care and annoyance. It was intensely cold, and in order to have a fire we were compelled to hold the pipe down on the little conical camp stove, for with the flopping of the tent and fly, the pipe was in constant motion. Faye would hold it for a while, then I would relieve him, and so on. The holding-down business was very funny for an hour or two, but in time it became monotonous.

We got through the night very well, but did not sleep much. The tearing and snapping of tents, and the shouting of the men when a tent would fall upon them was heard frequently, and when we looked out in the morning the camp had the appearance of having been struck by a cyclone! Two thirds of the tents were flat on the ground, others were badly torn, and the unfinished log quarters only added to the desolation. Snow was over everything ten or twelve inches deep. But the wind had gone down and the atmosphere was wonderfully clear, and sparkling, and full of frost.

Dinner the evening before had not been a success, so we were very prompt to the nice hot breakfast Charlie gave us. That Chinaman has certainly been a great comfort on this trip. The doctor came over looking cross and sick. He said at once that we had been wise in remaining in our comfortable tents, that everybody in the log houses was sneezing and complaining of stiff joints. The logs have not been chinked yet, and, as might have been expected, wind and snow swept through them. The stoves have not been set up, so even one fire was impossible. Two or three of their tents did go down, however, the doctor's included, and perhaps they were safer in a breezy house, after all.

The mail has been held back, and will start with us. The time of going was determined at Department

Headquarters, and we will have to leave here on the first—day after to-morrow—if such a thing is possible. We return by the way of Benton. It is perfectly exasperating to see prairie chicken all around us on the snow. Early this morning there was a large covey up in a tree just across the creek from our tent, looking over at us in a most insolent manner. They acted as though they knew there was not a shotgun within a hundred miles of them. They were perfectly safe, for everyone was too nearly frozen to trouble them with a rifle.

Camping on the snow will not be pleasant, and we regret very much that the storm came just at this time. Charlie is busy cooking all sorts of things for the trip, so he will not have much to do on the little camp stove. He is a treasure, but says that he wishes we could stay here; that he does not want to return to Fort Shaw. This puzzles me very much, as there are so many Chinamen at Shaw and not one here. The doctor will not go back with us, as he has received orders to remain at this post during the winter.

FORT SHAW, MONTANA TERRITORY,
November, 1880.

THE past few days have been busy ones. The house has received much needed attention and camp things have been looked over and put away, ready for the next move. The trip back was a disappointment to me and not at all pleasant. The wagons were very lightly loaded, so the men rode in them all the way, and we came about forty miles each day, the mules keeping up a steady slow trot. Of course I could not ride those distances at that gait, therefore

I was compelled to come in the old, jerky ambulance.

The snow was still deep when we left Maginnis, and at the first camp snow had to be swept from the ground where our tent was pitched. But after that the weather was warm and sunny. We saw the greatest number of feathered game—enormous flocks of geese, brant, and ducks. Our camp one night was near a small lake just the other side of Benton, and at dusk hundreds of geese came and lit on the water, until it looked like one big mass of live, restless things, and the noise was deafening. Some of the men shot at them with rifles, but the geese did not seem to mind much.

Charlie told me at Maginnis that he did not want to return to Shaw, and I wondered at that so many times. I went in the kitchen two miserable mornings back and found him sitting down looking unhappy and disconsolate. I do not remember to have ever seen a Chinaman sitting down that way before, and was afraid he might be sick, but he said at once and without preamble, " Me go 'way! " He saw my look of surprise and said again, " Me go 'way—Missee Bulk's Chineeman tellee me go 'way." I said, " But, Charlie, Lee has no right to tell you to go; I want you to stay." He hesitated one second, then said in the most mournful of voices, " Yes, me know, me feel vellee blad, but Lee, he tellee me go—he no likee mason-man." No amount of persuasion could induce him to stay, and that evening after dinner he packed his bedding on his back and went away—to the Crossing, I presume. Charlie called himself a mason, and has a book that he made himself which he said was a " mason-man blook," but I learned yesterday that he is a "high-binder," no mason at all, and for that reason the Chinamen in the garrison would not permit him to remain here. They were afraid of him, yet he seemed so very trustworthy in every way. But a highbinder in one's own house!

There has been another departure from the family—Bettie has been sold! Lieutenant Warren wanted her to match a horse he had recently bought. The two make a beautiful little team, and Bettie is already a great pet, and I am glad of that, of course, but I do not see the necessity of Lieutenant Warren's giving her sugar right in front of our windows! His quarters are near ours. He says that Bettie made no objections to the harness, but drove right off with her mate.

There was a distressing occurrence in the garrison yesterday that I cannot forget. At all army posts the prisoners do the rough work, such as bringing the wood and water, keeping the yards tidy, bringing the ice, and so on. Yesterday morning one of the general prisoners here escaped from the sentry guarding him. The long-roll was beaten, and as this always means that something is wrong and calls out all the troops, officers and men, I ran out on the porch to see what was the matter, fearing there might be a fire some place. It seemed a long time before the companies got in line, and then I noticed that instead of fire buckets they were carrying rifles. Directly every company started off on double time and disappeared in between two sets of barracks at one corner of the parade ground. Then everything was unusually quiet; not a human being to be seen except the sentry at the guardhouse, who was walking post.

It was pleasant, so I sat down, still feeling curious about the trouble that was serious enough to call out all the troops. It was not so very long before Lieutenant Todd, who was officer of the day, came from the direction the companies had gone, pistol in hand, and in front of him was a man with ball and chain. That means that his feet were fastened together by a large chain, just long enough to permit him to take short steps, and to that short chain was riveted a long one, at the end of which was a heavy iron ball hanging below his belt. When we see a prisoner carrying a ball and chain we know that he is a deserter, or that he has done something very bad, which will probably send him to the penitentiary, for these balls are never put on a prisoner who has only a short time in the guardhouse.

The prisoner yesterday—who seemed to be a young man—walked slowly to the guardhouse, the officer of the day following closely. Going up the steps and on in the room to a cot, he unfastened the ball from his belt and let it thunder down on the floor, and then throwing himself down on the cot, buried his face in the blankets, an awful picture of woe and despair. On the walk by the door, and looking at him with contempt, stood a splendid specimen of manhood—erect, broad-chested, with clear, honest eyes and a weather-beaten face—a typical soldier of the United States Army, and such as he, the prisoner inside might have become in time. Our house is separated from the guardhouse by a little park only, and I could plainly see the whole thing—the strong man and the weakling.

In the meantime, bugles had called the men back to quarters, and very soon I learned all about the

19

wretched affair. The misguided young man had deserted once before, was found guilty by a general
court-martial, and sentenced to the penitentiary at
Leavenworth for the regulation time for such an
offense, and to-morrow morning he was to have
started for the prison. Now he has to stand a second
court-martial, and serve a double sentence for desertion!

He was so silly about it too. The prisoners were at
the large ice house down by the river, getting ice out
for the daily delivery. There were sentinels over
them, of course, but in some way that man managed
to sneak over the ice through the long building to an
open door, through which he dropped down to the
ground, and then he ran. He was missed almost
instantly and the alarm given, but the companies were
sent to the lowland along the river, where there are
bushes, for there seemed to be no other place where
he could possibly secrete himself.

The officer of the day is responsible, in a way, for
the prisoners, so of course Lieutenant Todd went to
the ice house to find out the cause of the trouble, and on
his way back he accidentally passed an old barrel-
shaped water wagon. Not a sound was heard, but
something told him to look inside. He had to climb
up on a wheel in order to get high enough to look
through the little square opening at the top, but he is
a tall man and could just see in, and peering down
he saw the wretched prisoner huddled at one end,
looking more like an animal than a human being. He
ordered him to come out, and marched him to the
guardhouse.

It was a strange coincidence, but the officer of the

day happened to have been promoted from the ranks, had served his three years as an enlisted man, and then passed a stiff examination for a commission. One could see by his walk that he had no sympathy for the mother's baby. He knew from experience that a soldier's life is not hard unless the soldier himself makes it so. The service and discipline develop all the good qualities of the man, give him an assurance and manly courage he might never possess otherwise, and best of all, he learns to respect law and order.

The Army is not a rough place, and neither are the men starved or abused, as many mothers seem to think. Often the company commanders receive the most pitiful letters from mothers of enlisted men, beseeching them to send their boys back to them, that they are being treated like dogs, dying of starvation, and so on. As though these company commanders did not know all about those boys and the life they had to live.

It is such a pity that these mothers cannot be made to realize that army discipline, regular hours, and plain army food is just what those " boys " need to make men of them. Judging by several letters I have read, sent to officers by mothers of soldiers, I am inclined to believe that weak mothers in many cases are responsible for the desertion of their weak sons. They sap all manhood from them by " coddling " as they grow up, and send them out in the world wholly unequal to a vigorous life—a life without pie and cake at every meal. Well! I had no intention of moralizing this way, but I have written only the plain truth.

FORT SHAW, MONTANA TERRITORY,
September, 1881.

THERE has been quite a little flutter of excitement in the garrison during the past week,
brought about by a short visit from the Marquis of
Lorne and his suite. As governor general of Canada,
he had been inspecting his own military posts, and then
came on down across the line to Shaw, *en route* to
Dillon, where he will take the cars for the East.
Colonel Knight is in command, so it fell upon him
to see that Lord Lorne was properly provided for,
which he did by giving up absolutely for his use his
own elegantly furnished quarters. Lord Lorne took
possession at once and quietly dined there that evening with one or two of his staff, and Colonel Knight
as his guest.

The members of the suite were entertained by different officers of the garrison, and Captain Percival of
the Second Life Guards was our guest. They were
escorted across the line to this post by a company of
Canadian mounted police, and a brave appearance
those redcoats made as they rode on the parade
ground and formed two lines through which the governor general and his staff rode, with the booming of
cannon. Colonel Knight went out to meet them, escorted by our mounted infantry in command of Lieutenant Todd.

The horses of the mounted police were very small,
and inferior in every way to the animals one would
expect the Canadian government to provide, and it
did look very funny to see the gorgeously dressed
police with their jaunty, side-tilted caps riding such
wretched little beasts!

Our officers were on the parade to receive the governor general, and the regimental band was there also, playing all sorts of things. Presently, without stop, and as though it was the continuation of a melody, the first notes of " God Save the Queen " were heard. Instantly the head of every Englishman and Canadian was uncovered—quietly, and without ostentation or slightest break in hand-shaking and talking. It was like a military movement by bugle call! Some of us who were looking on through filmy curtains thought it a beautiful manifestation of loving loyalty. They were at a military post of another nation, in the midst of being introduced to its officers, yet not one failed to remember and to remind, that he was an Englishman ever!

Mrs. Gordon saved me the worry of preparing an elaborate dinner at this far-away place, by inviting us and our guest to dine with her and her guests. I am inclined to think that this may have been a shrewd move on the part of the dear friend, so she could have Hang to assist her own cook at her dinner. It was a fine arrangement, at all events, and pleased me most of all. I made the salad and arranged the table for her. Judging from what I saw and heard, Hang was having a glorious time. He had evidently frightened the old colored cook into complete idiocy, and was ordering her about in a way that only a Chinaman knows.

The dinner was long, but delicious and enjoyable in every way. Lord Bagot, the Rev. Dr. MacGregor, Captain Chater, and others of the governor general's staff were there—sixteen of us in all. Captain Percival sat at my right, of course, and the amount he ate was simply appalling! And the appetites of Lord Bagot and the others were equally fine. Course after course disappeared from their plates—not a scrap left on them—until one wondered how it was managed. Soon after dinner everyone went to Colonel Knight's quarters, where Lord Lorne was holding a little reception. He is a charming man, very simple in his manner, and one could hardly believe that he is the son-in-law of a great queen and heir to a splendid dukedom.

He had announced that he would start at ten o'clock the next morning, so I ordered breakfast at nine. A mounted escort from the post was to go with him to Dillon in command of Faye. It has always seemed so absurd and really unkind for Americans to put aside our own ways and customs when entertaining foreigners, and bore them with wretched representations of things of their own country, thereby preventing them from seeing life as it is here. So I decided to give our English captain an out and out American breakfast—not long, or elaborate, but dainty and nicely served. And I invited Miss Mills to meet him, to give it a little life.

Well, nine o'clock came, so did Miss Mills, so did half after nine come, and then, finally ten o'clock, but Captain Percival did not come! I was becoming very cross—for half an hour before I had sent Hang up to call him, knowing that he and Faye also, were obliged to be ready to start at ten o'clock. I was worried, too, fearing that Faye would have to go without any breakfast at all. Of course the nice little breakfast was ruined! Soon after ten, however, our guest came down and apologized very nicely—said that the bed was so very delightful he simply could

not leave it. Right there I made a mental resolution
to the effect that if ever a big Englishman should
come to my house to remain overnight, I would have
just one hour of delight taken from that bed!

To my great amusement, also pleasure, Captain Percival ate heartily of everything, and kept on eating,
and with such apparent relish I began to think that
possibly it might be another case of " delight," and
finally to wonder if Hang had anything in reserve.
Once he said, " What excellent cooks you have here! "
This made Miss Mills smile, for she knew that Hang
had been loaned out the evening before. Faye soon
left us to attend to matters in connection with the
trip, but the three of us were having a very merry
time—for Captain Percival was a most charming man
—when in the room came Captain Chater, his face
as black as the proverbial thundercloud, and after
speaking to me, looked straight and reprovingly at
Captain Percival and said, " You are keeping his
excellency waiting! " That was like a bomb to all,
and in two seconds the English captains had shaken
hands and were gone.

The mounted police are still in the post, and I suspect that this is because their commander is having
such a pleasant time driving and dining with his hostess, who is one of our most lovely and fascinating
women. I received a note from Faye this morning
from Helena. He says that so far the trip has been
delightful, and that in every way and by all he is
being treated as an honored guest. Lord Lorne de-
clined a large reception in Helena, because the United
States is in mourning for its murdered President.
What an exquisite rebuke to some of our ignorant

Americans! Faye writes that Lord Lorne and members of his staff are constantly speaking in great praise of the officers' wives at Shaw, and have asked if the ladies throughout the Army are as charming and cultured as those here.

Our young horses are really very handsome now, and their red coats are shining from good grooming and feeding. They are large, and perfectly matched in size, color, and gait, as they should be, since they are half brothers. I am learning to drive now, a single horse, and find it very interesting—but not one half as delightful as riding—I miss a saddle horse dreadfully. Now and then I ride George—my own horse—but he always reminds me that his proper place is in the harness, by making his gait just as rough as possible.

FORT SHAW, MONTANA TERRITORY,
December, 1881.

YOU will be greatly surprised to hear that Faye has gone to Washington! His father is very ill —so dangerously so that a thirty-days' leave was telegraphed Faye from Department Headquarters, without his having applied for it so as to enable him to get to Admiral Rae without delay. Some one in Washington must have asked for the leave. It takes so long for letters to reach us from the East that one never knows what may be taking place there. Faye started on the next stage to Helena and at Dillon will take the cars for Washington.

Faye went away the night before the entertainment, which made it impossible for me to be in the pantomime " Villikens and Dinah," so little Miss Gordon took my place and acted remarkably well, not-

withstanding she had rehearsed only twice. The very
stage that carried Faye from the post, brought to
us Mr. Hughes of Benton for a few days. But this
turned out very nicely, for Colonel and Mrs. Mills,
who know him well, were delighted to have him go
to them, and there he is now. The next day I invited Miss Mills and Mr. Hughes to dine with me in-
formally, and while I was in the dining room attending to the few pieces of extra china and silver that
would be required for dinner (a Chinaman has no
idea of the fitness of things), Volmer, our striker,
came in and said to me that he would like to take the
horses and the single buggy out for an hour or so, as
he wanted to show them to a friend.

I saw at once that he and I were to have our usual
skirmish. There is one, always, whenever Faye is
away any length of time. The man has a frightful temper, and a year ago shot and killed a deserter.
He was acquitted by military court, and later by civil
court, both courts deciding that the shooting was accidental. But the deserter was a catholic and Volmer
is a quaker, so the feeling in the company was so hostile toward him that for several nights he was put in
the guardhouse for protection. Then Faye took him as
striker, and has befriended him in many ways. But
those colts he could not drive. So I told him that the
horses could not go out during the lieutenant's absence,
unless I went with them. He became angry at once,
and said that it was the first team he had ever taken
care of that he was not allowed to drive as often as he
pleased. A big story, of course, but I said to him
quietly, " You heard what I said, Volmer, and further
discussion will be quite useless. You were never per-

mitted to take the colts out when Lieutenant Rae was here, and now that he is away, you certainly cannot do so." And I turned back to my spoons and forks.

Volmer went out of the room, but I had an uncomfortable feeling that matters were not settled. In a short time I became conscious of loud talking in the kitchen, and could distinctly hear Volmer using most abusive language about Faye and me. That was outrageous and not to be tolerated a second, and without stopping to reason that it would be better not to hear, and let the man talk his anger off, out to the kitchen I went. I found Volmer perched upon one end of a large wood box that stands close to a door that leads out to a shed. I said: " Volmer, I heard what you have been saying, as you intended I should, and now I tell you to go out of this house and stay out, until you can speak respectfully of Lieutenant Rae and of me." But he sat still and looked sullen and stubborn. I said again, " Go out, and out of the yard too." But he did not move one inch.

By that time I was furious, and going to the door that was so close to the man he could have struck me, I opened it wide, and pointing out with outstretched arm I said, " You go instantly! " and instantly he went. Chinamen are awful cowards, and with the first word I said to the soldier, Hang had shuffled to his own room, and there he had remained until he heard Volmer go out of the house. Then he came back, and looking at me with an expression of the most solemn pity, said, " He vellee blad man—he killee man—he killee you, meb-bee! " The poor little heathen was evidently greatly disturbed, and so was I, too. Not because I was at all afraid of being

killed, but because of the two spirited young horses
that still required most careful handling. And Faye
might be away several months! I knew that the commanding officer, also the quartermaster, would look
after them and do everything possible to assist me, but
at the same time I knew that there was not a man
in the post who could take Volmer's place with the
horses. He is a splendid whip and perfect groom.
I could not send them to Mr. Vaughn's to run, as
they had been blanketed for a long time, and the
weather was cold.

Of course I cried a little, but I knew that I had done
quite right, that it was better for me to regulate my
own affairs than to call upon the company commander
to do so for me. I returned to the dining room, but
soon there was a gentle knock on the door, and opening it, I saw Volmer standing in front of me, cap in
hand, looking very meek and humble. Very respectfully he apologized, and expressed his regret at having
offended me. That was very pleasant, but knowing
the man's violent temper, and thinking of coming
days, I proceeded to deliver a lecture to the effect
that there was not another enlisted man in the regiment who would use such language in our house, or
be so ungrateful for kindness that we had shown him.
Above all, to make it unpleasant for me when I was
alone.

I was so nervous, and talking to a soldier that way
was so very disagreeable, I might have broken down
and cried again—an awful thing to have done at that
time—if I had not happened to have seen Hang's head
sticking out at one side of his door. He had run
to his room again, but could not resist keeping watch

to see if Volmer was really intending to " killee "
me.   He is afraid of the soldier, and consequently
hates him.   Soon after he came, Volmer, who is a
powerful man, tied him down to his bed with a picket
rope, and such yells of fury and terror were never
heard, and when I ran out to see what on earth was
the matter, the Chinaman's eyes were green, and he
was frothing at the mouth.   For days after I was
afraid that Hang would do some mischief to the man.

It is the striker's duty always to attend to the fires
throughout the house, and this Volmer is doing very
nicely.   But when Faye went away he told Hang to
take good care of me—so he, also, fixes the fires,
and at the same time shows his dislike for Volmer, who will bring the big wood in and make the
fires as they should be.   Just as soon as he goes out,
however, in marches Hang, with one or two small
pieces of wood on his silk sleeve, and then, with much
noise, he turns the wood in the stove upside down, and
stirs things up generally, after which he will put in
the little sticks and let it all roar until I am quite as
stirred up as the fire.   After he closes the dampers
he will say to me in his most amiable squeak, " Me
flixee him—he vellee glood now."   This is all very
nice as long as the house does not burn.

Night before last Mrs. Mills invited me to a family dinner.   Colonel Mills was away, but Mr. Hughes
was there, also Lieutenant Harvey to whom Miss
Mills is engaged, and the three Mills boys, making
a nice little party.   But I felt rather sad—Faye was
still *en route* to Washington, and going farther from
home every hour, and it was impossible to tell when
he would return.   Mrs. Mills seemed *distraite*, too,

when I first got to the house, but she soon brightened up and was as animated as ever. The dinner was perfect. Colonel Mills is quite an epicure, and he and Mrs. Mills have a reputation for serving choice and dainty things on their table. We returned to the little parlor after dinner, and were talking and laughing, when something went bang! like the hard shutting of a door.

Mrs. Mills jumped up instantly and exclaimed, " I knew it—I knew it!" and rushed to the back part of the house, the rest of us running after her. She went on through to the Chinaman's room, and there, on his cot, lay the little man, his face even then the color of old ivory. He had fired a small Derringer straight to his heart and was quite dead. I did not like to look at the dying man, so I ran for the doctor and almost bumped against him at the gate as he was passing. There was nothing that he could do, however.

Mrs. Mills told us that Sam had been an inveterate gambler—that he had won a great deal of money from the soldiers, particularly one, who had that very day threatened to kill him, accusing the Chinaman of having cheated. The soldier probably had no intention of doing anything of the kind, but said it to frighten the timid heathen, just for revenge. Sam had eaten a little dinner, and was eating ice-cream, evidently, when something or somebody made him go to his room and shoot himself. The next morning the Chinamen in the garrison buried him—not in the post cemetery, but just outside. Upon the grave they laid one or two suits of clothing, shoes—all Chinese, of course—and a great quantity of food—much of it their own fruits. That was for his spirit until it reached the Happy Land.

The coyotes ate the food, but a Chinaman would never believe that, so more food was taken out this morning.

They are such a queer people! Hang's breakfast usually consists of a glass of cold water with two or three lumps of sugar dissolved in it and a piece of bread broken in it also. When it is necessary for Hang to be up late and do much extra work, I always give him a can of salmon, of which he seems very fond—or a chicken, and tell him to invite one or two friends to sit with him. This smooths away all little frowns and keeps things pleasant. Volmer killed the chicken once, and Hang brought it to me with eyes blazing—said it was poor—and " He ole-ee hin," so I found that the only way to satisfy the suspicious man was to let him select his own fowl. He always cooks it in the one way—boils it with Chinese fruits and herbs, and with the head and feet on—and I must admit that the odor is appetizing. But I have never tasted it, although Hang has never failed to save a nice piece for me. He was with Mrs. Pierce two years, and it was some time before I could convince him that this house was regulated my way and not hers. Major Pierce was promoted to another regiment and we miss them very much.

FORT SHAW, MONTANA TERRITORY,
July, 1882.

THE garrison seems lonesome since the two companies have been out, and I am beginning to feel that I am at home alone quite too much. Faye was in Washington two months, and almost immediately after he got back he was ordered to command the paymaster's escort from Helena here, and now he is

off again for the summer! The camp is on Birch
Creek not far from the Piegan Agency. The agents
become frightened every now and then, and ask for
troops, more because they know the Indians would be
justified in giving trouble than because there is any.

An officer is sent from the post to inspect all the
cattle and rations that are issued to them—yet there
is much cheating. Once it was discovered that a very
inferior brand of flour was being given the Indians
—that sacks with the lettering and marks of the brand
the government was supposed to issue to them had
been slipped over the sacks which really held the inferior flour, and carefully tied. Just imagine the
trouble some one had taken, but there had been a fat
reward, of course, and then, where had those extra
sacks come from—where had the fine flour gone?

Some one could have explained it all. I must admit, however, that anyone who has seen an Indian
use flour would say that the most inferior grade would
be good enough for them, to be mixed in dirty old
pans, with still dirtier hands. This lack of cleanliness
and appreciation of things by the Indians makes
stealing from them very tempting.

The very night after the troops had gone out there
was an excitement in the garrison, and, as usual, I was
mixed up in it, not through my own choosing, however. I had been at Mrs. Palmer's playing whist during the evening, and about eleven o'clock two of the
ladies came down to the house with me. The night
was the very darkest I ever saw, and of this we spoke
as we came along the walk. Almost all the lights
were out in the officers' quarters, making the whole
post seem dismal, and as I came in the house and

locked the door, I felt as if I could never remain here until morning. Hang was in his room, of course, but would be no protection whatever if anything should happen.

Major and Mrs. Stokes have not yet returned from the East, so the adjoining house is unoccupied, and on my right is Mrs. Norton, who is alone also, as Doctor Norton is in camp with the troops. She had urged me to go to her house for the night, but I did not go, because of the little card party. I ran upstairs as though something evil was at my heels and bolted my door, but did not fasten the dormer windows that run out on the roof in front. Before retiring, I put a small, lighted lantern in a closet and left the door open just a little, thinking that the streak of light would be cheering and the lantern give me a light quickly if I should need one.

Our breakfast had been very early that morning, on account of the troops marching, and I was tired and fell asleep immediately, I think. After a while I was conscious of hearing some one walking about in the room corresponding to mine in the next house, but I dozed on, thinking to myself that there was no occasion for feeling nervous, as the people next door were still up. But suddenly I remembered that the house was closed, and just then I distinctly heard some one go down the stairs. I kept very still and listened, but heard nothing more and soon went to sleep again, but again I was awakened—this time by queer noises—like some one walking on a roof. There were voices, too, as if some one was mumbling to himself.

I got the revolver and ran to the middle of the room,

where I stood ready to shoot or run—it would probably have been run—in any direction. I finally got courage to look through a side window, feeling quite sure that Mrs. Norton was out with her Chinaman, looking after some choice little chickens left in her care by the doctor. But not one light was to be seen in any place, and the inky blackness was awful to look upon, so I turned away, and just as I did so, something cracked and rattled down over the shingles and then fell to the ground. But which roof those sounds came from was impossible to tell. With "goose flesh" on my arms, and each hair on my head trying to stand up, I went back to the middle of the room, and there I stood, every nerve quivering.

I had been standing there hours—or possibly it was only two short minutes—when there was one loud, piercing shriek, that made me almost scream, too. But after it was perfect silence, so I said to myself that probably it had been a cat—that I was nervous and silly. But there came another shriek, another, and still another, so expressive of terror that the blood almost froze in my veins. With teeth chattering and limbs shaking so I could hardly step, I went to a front window, and raising it I screamed, "Corporal of the guard!"

I saw the sentinel at the guardhouse stop, as though listening, in front of a window where there was a light, and seeing one of the guard gave strength to my voice, and I called again. That time the sentry took it up, and yelled, "Corporal of the guard, No. 1!" Instantly lanterns were seen coming in our direction—ever so many of the guard came, and to our gate as they saw me at a window. But I sent them

20

on to the next house where they found poor Mrs. Norton in a white heap on the grass, quite unconscious.

The officer of the day was still up and came running to see what the commotion was about—and several other officers came. Colonel Gregory, a punctilious gentleman of the old school—who is in command just now—appeared in a striking costume, consisting of a skimpy evening gown of white, a dark military blouse over that, and a pair of military riding boots, and he carried an unsheathed saber. He is very tall and thin and his hair is very white, and I laugh now when I think of how funny he looked. But no one thought of laughing at that time. Mrs. Norton was carried in, and her house searched throughout. No one was found, but burned matches were on the floor of one or two rooms, which gave evidence that some one had been there.

In the yard back of the house a pair of heavy overshoes, also government socks, were found, so it was decided that the man had climbed up on the roof and entered the house through a dormer window that had not been fastened. No one would look for the piece of shingle that night, but in the morning I found it on the ground close to the house.

All the time the search was being made I had been in the window. Colonel Mills insisted that I should go to his house for the remainder of the night, but suggested that I put some clothes on first! It occurred to me then, for the first time, that my own costume was rather striking—not quite the proper thing for a balcony scene. Everyone was more than kind, but for a long time after Miss Mills and I had gone to her room my teeth chattered and big tears rolled down my face. Mrs. Norton declares that I was more frightened than she was, and I say, " Yes, probably, but you did not stop to listen to your own horrible screams, and then, after making us believe that you were being murdered, you quietly dropped into oblivion and forgot the whole thing."

Just as the entire garrison had become quiet once more—bang! went a gun, and then again we heard people running about to see what was the matter, and if the burglar had been caught. But it proved to have been the accidental going off of a rifle at the guard-house. The instant that Colonel Gregory ascertained that a soldier had really been in Mrs. Norton's house, check roll-call was ordered—that is, the officer of the day went to the different barracks and ordered the first sergeants to get the men up and call the roll at once, without warning or preparation. In that way it was ascertained if the men were on their cots or out of quarters. But that night every man was " present or accounted for." At the hospital, roll-call was not necessary, but they found an attendant playing possum! A lantern held close to his face did not waken him, although it made his eyelids twitch, and they found that his heart was beating at a furious rate. His clothes had been thrown down on the floor, but socks were not to be found with them.

So he is the man suspected. He will get his discharge in three days, and it is thought that he was after a suit of citizen clothes of the doctor's. Not so very long ago he was their striker. No one in the garrison has ever heard of an enlisted man troubling the quarters of an officer, and it is something that rarely occurs. I spend every night with Mrs. Norton now, who seems to have great confidence in my ability to protect her, as I can use a revolver so well. She calmly sleeps on, while I remain awake listening for footsteps. The fact of my having been at a military post when it was attacked by Indians—that a man was murdered directly under my window, when I heard every shot, every moan—and my having had two unpleasant experiences with horse thieves, has not been conducive to normal nerves after dark.

During all the commotion at Mrs. Norton's the night the man got in her house, her Chinaman did not appear. One of the officers went to his room in search of the burglar and found him—the Chinaman—sitting up in his bed, almost white from fear. He confessed to having heard some one in the kitchen, and when asked why he did not go out to see who it was, indignantly replied, " What for?—he go way, what for I see him? "

I feel completely upset without a good saddle horse. George is developing quite a little speed in single harness, but I do not care for driving—feel too much as though I was part of the little buggy instead of the horse. Major and Mrs. Stokes are expected soon from the East, and I shall be so glad to have my old neighbors back.

CAMP ON BIRCH CREEK,
NEAR PIEGAN AGENCY, MONTANA TERRITORY,
September, 1882.

BY this time you must have become accustomed to getting letters from all sorts of out-of-the-way places, therefore I will not weary you with long explanations, but simply say that Major Stokes and Faye sent for Mrs. Stokes and me to come to camp,

thinking to give us a pleasant little outing. We came
over with the paymaster and his escort. Major Car-
penter seemed delighted to have us with him, and naturally Mrs. Stokes and I were in a humor to enjoy
everything. We brought a nice little luncheon with us
for everybody—that is, everyone in the ambulance.
The escort of enlisted men were in a wagon back of us,
but the officer in charge was with us.

The Indians have quieted down, and several of the
officers have gone on leave, so with the two companies
now here there are only Major Stokes, who is in command, Faye, Lieutenant Todd, and Doctor Norton.
Mrs. Stokes has seen much of camp life, and enjoys
it now and then as much as I do. The importance of
our husbands as hosts—their many efforts to make us
comfortable and entertain us—is amusing, yet very
lovely. They give us no rest whatever, but as soon as
we return from one little excursion another is immediately proposed. There is a little spring wagon in
camp with two seats, and there are two fine mules to
pull it, and with this really comfortable turn-out we
drive about the country. Major Stokes is military inspector of supplies at this agency, and every Piegan
knows him, so when we meet Indians, as we do often,
there is always a powwow.

Three days ago we packed the little wagon with
wraps and other things, and Major and Mrs. Stokes,
Faye, and I started for a two days' outing at a little
lake that is nestled far up on the side of a mountain.
It is about ten miles from here. There is only a wagon
trail leading to it, and as you go on up and up, and
see nothing but rocks and trees, it would never occur
to you that the steep slope of the mountain could be

broken, that a lake of good size could be hidden on its side. You do not get a glimpse of it once, until you drive between the bushes and boulders that border its banks, and then it is all before you in amazing beauty. The reflections are wonderful, the high lights showing with exquisite sharpness against the dark green and purple depths of the clear, spring water.

The lake is fearfully deep—the Indians insist that in places it is bottomless—and it is teeming with trout, the most delicious mountain trout that can be caught any place, and which come up so cold one can easily fancy there is an iceberg somewhere down below. Some of these fish are fourteen or more inches long.

It was rather late in the afternoon when we reached the lake, so we hurriedly got ourselves ready for fishing, for we were thinking of a trout dinner. Four enlisted men had followed us with a wagon, in which were our tents, bedding, and boxes of provisions, and these men busied themselves at once by putting up the little tents and making preparations for dinner, and we were anxious to get enough fish for their dinner as well as our own. At a little landing we found two row-boats, and getting in these we were soon out on the lake.

If one goes to Fish Lake just for sport, and can be contented with taking in two or three fish during an all day's hard work, flies should be used always, but if one gets up there when the shadows are long and one's dinner is depending upon the fish caught, one might as well begin at once with grasshoppers—at least, that is what I did. I carried a box of fine yellow grasshoppers up with me, and I cast one over before the boat had fairly settled in position. It was seized

the instant it had touched the water, and down, down
went the trout, its white sides glistening through the
clear water.   For some reason still unaccountable I
let it go, and yard after yard of line was reeled out.
Perhaps, after all, it was fascination that kept me from
stopping the plunge of the fish, that never stopped
until the entire line was let out.   That brought me to
my senses, and I reeled the fish up and got a fine
trout, but I also got at the same time an uncontrollable
longing for land.   To be in a leaky, shaky old boat
over a watery, bottomless pit, as the one that trout
had been down in, was more than I could calmly endure, so with undisguised disgust Faye rowed me
back to the landing, where I caught quite as many fish
as anyone out in the boats.

One of the enlisted men prepared dinner for us, and
fried the trout in olive oil, the most perfect way of
cooking mountain trout in camp.   They were delicious
—so fresh from the icy water that none of their delicate flavor had been lost, and were crisp and hot.
We had cups of steaming coffee and all sorts of nice
things from the boxes we had brought from the post.
A flat boulder made a grand table for us, and of
course each one had his little camp stool to sit upon.
Altogether the dinner was a success, the best part of
it being, perhaps, the exhilarating mountain air that
gave us such fine appetites, and a keen appreciation of
everything ludicrous.

While we were fishing, our tents had been arranged
for us in real soldier fashion.   Great bunches of long
grass had been piled up on each side underneath the
little mattresses, which raised the beds from the
ground and made them soft and springy.   Those " A "

tents are very small and low, and it is impossible to stand up in one except in the center under the ridge-pole, for the canvas is stretched from the ridgepole to the ground, so the only walls are back and front, where there is an opening. I had never been in one before and was rather appalled at its limitations, and neither had I ever slept on the ground before, but I had gone prepared for a rough outing. Besides, I knew that everything possible had been done to make Mrs. Stokes and me comfortable. The air was chilly up on the mountain, but we had any number of heavy blankets that kept us warm.

The night was glorious with brilliant moonlight, and the shadows of the pine trees on the white canvas were black and wonderfully clear cut, as the wind swayed the branches back and forth. The sounds of the wind were dismal, soughing and moaning as all mountain winds do, and made me think of the Bogy-man and other things. I found myself wondering if anything could crawl under the tent at my side. I wondered if snakes could have been brought in with the grass. I imagined that I heard things moving about, but all the time I was watching those exquisite shadows of the pine needles in a dreamy sort of way.

Then all at once I saw the shadow of one, then three, things as they ran up the canvas and darted this way and that like crazy things, and which could not possibly have grown on a pine tree. And almost at the same instant, something pulled my hair! With a scream and scramble I was soon out of that tent, but of course when I moved all those things had moved, too, and wholly disappeared. So I was called foolish to be afraid in a tent after the weeks and months I had

lived in camp. But just then Mrs. Stokes ran from her
tent, Major Stokes slowly following, and then it came
out that there had been trouble over there also, and
that I was not the only one in disgrace. Mrs. Stokes
had seen queer shadows on her canvas, and coming to
me, said, " Will says those things are squirrels! "
That was too much, and I replied with indignation,
" They are not squirrels at all; they are too small and
their tails are not bushy."

Well, there was a time! We refused absolutely,
positively, to go back to our tents until we knew all
about those darting shadows. We saw that those two
disagreeable men had an understanding with each
other and were much inclined to laugh. It was cold
and our wrappers not very warm, but Mrs. Stokes and
I finally sat down upon some camp stools to await
events. Then Faye, who can never resist an opportunity to tease, said to me, " You had better take care,
mice might run up that stool! " So the cat was out!
I have never been afraid of mice, and have always
considered it very silly in women to make such a fuss
over them. But those field mice were different; they
seemed inclined to take the very hair from your head.
Of course we could not sit up all night, and after a
time had to return to our tents. I wrapped my head
up securely, so my hair could not be carried off without my knowing something about it. Ever so many
times during the night I heard talking and smothered
laughter, and concluded that the soldiers also were
having small visitors with four swift little legs.

We had more delicious trout for our breakfast; that
time fried with tiny strips of breakfast bacon. The
men had been out on the lake very early, and had

caught several dozen beautiful fish. The dinner the evening before had been much like an ordinary picnic, but the early breakfast up on the side of a mountain, with big boulders all around, was something to remember. One can never imagine the deliciousness of the air at sunrise up on the Rocky Mountains. It has to be breathed to be appreciated.

Everyone fished during the morning and many fish were caught, every one of which were carefully packed in wet grass and brought to Birch Creek, to the unfortunates who had not been on that most delightful trip to Fish Lake. After luncheon we came down from the mountain and drove to the Piegan Agency. The heavy wagon came directly to camp, of course. There is nothing remarkable to be seen at the agency—just a number of ordinary buildings, a few huts, and Indians standing around the door of a store that resembles a post trader's. Every Indian had on a blanket, although Major Stokes said there were several among them who had been to the Carlisle School.

Along the road before we reached the agency, and for some distance after we had left it, we passed a number of little one-room log huts occupied by Indians, often with two squaws and large families of children; and at some of these we saw wretched attempts at gardening. Those Indians are provided with plows, spades, and all sorts of implements necessary for the making of proper gardens, and they are given grain and seeds to plant, but seldom are any of these things made use of. An Indian scorns work of any kind—that is only for squaws. The squaws will scratch up a bit of ground with sticks, put a little seed in, and then leave it for the sun and rain to do with as it sees fit. No more attention will be paid to it, and half the time the seed is not covered.

One old chief raised some wheat one year—I presume his squaws did all the work—and he gathered several sackfuls, which was made into flour at the agency mill. The chief was very proud. But when the next quarterly issue came around, his ration of flour was lessened just the amount his wheat had made, which decided all future farming for him! Why should he, a chief, trouble himself about learning to farm and then gain nothing in the end! There is a fine threshing machine at the agency, but the Indians will have nothing whatever to do with it. They cannot understand its workings and call it the "Devil Machine."

As we were nearing the Indian village across the creek from us, we came to a most revolting spectacle. Two or three Indians had just killed an ox, and were slashing and cutting off pieces of the almost quivering flesh, in a way that left little pools of blood in places on the side. There were two squaws with them, squatted on the ground by the dead animal, and those hideous, fiendish creatures were scooping up the warm blood with their hands and greedily drinking it! Can one imagine anything more horrible? We stopped only a second, but the scene was too repulsive to be forgotten. It makes me shiver even now when I think of the flashing of those big knives and of how each one of the savages seemed to be reveling in the smell and taste of blood! I feel that they could have slashed and cut into one of us with the same relish. It was much like seeing a murder committed.

Major Stokes told us last evening that when he returned from the East a few weeks ago, he discovered that one of a pair of beautiful pistols that had been presented to him had been stolen, that some one had gone upstairs and taken it out of the case that was in a closet corresponding to mine, so that accounts for the footsteps I heard in that house the night the man entered Mrs. Norton's house. But how did the man know just where to get a pistol? The hospital attendant who was suspected that night got his discharge a few days later. He stayed around the garrison so long that finally Colonel Gregory ordered him to leave the reservation, and just before coming from the post we heard that he had shot a man and was in jail. A very good place for him, I think.

We expect to return to the post in a few days. I would like to remain longer, but as everybody and everything will go, I can't very well. The trout fishing in Birch Creek is very good, and I often go for a little fish, sometimes alone and sometimes Mrs. Stokes will go with me. I do not go far, because of the dreadful Indians that are always wandering about. They have a small village across the creek from us, and every evening we hear their " tom-toms " as they chant and dance, and when the wind is from that direction we get a smell now and then of their dirty tepees. Major Stokes and Mrs. Stokes, also, see the noble side of Indians, but that side has always been so covered with blankets and other dirty things I have never found it!

Fort Shaw, Montana Territory,
November, 1882.

YOU will be shocked, I know, when you hear that we are houseless—homeless—that for the second time Faye has been ranked out of quarters! At Camp Supply the turn out was swift, but this time it has been long drawn out and most vexatious. Last month Major Bagley came here from Fort Maginnis, and as we had rather expected that he would select our house, we made no preparations for winter previous to his coming. But as soon as he reached the post, and many times after, he assured Faye that nothing could possibly induce him to disturb us, and said many more sweet things.

Unfortunately for us, he was ordered to return to Fort Maginnis to straighten out some of his accounts while quartermaster, and Mrs. Bagley decided to remain as she was until Major Bagley's return. He was away one month, and during that time the gardener stored away in our little cellar our vegetables for the winter, including quantities of beautiful celery that was packed in boxes. All those things had to be taken down a ladder, which made it really very hard work. Having faith in Major Bagley's word, the house was cleaned from top to bottom, much painting and calcimining having been done. All the floors were painted and hard-oiled, and everyone knows what discomfort that always brings about. But at last everything was finished, and we were about to settle down to the enjoyment of a tidy, cheerful little home when Major Bagley appeared the second time, and within two hours Faye was notified that his quarters had been selected by him!

We are at present in two rooms and a shed that happened to be unoccupied, and I feel very much as though I was in a second-hand shop. Things are piled up to the ceiling in both rooms, and the shed is full also. All of the vegetables were brought up from the cellar, of course, and as the weather has been very cold, the celery and other tender things were frozen. General and Mrs. Bourke have returned, and at once insisted upon our going to their house, but as there was nothing definite about the time when we will get our house, we said " No." We are taking our meals with them, however, and Hang is there also, teaching their new Chinaman. But I can assure you that I am more than cross. If Major Bagley had selected the house the first time he came, or even if he had said nothing at all about the quarters, much discomfort and unpleasantness would have been avoided. They will get our nice clean house, and we will get one that will require the same renovating we have just been struggling with. I have made up my mind unalterably to one thing—the nice little dinner I had expected to give Major and Mrs. Bagley later on, will be for other people, friends who have had less honey to dispose of.

The splendid hunting was interrupted by the move, too. Every October in this country we have a snowstorm that lasts usually three or four days; then the snow disappears and there is a second fall, with clear sunny days until the holidays. This year the weather remained warm and the storm was later than usual, but more severe when it did come, driving thousands of water-fowl down with a rush from the mountain streams and lakes. There is a slough around a little plateau near the post, and for a week or more this was teeming with all kinds of ducks, until it was frozen over. Sometimes we would see several species quietly feeding together in the most friendly way. Faye and I would drive the horses down in the cutter, and I would hold them while he walked on ahead hunting.

One day, when the snow was falling in big moist flakes that were so thick that the world had been narrowed down to a few yards around us, we drove to some tall bushes growing on the bank of the slough. Faye was hunting, and about to make some ducks rise when he heard a great whir over his head, and although the snow was so thick he could not see just what was there, he quickly raised his gun and fired at something he saw moving up there. To his great amazement and my horror, an immense swan dropped down and went crashing through the bushes. It was quite as white as the snow on the ground, and coming from the dense cloud of snow above, where no warning of its presence had been given, no call sounded, one felt that there was something queer about it all. With its enormous wings spread, it looked like an angel coming to the earth.

The horses thought so, also, for as soon as it touched the bushes they bolted, and for a few minutes I was doubtful if I could hold them. I was so vexed with them, too, for I wanted to see that splendid bird. They went around and around the plateau, and about all I was able to do at first was to keep them from going to the post. They finally came down to a trot, but it was some time before I could coax them to go to the bushes where the swan had fallen. I did not blame them much, for when the big bird came down, it seemed as if the very heavens were falling. We supplied our friends with ducks several days, and upon our own dinner table duck was served ten successive days. And it was just as acceptable the last day as the first, for almost every time there was a different variety, the cinnamon, perhaps, being the most rare.

Last year Hang was very contrary about the packing down of the eggs for winter use. I always put them in salt, but he thought they should be put in oats because Mrs. Pierce had packed hers that way. You know he had been Mrs. Pierce's cook two years before he came to me, and for a time he made me weary telling how she had things done. Finally I told him he must do as I said, that he was my cook now. There was peace for a while, and then came the eggs.

He would not do one thing to assist me, not even take down the eggs, and looked at Volmer with scorn when he carried down the boxes and salt. I said nothing, knowing what the result would be later on if Hang remained with me. When the cold weather came and no more fresh eggs were brought in, it was astonishing to see how many things that stubborn Chinaman could make without any eggs at all. Get them out of the salt he simply would not. Of course that could not continue forever, so one day I brought some up and left them on his table without saying a word. He used them, and after that there was no trouble, and one day in the spring he brought in to show me some beautifully beaten eggs, and said, " Velly glood—allee same flesh."

This fall when the time came to pack eggs, I said, " Hang, perhaps we had better pack the eggs in oats

this year." He said, " Naw, loats no glood!" Then
came my revenge. I said, " Mrs. Pierce puts hers in
oats," but he became angry and said, " Yes, me know
—Missee Pleese no know—slalt makee him allee
same flesh." And in salt they are, and Hang packed
every one. I offered to show him how to do it, but
he said, " Me know—you see." It gave him such a
fine opportunity to dictate to Volmer! If the striker
did not bring the eggs the very moment he thought
they should be in, Hang would look him up and say,
" You bling leggs!" Just where these boxes of eggs
are I do not know. The Chinaman has spirited them
off to some place where they will not freeze. He cannot understand all this ranking out of quarters, particularly after he had put the house in perfect order.
When I told him to sweep the rooms after everything
had been carried out, he said: " What for? You
cleanee house nuff for him; he no care," and off he
went. I am inclined to think that the little man was
right, after all.

There have been many changes in the garrison during the past few months, and a number of our friends
have gone to other posts. Colonel and Mrs. Palmer,
Major and Mrs. Pierce, and Doctor and Mrs. Gordon
are no longer here. We have lost, consequently, both
of our fine tenors and excellent organist, and our little
choir is not good now. Some of us will miss in other
ways Colonel Palmer's cultivated voice. During the
summer four of us found much pleasure in practicing
together the light operas, each one learning the one
voice through the entire opera.

When we get settled, if we ever do, we will be at
our old end of the garrison again, and our neighbors

21

on either side will be charming people. There is some consolation in that; nevertheless, I am thinking all the time of the pretty walls and shiny floors we had to give up, and to a very poor housekeeper, too. After we get our house, it will take weeks to fix it up, and it will be impossible to take the same interest in it that we found in the first. If Faye gets his first lieutenancy in the spring, it is possible that we may have to go to another post, which will mean another move. But I am tired and cross; anyone would be under such uncomfortable conditions.

FORT ELLIS, MONTANA TERRITORY,
March, 1883.

THE trip over was by far the most enjoyable of any we have taken between Fort Shaw and this post, and we were thankful enough that we could come before the snow began to melt on the mountains. Our experience with the high water two years ago was so dreadful that we do not wish to ever encounter anything of the kind again. The weather was delightful—with clear, crisp atmosphere, such as can be found only in this magnificent Territory. It was such a pleasure to have our own turn-out, too, and to be able to see the mountains and cañons as we came along, without having our heads bruised by an old ambulance.

Faye had to wait almost twelve years for a first lieutenancy, and now, when at last he has been promoted, it has been the cause of our leaving dear friends and a charming garrison, and losing dear yellow Hang, also. The poor little man wept when he said good-by to me in Helena. We had just arrived and

were still on the walk in front of the hotel, and of
course all the small boys in the street gathered around
us. I felt very much like weeping, too, and am afraid
I will feel even more so when I get in my own home.
Hang is going right on to China, to visit his mother
one year, and I presume that his people will consider
him a very rich man, with the twelve hundred dollars he has saved. He has never cut his hair, and
has never worn American clothes. Even in the winter, when it has been freezing cold, he would shuffle
along on the snow with his Chinese shoes.

I shall miss the pretty silk coats about the house,
and his swift, almost noiseless going around. That
Chinamen are not more generally employed I cannot
understand, for they make such exceptional servants.
They are wonderfully economical, and can easily do
the work of two maids, and if once you win their confidence and their affection they are your slaves. But
they are very suspicious. Once, when Bishop Tuttle
was with us, he wanted a pair of boots blackened, and
set them in his room where Hang could see them, and
on the toe of one he put a twenty-five cent piece.
Hang blackened the boots beautifully, and then put
the money back precisely where it was in the first
place. Then he came to me and expressed his opinion
of the dear bishop. He said, " China-man no stealee
—you tellee him me no stealee—he see me no takee
him "—and then he insisted upon my going to see
for myself that the money was on the boot. I was
awfully distressed. The bishop was to remain with
us several days, and no one could tell how that Chinaman might treat him, for I saw that he was deeply
hurt, but it was utterly impossible to make him believe

otherwise than that the quarter had been put there to test his honesty. I finally concluded to tell the bishop all about it, knowing that his experience with all kinds of human nature had been great in his travels about to his various missions, and his kindness and tact with miner, ranchman, and cowboy; he is now called by them lovingly " The Cowboy Bishop." He laughed heartily about Hang, and said, " I'll fix that," which he must have done to Hang's entire satisfaction, for he fairly danced around the bishop during the remainder of his stay with us.

Faye was made post quartermaster and commissary as soon as he reported for duty here, and is already hard at work. The post is not large, but the office of quartermaster is no sinecure. An immense amount of transportation has to be kept in readiness for the field, for which the quartermaster alone is held responsible, and this is the base of supplies for outfits for all parties—large and small—that go to the Yellowstone Park, and these are many, now that Livingstone can be reached from the north or the south by the Northern Pacific Railroad. Immense pack trains have to be fitted out for generals, congressmen, even the President himself, during the coming season. These people bring nothing whatever with them for camp, but depend entirely upon the quartermaster here to fit them out as luxuriously as possible with tents and commissaries—even to experienced camp cooks!

The railroad has been laid straight through the post, and it looks very strange to see the cars running directly back of the company quarters. The long tunnel—it is to be called the Bozeman tunnel—that has been cut through a large mountain is not quite finished, and the cars are still run up over the mountain upon a track that was laid only for temporary use. It requires two engines to pull even the passenger trains up, and when the divide is reached the "pilot" is uncoupled and run down ahead, sometimes at terrific speed. One day, since we came, the engineer lost control, and the big black thing seemed almost to drop down the grade, and the shrieking of the con-

"The 'pilot' is uncoupled and run down ahead."

tinuous whistle was awful to listen to; it seemed as if it was the wailing of the souls of the two men being rushed on—perhaps to their death. The thing came on and went screaming through the post and on through Bozeman, and how much farther we do not know. Some of the enlisted men got a glimpse of the engineer as he passed and say that his face was like chalk.

We will not be settled for some time, as Faye is

to take a set of vacant quarters on the hill until one of the officers goes on leave, when we will move to that house, as it is nicer and nearer the offices. He could have taken it when we came had he been willing to turn anyone out. It seems to me that I am waiting for a house about half the time, yet when anyone wants our house it is taken at once!

For a few days we are with Lieutenant and Mrs. Fiske. They gave us an elegant dinner last evening. Miss Burt and her brother came up from Bozeman. This evening we dine with Major and Mrs. Gillespie of the cavalry. He is in command of the post—and to-morrow we will dine with Captain and Mrs. Spencer. And so it will go on, probably, until everyone has entertained us in some delightful manner, as this is the custom in the Army when there are newcomers in the garrison. I am so sorry that these courtesies cannot be returned for a long time—until we get really settled, and then how I shall miss Hang! How I am to do without him I do not quite see.

FORT ELLIS, MONTANA TERRITORY,
July, 1884.

THIS post is in a most dilapidated condition, and it—also the country about—looks as though it had been the scene of a fierce bombardment. And bombarded we certainly have been—by a terrific hailstorm that made us feel for a time that our very lives were in danger. The day had been excessively warm, with brilliant sunshine until about three o'clock, when dark clouds were seen to be coming up over the Bozeman Valley, and everyone said that perhaps at last we would have the rain that was so much needed. I

have been in so many frightful storms that came from
innocent-looking clouds, that now I am suspicious of
anything of the kind that looks at all threatening.
Consequently, I was about the first person to notice
the peculiar unbroken gray that had replaced the black
of a few minutes before, and the first, too, to hear the
ominous roar that sounded like the fall of an immense
body of water, and which could be distinctly heard fifteen minutes before the storm reached us.

While I stood at the door listening and watching, I
saw several people walking about in the garrison, each
one intent upon his own business and not giving the
storm a thought. Still, it seemed to me that it would
be just as well to have the house closed tight, and
calling Hulda we soon had windows and doors closed
—not one minute too soon, either, for the storm came
across the mountains with hurricane speed and struck
us with such force that the thick-walled log houses
fairly trembled. With the wind came the hail at the
very beginning, changing the hot, sultry air into the
coldness of icebergs. Most of the hailstones were the
size of a hen's egg, and crashed through windows and
pounded against the house, making a noise that was
not only deafening but paralyzing. The sounds of
breaking glass came from every direction and Hulda
and I rushed from one room to the other, not knowing what to do, for it was the same scene everyplace
—floors covered with broken glass and hail pouring
in through the openings.

The ground upon which the officers' quarters are
built is a little sloping, therefore it had to be cut away,
back of the kitchen, to make the floor level for a large
shed where ice chest and such things are kept, and

there are two or three steps at the door leading from the shed up to the ground outside. This gradual rise continues far back to the mountains, so by the time the hail and water reached us from above they had become one broad, sweeping torrent, ever increasing in volume. In one of the boards of our shed close to the steps, and just above the ground, there happened to be a large " knot " which the pressure of the water soon forced out, and the water and hailstones shot through and straight across the shed as if from a fire hose, striking the wall of the main building! The sight was most laughable—that is, at first it was; but we soon saw that the awful rush of water that was coming in through the broken sash and the remarkable hose arrangement back of the kitchen was rapidly flooding us.

So I ran to the front door, and seeing a soldier at one of he barrack windows, I waved and waved my hand until he saw me. He understood at once and came running over, followed by three more men, who brought spades and other things. In a short time sods had been banked up at every door, and then the water ceased to come in. By that time the heaviest of the storm had passed over, and the men, who were most willing and kind, began to shovel out the enormous quantity of hailstones from the shed. They found by actual measurement that they were eight inches deep—solid hail, and over the entire floor. Much of the water had run into the kitchen and on through to the butler's pantry, and was fast making its way to the dining room when it was cut off. The scenes around the little house were awful. More or less water was in each room, and there was not one unbroken pane of glass to be found, and that was not all—there was not one unbroken pane of glass in the whole post. That night Faye telegraphed to St. Paul for glass to replace nine hundred panes that had been broken.

Faye was at the quartermaster's office when the storm came up, and while it was still hailing I happened to look across the parade that way, and in the door I saw Faye standing. He had left the house not long before, dressed in a suit of immaculate white linen, and it was that suit that enabled me to recognize him through the veil of rain and hail. Sorry as I was, I had to laugh, for the picture was so ludicrous —Faye in those chilling white clothes, broken windows each side of him, and the ground covered with inches of hailstones and ice water! He ran over soon after the men got here, but as he had to come a greater distance his pelting was in proportion. Many of the stones were so large it was really dangerous to be hit by them.

When the storm was over the ground was white, as if covered with snow, and the high board fences that are around the yards back of the officers' quarters looked as though they had been used for targets and peppered with big bullets. Mount Bridger is several miles distant, yet we can distinctly see from here the furrows that were made down its sides. It looks as if deep ravines had been cut straight down from peak to base. The gardens are wholly ruined— not one thing was left in them. The poor little gophers were forced out of their holes by the water, to be killed by the hail, and hundreds of them are lying around dead. I wondered and wondered why Dryas did not come to our assistance, but he told us afterward that when the storm first came he went to the stable to fasten the horses up snug, and was then afraid to come away, first because of the immense hailstones, and later because both horses were so terrified by the crashing in of their windows, and the awful cannonade of hail on the roof. A new cook had come to us just the day before the storm, and I fully expected that she would start back to Bozeman that night, but she is still here, and was most patient over the awful condition of things all over the house. She is a Pole and a good cook, so there is a prospect of some enjoyment in life after the house gets straightened out. There was one thing peculiar about that storm. Bozeman is only three miles from here, yet not one hailstone, not one drop of rain did they get there. They saw the moving wall of gray and heard the roar, and feared that something terrible was happening up here.

The storm has probably ruined the mushrooms that we have found so delicious lately. At one time, just out of the post, there was a long, log stable for cavalry horses which was removed two or three years ago, and all around, wherever the decayed logs had been, mushrooms have sprung up. When it rains is the time to get the freshest, and many a time Mrs. Fiske and I have put on long storm coats and gone out in the rain for them, each bringing in a large basket heaping full of the most delicate buttons. The quantity is no exaggeration whatever—and to be very exact, I would say that we invariably left about as many as we gathered. Usually we found the buttons massed together under the soft dirt, and when we came to an umbrella-shaped mound with little cracks on top, we would carefully lift the dirt with a stick and uncover big clusters of buttons of all sizes. We always broke the large buttons off with the greatest care and settled the spawn back in the loose dirt for a future harvest. We often found large mushrooms above ground, and these were delicious baked with cream sauce. They would be about the size of an ordinary saucer, but tender and full of rich flavor—and the buttons would vary in size from a twenty-five-cent piece to a silver dollar, each one of a beautiful shell pink underneath. They were so very superior to mushrooms we had eaten before—with a deliciousness all their own.

We are wondering if the storm passed over the Yellowstone Park, where just now are many tents and considerable transportation. The party consists of the general of the Army, the department commander, members of their staffs, and two justices of the supreme court. From the park they are to go across country to Fort Missoula, and as there is only a narrow trail over the mountains they will have to depend entirely upon pack mules. These were sent up from Fort Custer for Faye to fit out for the entire trip. I went down to the corral to see them start out, and it was a sight well worth going to see. It was wonderful, and laughable, too, to see what one mule could carry upon his back and two sides.

The pack saddles are queer looking things that are strapped carefully and firmly to the mules, and then the tents, sacks, boxes, even stoves are roped to the saddle. One poor mule was carrying a cooking stove. There were forty pack mules and one " bell horse " and ten packers—for of course it requires an expert packer to put the things on the saddle so they are perfectly balanced and will not injure the animal's back. The bell horse leads, and wherever it goes the mules will follow.

At present Faye is busy with preparations for two more parties of exceedingly distinguished *personnel.* One of these will arrive in a day or two, and is called the "Indian Commission," and consists of senator Dawes and fourteen congressmen. The other party for whom an elaborate camp outfit is being put in readiness consists of the President of the United States, the lieutenant general of the Army, the governor of Montana, and others of lesser magnitude. A troop of cavalry will escort the President through the park. Now that the park can be reached by railroad, all of the generals, congressmen, and judges are seized with a desire to inspect it—in other words, it gives them a fine excuse for an outing at Uncle Sam's expense.

CAMP ON YELLOWSTONE RIVER, YELLOWSTONE PARK,
August, 1884.

OUR camp is in a beautiful pine grove, just above the Upper Falls and close to the rapids; from out tent we can look out on the foaming river as it rushes from one big rock to another. Far from the bank on an immense boulder that is almost surrounded by water is perched my tent companion, Miss Hayes. She says the view from there is grand, but how she can have the nerve to go over the wet, slippery rocks is a mystery to all of us, for by one little misstep she would be swept over the falls and to eternity.

Our party consists of Captain and Mrs. Spencer, their little niece, Miss Hayes, and myself—oh, yes, Lottie, the colored cook, and six or eight soldiers. We have part of the transportation that Major General Schofield used for this same trip two weeks ago, and which we found waiting for us at Mammoth Hot Springs. We also have two saddle horses. By having tents and our own transportation we can remain as long as we wish at any one place, and can go to many out-of-the-way spots that the regular tourist does not even hear of. But I do not intend to weary you with long descriptions of the park, the wonderful geysers, or the exquisitely tinted water in many of the springs, but to tell you of our trip, that has been most enjoyable from the very minute we left Livingstone.

We camped one night by the Fire-Hole River, where there is a spring I would like to carry home with me! The water is very hot—boils up a foot or so all the year round, and is so buoyant that in a porcelain tub of ordinary depth we found it difficult to do otherwise than float, and its softening effect upon the skin is delightful. A pipe has been laid from the spring to the little hotel, where it is used for all sorts of household purposes. Just fancy having a stream of water that a furnace somewhere below has brought to boiling heat, running through your house at any and all times. They told us that during the winter when everything is frozen, all kinds of wild animals come to drink at the overflow of the spring. There are hundreds of hot springs in the park, I presume, but that one at Marshall's is remarkable for the purity of its water.

Captain Spencer sent to the hotel for fresh meat and

was amazed when the soldier brought back, instead of meat, a list from which he was asked to select. At that little log hotel of ten or twelve rooms there were seven kinds of meat—black-tail deer, white-tail deer, bear, grouse, prairie chicken, squirrels, and domestic fowl—the latter still in possession of their heads. Hunting in the park is prohibited, and the proprietor of that fine game market was most careful to explain to the soldier that everything had been brought from the other side of the mountain. That was probably true, but nevertheless, just as we were leaving the woods by " Hell's Half Acre," and were coming out on a beautiful meadow surrounded by a thick forest, we saw for one instant a deer standing on the bank of a little stream at our right, and then it disappeared in the forest. Captain Spencer was on horseback, and happening to look to the left saw a man skulking to the woods with a rifle in his hand. The poor deer would undoubtedly have been shot if we had been a minute or two later.

For two nights our camp was in the pine forest back of " Old Faithful," and that gave us one whole day and afternoon with the geysers. Our colored cook was simply wild over them, and would spend hours looking down in the craters of those that were not playing. Those seemed to fascinate her above all things there, and at times she looked like a wild African when she returned to camp from one of them. Not far from the tents of the enlisted men was a small hot spring that boiled lazily in a shallow basin. It occurred to one of the men that it would make a fine laundry, so he tied a few articles of clothing securely to a stick and swished them up and down in the hot sulphur water and then hung them up to dry. Another soldier, taking notice of the success of that washing, decided to do even better, so he gathered all the underwear he had with him, except those he had on, and dropped them down in the basin. He used the stick, but only to push them about with, and alas! did not fasten them to it. They swirled about for a time, and then all at once every article disap-

"The poor deer would undoubtedly have been shot if we had been a minute later."

peared, leaving the poor man in dumb amazement. He sat on the edge of the spring until dark, watching and waiting for his clothes to return to him; but come back they did not. Some of the men watched with him, but most of them teased him cruelly. Such a loss on a trip like this was great.

When we got to Obsidian Mountain, Miss Hayes and I decided that we would like to go up a little distance and get a few specimens to carry home with us. Our camp for the night was supposed to be only one mile farther on, and the enlisted men and two wagons were back of us, so we thought we could safely stay there by ourselves. The so-called mountain is really only a foothill to a large mountain, but is most interesting from the fact that it is covered with pieces of obsidian, mostly smoke-color, and that long ago Indians came there for arrowheads.

A very narrow road has been cut out of the rocks at the base of the mountain, and about four feet above a small stream. It has two very sharp turns, and all around, as far as we could see, it would be exceedingly dangerous, if not impossible, for large wagons to pass. Miss Hayes and I went on up, gathering and rejecting pieces of obsidian that had probably been gathered and rejected by hundreds of tourists before us, and we were laughing and having a beautiful time when, for some reason, I looked back, and down on the point where the road almost doubles on itself I saw an old wagon with two horses, and standing by the wagon were two men. They were looking at us, and very soon one beckoned. I looked all around, thinking that some of their friends must certainly be near us, but no one was in sight. By that time one man was waving his hat to us, and then they actually called, " Come on down here—come down, it is all right ! "

Miss Hayes is quite deaf, and I was obliged to go around rocks before I could get near enough to tell her of the wagon below, and the men not hear me. She gave the men and wagon an indifferent glance, and then went on searching for specimens. I was so vexed I could have shaken her. She will scream over

a worm or spider, and almost faint at the sight of a
snake, but those two men, who were apparently real
tramps, she did not mind. The situation was critical,
and for just one instant I thought hard. If we were to
go over the small mountain we would probably be lost,
and might encounter all sorts of wild beasts, and if
those men were really vicious they could easily overtake us. Besides, it would never do to let them suspect
that we were afraid. So I decided to go down—and
slowly down I went, almost dragging Miss Hayes
with me. She did not understand my tactics, and I
did not stop to explain.

I went right to the men, taking care to get between
them and the road to camp. I asked them if they were
in trouble of any kind, and they said " No." I could
hardly control my voice, but it seemed important that
I should give them to understand at once who we
were. So I said, " Did you meet our friends in the
army ambulance just down the road? " The two
looked at each other and then one said " Yes! " I
continued with, " There are two very large and
heavily loaded army wagons, and a number of soldiers
coming down the other road that should be here right
now." They smiled again, and said something to each
other, but I interrupted with, " I do not see how those
big wagons and four mules can pass you here, and it
seems to me you had better get out of their way, for
soldiers can be awfully cross if things are not just to
suit them."

Well, those two men got in the old wagon without
saying one word and started on, and we watched them
until they had disappeared from sight around a bend,
and then I said to Miss Hayes, " Come! " and lifting

22

my skirts, I started on the fastest run I ever made in my life, and I kept it up until I actually staggered. Then I sat upon a rock back of some bushes and waited for Miss Hayes, who appeared after a few minutes. We rested for a short time and then went on and on, and still there was nothing to be seen of the meadow where the camp was supposed to be. Finally, after we had walked miles, it seemed to us, we saw an opening far ahead, and the sharp silhouette of a man under the arch of trees, and when we reached the end of the wooded road we found Captain Spencer waiting for us. He at once started off on a fine inspection-day reprimand, but I was tired and cross and reminded him that it was he who had told us that the camp would be only one mile from us, and if we had not listened to him we would not have stopped at all. Then we all laughed!

Captain and Mrs. Spencer had become worried, and the ambulance was just starting back for us when fortunately we appeared. Miss Hayes cannot understand yet why I went down to that wagon. The child does not fear tramps and desperadoes, simply because she has never encountered them. Whether my move was wise or unwise, I knew that down on the road we could run—up among the rocks we could not. Besides, I have the satisfaction of knowing that once in my life I outgeneraled a man—two men—and whether they were friends or foes I care not now. I was wearing an officer's white cork helmet at the time, and possibly that helped matters a little. But why did they call to us—why beckon for us to come down? It was my birthday too. That evening Mrs. Spencer made some delicious punch and brought out

the last of the huge fruit cake she made for the trip.
We had bemoaned the fact of its having all been
eaten, and all the time she had a piece hidden away for
my birthday, as a great surprise.

We have had one very stormy day. It began to
rain soon after we broke camp in the morning, not
hard, but in a cold, penetrating drizzle. Captain and
Mrs. Spencer were riding that day and continued to
ride until luncheon, and by that time they were wet to
the skin and shaking from the cold. We were nearing the falls, the elevation was becoming greater and
the air more chilling every minute. We had expected
to reach the Yellowstone River that day, but it was so
wet and disagreeable that Captain Spencer decided to
go into camp at a little spring we came to in the early
afternoon, and which was about four miles from here.
The tents were pitched just above the base of a hill—
you would call it a mountain in the East—and in a
small grove of trees. The ground was thickly car-
peted with dead leaves, and everything looked most
attractive from the ambulance.

When Miss Hayes and I went to our tent, however,
to arrange it, we found that underneath that thick
covering of leaves a sheet of water was running down
the side of the hill, and with every step our feet sank
down almost ankle deep in the wet leaves and water.
Each has a little iron cot, and the two had been set up
and the bedding put upon them by the soldiers, and
they looked so inviting we decided to rest a while and
get warm also. But much to our disgust we found that
our mattresses were wet and all of our blankets more
or less wet, too. It was impossible to dry one thing in
the awful dampness, so we folded the blankets with the

dry part on top as well as we could, and then " crawled in." We hated to get up for dinner, but as we were guests, we felt that we must do so, but for that meal we waited in vain—not one morsel of dinner was prepared that night, and Miss Hayes and I envied the enlisted men when we got sniffs of their boiling coffee. Only a soldier could have found dry wood and a place for making coffee that night.

When it is at all wet Faye always has our tents " ditched," that is, the sod turned up on the canvas all around the bottom. So just before dark I asked Captain Spencer if the men could not do that to our tent, and it was done without delay. It made a great difference in our comfort, for at once the incoming of the water was stopped. We all retired early that night, and notwithstanding our hunger, and the wet below and above us, our sleep was sound. In the morning we found several inches of snow on the ground and the whole country was white. The snow was so moist and clinging, that the small branches of trees were bent down with its weight, and the effect of the pure white on the brilliant greens was enchanting. Over all was the glorious sunshine that made the whole grand scene glisten and sparkle like fairyland. And that day was the twenty-sixth of August!

It was wretchedly cold, and our heaviest wraps seemed thin and light. Lottie gave us a nice hot breakfast, and after that things looked much more cheerful. By noon most of the snow had disappeared, and after an early luncheon we came on to these dry, piney woods, that claim an elevation of nine thousand feet. The rarefied air affects people so differently. Some breathe laboriously and have great difficulty in walking at all, while to others it is most exhilarating, and gives them strength to walk great distances. Fortunately, our whole party is of the latter class.

Yesterday morning early we all started for a tramp down the cañon. I do not mean that we were in the cañon by the river, for that would have been impossible, but that we went along the path that runs close to the edge of the high cliff. We carried our luncheon with us, so there was no necessity for haste, and every now and then we sat upon the thick carpet of pine needles to rest, and also study the marvelous coloring of the cliffs across the river. The walls of the cañon are very high and very steep—in many places perpendicular—and their strata of brilliant colors are a marvel to everyone. It was a day to be remembered, and no one seemed to mind being a little tired when we returned late in the afternoon. The proprietor of the little log hotel that is only a short distance up the river, told Captain Spencer that we had gone down six good miles—giving us a tramp altogether, of twelve miles. It seems incredible, for not one of us could walk one half that distance in less rarefied air.

Just below the big falls, and of course very near our camp, is a nature study that we find most interesting. An unusually tall pine tree has grown up from between the boulders at the edge of the river. The tree is now dead and its long branches have fallen off, but a few outspreading short ones are still left, and right in the center of these a pair of eagles have built a huge nest, and in that nest, right now, are two dear eaglets! The tree is some distance from the top of the cliff, but it is also lower, otherwise we would not have such a fine view of the nest and the big babies.

They look a little larger than mallard ducks, and are well feathered. They fill the nest to overflowing, and seem to realize that if they move about much, one would soon go overboard. The two old birds—immense in size—can be seen soaring above the nest at almost any time, but not once have we seen them come to the nest, although we have watched with much patience for them to do so. The great wisdom shown by those birds in the selection of a home is wonderful. It would be utterly impossible for man or beast to reach it.

Another nature study that we have seen in the park, and which, to me, was most wonderful, was a large beaver village. Of course most people of the Northwest have seen beaver villages of various sizes, but that one was different, and should be called a city. There were elevated roads laid off in squares that run with great precision from one little house to the other. There are dozens and dozens of houses —perhaps a hundred—in the marshy lake, and the amount of intelligence and cunning the little animals have shown in the construction of their houses and elevated roads is worth studying. They are certainly fine engineers.

We take the road home from here, but go a much more direct route, which will be by ambulance all the way to Fort Ellis, instead of going by the cars from Mammoth Hot Springs. I am awfully glad of this, as it will make the trip one day longer, and take us over a road that is new to us, although it is the direct route from Ellis to the Park through Rocky Cañon.

FORT ELLIS, MONTANA TERRITORY,
November, 1884.

ONLY a few days more, and then we will be off for the East! It is over seven years since we started from Corinne on that long march north, and I never dreamed at that time that I would remain right in this territory, until a splendid railroad would be built to us from another direction to take us out of it. Nearly everything is packed. We expect to return here in the spring, but in the Army one never knows what destiny may have waiting for them at the War Department. Besides, I would not be satisfied to go so far away and leave things scattered about.

The two horses, wagons, and everything of the kind have been disposed of—not because we wanted to sell them, but because Faye was unwilling to leave the horses with irresponsible persons during a long winter in this climate, when the most thoughtful care is absolutely necessary to keep animals from suffering. Lieutenant Gallagher of the cavalry bought them, and we are passing through our second experience of seeing others drive around horses we have petted, and taught to know us apart from all others. George almost broke my heart the other day. He was standing in front of Lieutenant Gallagher's quarters, that are near ours, when I happened to go out on the walk, not knowing the horses were there. He gave a loud, joyous whinnie, and started to come to me, pulling Pete and the wagon with him. I ran back to the house, for I could not go to him! He had been my own horse, petted and fed lumps of sugar every day with my own hands, and I always drove him in single harness, because his speed was so much greater than Pete's.

My almost gownless condition has been a cause of great worry to me, but Pogue has promised to fix up my wardrobe with a rush, and after the necessary time for that in Cincinnati, I will hurry on to Columbus Barracks for my promised visit to Doctor and Mrs. Gordon. Then on home! Faye will go to Cincinnati with me, and from there to the United States Naval Home, of which his father is governor at present. I will have to go there, too, before so very long.

We attended a pretty cotillon in Bozeman last evening and remained overnight at the hotel. Faye led, and was assisted by Mr. Ladd, of Bozeman. It was quite a large and elaborate affair, and there were present " the butcher, the baker, and candlestick maker." Nevertheless, everything was conducted with the greatest propriety. There are five or six very fine families in the small place—people of culture and refinement from the East—and their influence in the building up of the town has been wonderful. The first year we were at Fort Ellis one would see every now and then a number, usually four numerals, painted in bright red on the sidewalk. Everyone knew that to have been the work of vigilantes, and was a message to some gambler or horse thief to get himself out of town or stand the shotgun or rope jury. The first time I saw those red figures—I knew what they were for—it seemed as if they had been made in blood, and step over them I could not. I went out in the road around them. We have seen none of those things during the past two years, and for the sake of those who have worked so hard for law and order, we hope the desperado element has passed on.

FORT SHAW, MONTANA TERRITORY,
May, 1885.

IT is nice to be once more at this dear old post, particularly under such very pleasant circumstances. The winter East was enjoyable and refreshing from first to last, but citizens and army people have so little in common, and this one feels after being with them a while, no matter how near and dear the relationship may be. Why, one half of them do not know the uniform, and could not distinguish an officer of the Army from a policeman! I love army life here in the West, and I love all the things that it brings to me—the grand mountains, the plains, and the fine hunting. The buffalo are no longer seen; every one has been killed off, and back of Square Butte in a rolling valley, hundreds of skeletons are bleaching even now. The valley is about two miles from the post.

We are with the commanding officer and his wife, and Hulda is here also. She was in Helena during the winter and came from there with us. I am so glad to have her. She is so competent, and will be such a comfort a little later on, when there will be much entertaining for us to do. We stopped at Fort Ellis two days to see to the crating of the furniture and to get all things in readiness to be shipped here, this time by the cars instead of by wagon, through mud and water. We were guests of Captain and Mrs. Spencer, and enjoyed the visit so much. Doctor and Mrs. Lawton gave an informal dinner for us, and that was charming too.

But the grand event of the stop-over was the champagne supper that Captain Martin gave in our honor —that is, in honor of the new adjutant of the regiment. He is the very oldest bachelor and one of the oldest officers in the regiment—a very jolly Irishman. The supper was old-fashioned, with many good things to eat, and the champagne frappé was perfect. I do believe that the generous-hearted man had prepared at least two bottles for each one of us. Every member of the small garrison was there, and each officer proposed something pleasant in life for Faye, and often I was included. There was not the least harm done to anyone, however, and not a touch of headache the next day.

As usual, we are waiting for quarters to avoid turning some one out. But for a few days this does not matter much, as our household goods are not here, except the rugs and things we sent out from Philadelphia. Faye entered upon his new duties at guard mounting this morning, and I scarcely breathed until the whole thing was over and the guard was on its way to the guardhouse! It was so silly, I knew, to be afraid that Faye might make a mistake, for he has mounted the guard hundreds of times while post adjutant. But here it was different. I knew that from almost every window that looked out on the parade ground, eyes friendly and eyes envious were peering to see how the new regimental adjutant conducted himself, and I knew that there was one pair of eyes green from envy and pique, and that the least *faux-pas* by Faye would be sneered at and made much of by their owner. But Faye made no mistake, of course. I knew all the time that it was quite impossible for him to do so, as he is one of the very best tacticians in the regiment—still, it is the unexpected that so often happens.

The band and the magnificent drum major, watching their new commander with critical eyes, were quite enough in themselves to disconcert any man. I never told you what happened to that band once upon a time! It was before we came to the regiment, and when headquarters were at Fort Dodge, Kansas. Colonel Mills, at that time a captain, was in command. It had been customary to send down to the river every winter a detail of men from each company to cut ice for their use during the coming year. Colonel Mills ordered the detail down as usual, and also ordered the band down. It seems that Colonel Fitz-James, who had been colonel of the regiment for some time, had babied the bandsmen, one and all, until they had quite forgotten the fact of their being enlisted men.

So over to Colonel Mills went the first sergeant with a protest against cutting ice, saying that they were musicians and could not be expected to do such work, that it would chap their lips and ruin their delicate touch on the instruments. Colonel Mills listened patiently and then said, " But you like ice during the summer, don't you? " The sergeant said, " Yes, sir, but they could not do such hard work as the cutting of ice." Colonel Mills said, " You are musicians, you say? " The unsuspicious sergeant, thinking he had gained his point, smilingly said, " Yes, sir! " But there must have been an awful weakness in his knees when Colonel Mills said, " Very well, since you are musicians and cannot cut ice, you will go to the river and play for the other men while they

cut it for you!" The weather was freezing cold, and
the playing of brass instruments in the open air over
two feet of solid ice, would have been painful and difficult, so it was soon decided that it would be better
to cut ice, after all, and in a body the band went down
with the other men to the river without further complaint or protest.

It is a splendid band, and has always been regarded
as one of the very best in the Army, but there are a
few things that need changing, which Faye will attend to as quickly as possible, and at the same time
bring criticism down upon his own head. The old
adjutant is still in the post, and—"eyes green" are
here!

FORT SHAW, MONTANA TERRITORY,
August, 1885.

MY ride this morning was grand! My new horse
is beginning to see that I am really a friend, and
is much less nervous. It is still necessary, however,
for Miller, our striker, to make blinders with his hands
back of Rollo's eyes so he will not see me jump to the
saddle, otherwise I might not get there. I mount in
the yard back of the house, where no one can see me.
The gate is opened first, and that the horse always
stands facing, for the instant he feels my weight upon
his back there is a little flinch, then a dash down the
yard, a jump over the *acéquia*, then out through the
gate to the plain beyond, where he quiets down and
I fix my stirrup.

There is not a bit of viciousness about this, as the
horse is gentle and most affectionate at all times, but
he has been terribly frightened by a saddle, and it is
distressing to see him tremble and his very flesh quiver

when one is put upon his back, no matter how gently. He had been ridden only three or four times when we bought him, and probably by a " bronco breaker," who slung on his back a heavy Mexican saddle, cinched it tight without mercy, then mounted with a slam over of a leather-trousered leg, let the almost crazy horse go like the wind, and if he slackened his speed, spurs or " quirt," perhaps both, drove him on again. I know only too well how the so-called breaking is done, for I have seen it many times, and the whole perform-ance is cruel and disgraceful. There are wicked horses, of course, but there are more wicked men, and many a fine, spirited animal is ruined, made an " out-law " that no man can ride, just by the fiendish way in which they are first ridden. But the more crazy the poor beast is made, the more fun and glory for the breaker.

Rollo is a light sorrel and a natural pacer; he can-not trot one step, and for that reason I did not want him, but Faye said that I had better try him, so he was sent up. The fact of his being an unbroken colt, Faye seemed to consider a matter of no consequence, but I soon found that it was of much consequence to me, inasmuch as I was obliged to acquire a more pre-cise balance in the saddle because of his coltish ways, and at the same time make myself—also the horse—perfectly acquainted with the delicate give and take of bit and bridle, for with a pacer the slightest tightening or slackening at the wrong time will make him break. When Rollo goes his very fastest, which is about 2:50, I never use a stirrup and never think of a thing but his mouth! There is so little motion to his body I could almost fancy that he had no legs at all—that we are being rushed through the air by some unseen force. It is fine!

Faye has reorganized the band, and the instrumentation is entirely new. It was sent to him by Sousa, director of the Marine Band, who has been most kind and interested. The new instruments are here, so are the two new sets of uniform—one for full dress, the other for concerts and general wear. Both have white trimmings to correspond with the regiment, which are so much nicer than the old red facings that made the band look as if it had been borrowed from the artillery. All this has been the source of much comment along the officers' quarters and in the barracks across the parade ground, and has caused several skirmishes between Faye and the band. It was about talked out, however, when I came in for my share of criticism!

The post commander and Faye came over from the office one morning and said it was their wish that I should take entire charge of the music for services in church, that I could have an orchestra of soft-toned instruments, and enlisted men to sing, but that all was to be under my guidance. I must select the music, be present at all practicings, and give my advice in any way needed. At first I thought it simply a very unpleasant joke, but when it finally dawned upon me that those two men were really in earnest, I was positive they must be crazy, and that I told them. The whole proposition seemed so preposterous, so ridiculous, so everything! I shall always believe that Bishop Brewer suggested church music by the soldiers. Faye is adjutant and in command of the band, so I was really the proper person to take charge of the church musicians if anybody did, but the undertaking was simply appalling. But the commanding officer insisted and Faye insisted, and both gave many reasons for doing so. The enemy was too strong, and I was forced to give in, the principal reason being, however, that I did not want some one else to take charge!

In a short time the little choir was organized and some of the very best musicians in the band were selected for the orchestra. We have two violins (first and second), one clarinet, violoncello, oboe, and bassoon, the latter instrument giving the deep organ tones. There have been three services, and at one Sergeant Graves played an exquisite solo on the violin, " There is a green hill far away," from the oratorio of St. Paul. At another, Matijicek played Gounod's " Ave Maria " on the oboe, and last Sunday he gave us, on the clarinet, " Every valley shall be exalted." The choir proper consists of three sergeants and one corporal, and our tenor is his magnificence, the drum major!

Service is held in a long, large hall, at the rear end of which is a smaller room that can be made a part of the hall by folding back large doors. We were just inside this small room and the doors were opened wide. On a long bench sat the four singers, two each side of a very unhappy woman, and back of the bench in a half circle were the six musicians. Those musicians depended entirely upon me to indicate to them when to play and the vocalists when to sing, therefore certain signals had been arranged so that there would be no mistake or confusion. There I sat, on a hot summer morning, almost surrounded by expert musicians who were conscious of my every movement, and then, those men were soldiers accustomed to military precision, and the fear of making a mistake and leading them wrong was agonizing. At the farther end of the hall the Rev. Mr. Clark was standing, reading along in an easy, self-assured way that was positively irritating. And again, there was the congregation, each one on the alert, ready to criticise, probably condemn, the unheard-of innovation! Every man, woman, and child was at church that morning, too—many from curiosity, I expect—and every time we sang one half of them turned around and stared at us.

During the reading of the service I could not change my position, turn my head, or brush the flies that got upon my face, without those six hands back of me pouncing down for their instruments. It was impossible to sing the chants, as the string instruments could not hold the tones, so anthems were used instead—mostly Millard's—and they were very beautiful. Not one mistake has ever been made by anyone, but Sergeant Moore has vexed me much. He is our soprano, and has a clear, high-tenor voice and often sings solos in public, but for some unexplainable reason he would not sing a note in church unless I sang with him, so I had to hum along for the man's ear alone. Why he has been so frightened I do not know, unless it was the unusual condition of things, which have been quite enough to scare anyone.

Well, I lived through the three services, and suppose I can live through more. The men are not compelled to do this church work, although not one would think of refusing. There is much rehearsing to be done, and Sergeant Graves has to transpose the hymns and write out the notes for each instrument, and this requires much work. To show my appreciation of their obedience to my slightest request, a large cake and dozens of eggs have been sent to them after each service. It is funny how nice things to eat often make it easy for a man to do things that otherwise would be impossible!

FORT SHAW, MONTANA TERRITORY,
July, 1886.

MY trip to Helena was made alone, after all! The evening before I started Mrs. Todd told me that she could not go, frankly admitting that she was afraid to go over the lonesome places on the road with only the driver for a protector. It was important that I should see a dentist, and Mrs. Averill was depending upon me to bring her friend down from Helena who was expected from the East, so I decided to go alone. The quartermaster gave me the privilege of choosing my driver, and I asked for a civilian, a rather old man who is disliked by everyone because of his surly, disagreeable manner. Just why I chose him I cannot tell, except that he is a good driver and I felt that he could be trusted. The morning we started Faye said to him, "Driver, you must take good care of Mrs. Rae, for she asked for you to drive on this trip," which must have had its effect—that, and the nice lunch I had prepared for him—for he was kind and thoughtful at all times.

It takes two days to go to Helena from here, a ride of forty-five miles one day and forty the second; and on each long drive there are stretches of miles and miles over mountains and through cañons where one is far from a ranch or human being, and one naturally thinks of robbers and other unpleasant things. At

23

such places I rode on top with the driver, where I could at least see what was going on around us.

Just before we crossed the Bird-Tail divide we came to a wonderful sight, " a sight worth seeing," the driver said; and more to gratify him than because I wanted to, we stopped. An enormous corral had been put up temporarily, and in it were thousands of sheep, so closely packed that those in the center were constantly jumping over the others, trying to find a cooler place. In the winter, when the weather is very cold, sheep will always jump from the outer circle of the band to the center, where it is warm; they always huddle together in cold weather, and herders are frequently compelled to remain right with them, nights at a time, working hard every minute separating them so they will not smother. One of the men, owner of the sheep, I presume, met us and said he would show me where to go so I could see everything that was being done, which proved to be directly back of a man who was shearing sheep. They told me that he was the very fastest and most expert shearer in the whole territory. Anyone could see that he was an expert, for three men were kept busy waiting upon him. At one corner of the corral was a small, funnel-shaped " drive," the outer opening of which was just large enough to squeeze a sheep through, and in the drive stood a man, sheep in hand, ever ready to rush it straight to the hands of the shearer the instant he was ready for it.

The shearer, who was quite a young man, sat upon a box close to the drive, and when he received a sheep it was always the same way—between his knees—and he commenced and finished the shearing of each animal exactly the same way, every clip of the large shears counting to the best advantage. They told me that he gained much time by the unvarying precision that left no ragged strips to be trimmed off. The docility of those wild sheep was astonishing. Almost while the last clip was being made the sheep was seized by a second assistant standing at the shearer's left, who at once threw the poor thing down on its side, where he quickly painted the brand of that particular ranch, after which it was given its freedom. It was most laughable to see the change in the sheep—most of them looking lean and lanky, whereas in less than one short minute before, their sides had been broad and woolly. A third man to wait upon the shearer was kept busy at his right carefully gathering the wool and stuffing it in huge sacks. Every effort was made to keep it clean, and every tiny bit was saved.

About four o'clock we reached Rock Creek, where we remained overnight at a little inn. The house is built of logs, and the architecture is about as queer as its owner. Mrs. Gates, wife of the proprietor, can be, and usually is, very cross and disagreeable, and I rather dreaded stopping there alone. But she met me pleasantly—that is, she did not snap my head off—so I gathered courage to ask for a room that would be near some one, as I was timid at night. That settled my standing in her opinion, and with a " Humph! " she led the way across a hall and through a large room where there were several beds, and opening a door on the farther side that led to still another room, she told me I could have that, adding that I " needn't be scared to death, as the boys will sleep right there." I asked her how old the boys were, and she snapped,

"How old! why they's men folks," and out of the room she went. Upon looking around I saw that my one door opened into the next room, and that as soon as the " boys " occupied it I would be virtually a prisoner. To be sure, the windows were not far from the ground, and I could easily jump out, but to jump in again would require longer arms and legs than I possessed. But just then I felt that I would much prefer to encounter robbers, mountain lions, any gentle creatures of that kind, to asking Mrs. Gates for another room.

When I went out to supper that night I was given a seat at one end of a long table where were already sitting nine men, including my own civilian driver, who, fortunately, was near the end farthest from me. No one paid the slightest attention to me, each man attending to his own hungry self and trying to outdo the others in talking. Finally they commenced telling marvelous tales about horses that they had ridden and subdued, and I said to myself that I had been told all about sheep that day, and there it was about horses, and I wondered how far I would have to go to hear all sorts of things about cattle! But anything about a horse is always of interest to me, and those men were particularly entertaining, as it was evident that most of them were professional trainers.

There was sitting at the farther end of the table a rather young-looking man, who had been less talkative than the others, but who after a while said something about a horse at the fort. The mentioning of the post was startling, and I listened to hear what further he had to say. And he continued, " Yes, you fellers can say what yer dern please about yer broncos, but that little horse can corral any dern piece of horse-

flesh yer can show up. A lady rides him, and I guess
I'd put her up with the horse. The boys over there
say that she broke the horse herself, and I say! you
fellers orter see her make him go—and he likes it,
too."

By the time the man stopped talking, my excitement
was great, for I was positive that he had been speaking of Rollo, although no mention had been made of
the horse's color or gait. So I asked what gait the
horse had. He and two or three of the other men
looked at me with pity in their eyes—actual pity—
that plainly said, " Poor thing—what can you know
about gaits "; but he answered civilly, " Well, lady,
he is what we call a square pacer," and having done
his duty he turned again to his friends, as though
they only could understand him, and said, " No cow
swing about that horse. He is a light sorrel and has
the very handsomest mane yer ever did see—it waves,
too, and I guess the lady curls it—but don't know for
sure."

The situation was most unusual and in some ways
mose embarrassing, also. Those nine men were rough
and unkempt, but they were splendid horsemen—that
I knew intuitively—and to have one of their number
select my very own horse above all others to speak
of with unstinted praise, was something to be proud
of, but to have my own self calmly and complacently
disposed of with the horse—" put up," in fact—was
quite another thing. But not the slightest disrespect
had been intended, and to leave the table without
making myself known was not to be thought of. I
wanted the pleasure, too, of telling those men that I
knew the gait of a pacer very well—that not in the

least did I deserve their pity. My face was burning and my voice unnatural when I threw the bomb!

I said, " The horse you are speaking of I know very well. He is mine, and I ride him, and I thank you very much for the nice things you have just said about him!" Well, there was a sudden change of scene at that table—a dropping of knives and forks and various other things, and I became conscious of eyes—thousands of eyes—staring straight at me, as I watched my bronco friend at the end of the table. The man had opened his eyes wide, and almost gasped " Gee-rew-s'lum! "—then utterly collapsed. He sat back in his chair gazing at me in a helpless, bewildered way that was disconcerting, so I told him a number of things about Rollo—how Faye had taken him to Helena during race week and Lafferty, a professional jockey of Bozeman, had tested his speed, and had passed a 2:30 trotter with him one morning. The men knew Lafferty, of course. There was a queer coincidence connected with him and Rollo. The horse that he was driving at the races was a pacer named Rolla, while my horse, also a pacer, was named Rollo.

All talk about horses ceased at once, and the men said very little to each other during the remainder of the time we were at the table. It was almost pathetic, and an attention I very much appreciated, to see how bread, pickles, cold meat, and in fact everything else on that rough table, were quietly pushed to me, one after the other, without one word being said. That was their way of showing their approval of me. It was unpolished, but truly sincere.

I was not at all afraid that night, for I suspected

that the horsemen at the supper-table were the " boys "
referred to by Mrs. Gates. But it was impossible
to sleep. The partition between the two rooms must
have been very thin, for the noises that came through
were awful. It seemed as though dozens of men were
snoring at the same time, and that some of them were
dangerously "croupy," for they choked and gulped,
and every now and then one would have nightmare
and groan and yell until some one would tell him
to "shut up," or perhaps say something funny about
him to the others. No matter how many times those
men were wakened they were always cheerful and
good-natured about it. A statement that I cannot
truthfully make about myself on the same subject!

It was not necessary for me to leave my room
through the window the next morning, although my
breakfast was early. The house seemed deserted, and
I had the long table all to myself. At six o'clock we
started on our ride to Helena. I sat with the driver
going through the long Prickly-Pear cañon, and
had a fine opportunity of seeing its magnificent grandeur, while the early shadows were still long. The
sun was on many of the higher boulders, that made
them sparkle and show brilliantly in their high lights
and shadows. The trees and bushes looked unusually
fresh and green. We hear that a railroad will soon
be built through that cañon—but we hope not. It
would be positively wicked to ruin anything so grand.

We reached Helena before luncheon, and I soon
found Miss Duncan, who was expecting me. We did
not start back until the second day, so she and I
visited all the shops and then drove out to Sulphur Spring. The way everybody and everything

have grown and spread out since the Northern Pacific Railroad has been running cars through Helena is most amazing. It was so recently a mining town, just " Last Chance Gulch," where Chinamen were digging up the streets for gold, almost undermining the few little buildings, and Chinamen also were raising delicious celery, where now stand very handsome houses. Now Main street has many pretentious shops, and pretty residences have been put up almost to the base of Mount Helena.

The ride back was uneventful, greatly to Miss Duncan's disappointment. It is her first visit to the West, and she wants to see cowboys and all sorts of things. I should have said " wanted to see," for I think that already her interest in brass buttons is so great the cowboys will never be thought of again. There were two at Rock Creek, but they were uninteresting—did not wear " chaps," pistols, or even big spurs. At the Bird-Tail not one sheep was to be seen— every one had been sheared, and the big band driven back to its range. Miss Duncan is a pretty girl, and unaffected, and will have a delightful visit at this Western army post, where young girls from the East do not come every day. And then we have several charming young bachelors!

FORT SHAW, MONTANA TERRITORY,
December, 1887.

THE excitement is about over. Our guests have returned to their homes, and now we are settling down to our everyday garrison life. The wedding was very beautiful and as perfect in every detail as adoring father and mother and loving friends could

make it. It was so strictly a military wedding, too—
at a frontier post where everything is of necessity
"army blue"—the bride a child of the regiment, her
father an officer in the regiment many years, and the
groom a recent graduate from West Point, a lieutenant in the regiment. We see all sorts of so-called
military weddings in the East—some very magnificent
church affairs, others at private houses, and informal,
but there are ever lacking the real army surroundings
that made so perfect the little wedding of Wednesday
evening.

The hall was beautifully draped with the greatest
number of flags of all sizes—each one a "regulation,"
however—and the altar and chancel rail were thickly
covered with ropes and sprays of fragrant Western
cedars and many flowers, and from either side of the
reredos hung from their staffs the beautifully embroidered silken colors of the regiment. At the rear end
of the hall stood two companies of enlisted men—one
on each side of the aisle—in shining full-dress uniforms, helmets in hand. The bride's father is captain
of one of those companies, and the groom a lieutenant
in the other. As one entered the hall, after passing
numerous orderlies, each one in full-dress uniform,
of course, and walked up between the two companies,
every man standing like a statue, one became impressed by the rare beauty and military completeness
of the whole scene.

The bride is petite and very young, and looked almost a child as she and her father slowly passed us,
her gown of heavy ivory satin trailing far back of her.
The orchestra played several numbers previous to the
ceremony—the Mendelssohn March for processional,

and Lohengrin for recessional, but the really exquisite music was during the ceremony, when there came
to us softly, as if floating from afar over gold lace
and perfumed silks and satins, the enchanting strains
of Moszkowski's Serenade! Faye remained with the
orchestra all the time, to see that the music was
changed at just the right instant and without mistake.
The pretty reception was in the quarters of Major and
Mrs. Stokes, and there also was the delicious supper
served. Some of the presents were elegant. A case
containing sixty handsome small pieces of silver was
given by the officers of the regiment. A superb silver
pitcher by the men of Major Stokes's company, and
an exquisite silver after-dinner coffee set by the company in which the groom is a lieutenant. Several
young officers came down from Fort Assiniboine to
assist as ushers, and there were at the post four girls
from Helena. An army post is always an attractive
place to girls, but it was apparent from the first that
these girls came for an extra fine time. I think they
found it!

They were all at our cotillon Monday evening, and
kept things moving fast. It was refreshing to have
a new element, and a little variety in partners. We
have danced with each other so much that everyone
has become more or less like a machine. Faye led,
dancing with Miss Stokes, for whom the german was
given. The figures were very pretty—some of them
new—and the supper was good. To serve refresh-
ments of any kind at the hall means much work, for
everything has to be prepared at the house—even
coffee must be sent over hot; and every piece of
china and silver needed must be sent over also. Mrs.

Hughes came from Helena on Saturday and remained with me until yesterday.

You know something of the awful times I have had with servants since Hulda went away! First came the lady tourist—who did us the honor to consent to our paying her expenses from St. Paul, and who informed me upon her arrival that she was not obliged to work out—no indeed—that her own home was much nicer than our house—that she had come up to see the country, and so forth. We found her presence too great a burden, particularly as she could not prepare the simplest meal, and so invited her to return to her elegant home. Then came the two women—the mother to Mrs. Todd, the daughter to me—who were insulted because they were expected to occupy servant's rooms, and could not " eat with the family "— so Mrs. Todd and I gave them cordial invitations to depart. Then came my Russian treasure—a splendid cook, but who could not be taught that a breakfast or dinner an hour late mattered to a regimental adjutant, and wondered why guard mounting could not be held back while she prepared an early breakfast for Faye. After a struggle of two months she was passed on. A tall, angular woman with dull red hair drawn up tight and twisted in a knot as hard as her head, was my next trial. She was the wife of a gambler of the lowest type, but that I did not know while she was here.

One day I told her to do something that she objected to, and with her hands clinched tight she came up close as if to strike me. I stood still, of course, and quietly said, " You mustn't strike me." She looked like a fury and screamed, " I will if I want to! "

She was inches taller than I, but I said, "If you do, I will have you locked in the guardhouse." She became very white, and fairly hissed at me, "You can't do that—I ain't a soldier." I told her, "No, if you were a soldier you would soon be taught to behave yourself," and I continued, "you are in an army post, however, and if you do me violence I will certainly call the guard." Before I turned to go from the room I looked up at her and said, "Now I expect you to do what I have told you to do." I fully expected a strike on my head before I got very far, but she controlled herself. I went out of the house hoping she would do the same and never return, but she was there still, and we had to tell her to go, after all. I must confess, though, that the work she had objected to doing she did nicely while I was out. Miller told me that she had three pistols and two large watches in her satchel when she went away.

Then came a real treasure—Scotch Ellen—who has been with us six months, and has been very satisfactory every way. To be sure she has had awful headaches, and often it has been necessary for some one to do her work. She and the sergeant's wife prepared the supper for the german, and everything was sent to the hall in a most satisfactory way—much to my delight. Nothing wrong was noticed the next morning either, until she carried chocolate to Mrs. Hughes, when I saw with mortification that she looked untidy, but thinking of the confusion in her part of the house, I said nothing about it.

Our breakfast hour is twelve o'clock, and about eleven Mrs. Hughes and I went out for a little walk. In a short time Faye joined us, and just before twelve I came in to see if everything was in its proper place on the table. As I went down the hall I saw a sight in the dining room that sent shivers down my back. On the table were one or two doilies, and one or two of various other things, and at one side stood the Scotch treasure with a plate in one hand upon which were a few butter balls, and in the other she held a butter pick. The doors leading through pantry into the kitchen were open and all along the floor I could see here and there a little golden ball that had evidently rolled off the plate. I could also see the range—that looked black and cold and without one spark of fire!

Going to the side of the table opposite Ellen I said, " Ellen, what is the matter with you? "—and looking at me with dull, heavy eyes, she said, " And what is the matter wit' you? " Then I saw that she was drunk, horribly drunk, and told her so, but she could only say, " I'm drunk, am I? " I ran outside for Faye, but he and Mrs. Hughes had walked to the farther end of the officers' line, and I was compelled to go all that distance before I could overtake them and tell of my woes. I wanted the woman out of the house as quickly as possible, so that Miller—who is a very good cook—and I could prepare some sort of a breakfast. Faye went to the house with his longest strides and told the woman to go at once, and I saw no more of her. Mrs. Hughes was most lovely about the whole affair—said that not long ago she had tried a different cook each week for six in succession. That was comforting, but did not go far toward providing a breakfast for us. Miller proved to be a genuine treasure, however, and the sergeant's wife—who is

ever " a friend indeed "—came to our assistance so
soon we scarcely missed the Scotch creature. Still, it
was most exasperating to have such an unnecessary
upheaval, just at the very time we had a guest in the
house—a dainty, fastidious little woman, too—and
wanted things to move along smoothly. I wonder of
what nationality the next trial will be! If one gets
a good maid out here the chances are that she will
soon marry a soldier or quarrel with one, as was the
case with Hulda. For some unaccountable reason a
Chinese laundry at Sun River has been the cause of
all the Chinamen leaving the post.

Now I must tell of something funny that happened
to me.

The morning before Mrs. Hughes arrived I went
out for a little ride, and about two miles up the river
I left the road to follow a narrow trail that leads to a
bluff called Crown Butte. I had to go through a
large field of wild rosebushes, then across an alkali
bed, and then through more bushes. I had passed the
first bushes and was more than half way across the
alkali, Rollo's feet sinking down in the sticky mud at
every step, when there appeared from the bushes in
front of me, and right in the path, two immense gray
wolves. If they had studied to surprise me in the
worst place possible they could not have succeeded
better. Rollo saw them, of course, and stopped instantly, giving deep sighs, preparing to snort, I knew.
To give myself courage I talked to the horse, slowly
turning him around, so as to not excite him, or let
the timber wolves see that I was running from
them.

But the horse I could not deceive, for as soon as his

back was toward them, head and tail went up, and
there was snort after snort. He could not run, as we
were still in the alkali lick. I looked back and saw
that the big gray beasts were slowly moving toward
us, and I recognized the fact that the mud would not
stop them, if they chose to cross it. Once free of the

"The poor horse was terribly frightened."

awful stickiness, I knew that we would be out of danger, as the swiftest wolf could never overtake the
horse—but it seemed as if it were miles across that
white mud. But at last we got up on solid ground,
and were starting off at Rollo's best pace, when from
out of the bushes in front of us, there came a third
wolf! The horse stopped so suddenly it is a wonder I

was not pitched over his head, but I did not think of that at the time.

The poor horse was terribly frightened, and I could feel him tremble, which made me all the more afraid. The situation was not pleasant, and without stopping to think, I said, " Rollo, we must run him down—now do your best ! " and taking a firm hold of the bridle, and bracing myself in the saddle, I struck the horse hard with my whip and gave an awful scream. I never use a whip on him, so the sting on his side and yell in his ears frightened him more than the wolf had, and he started on again with a rush. But the wolf stood still—so did my heart—for the beast looked savage. When it seemed as though we were actually upon him I struck the horse again and gave scream after scream as fast as my lungs would allow me. The big gray thing must have thought something evil was coming, for he sprang back, and then jumped over in the bushes and did not show himself again. Rollo came home at an awful pace ; but I looked back once and saw, standing in the road near the bushes, five timber wolves, evidently watching us. Just where the other two had been I will never know, of course.

We have ridden and driven up that road many, many times, and I have often ridden through those rosebushes, but have never seen wolves or coyotes. Down in the lowland on the other side of the post we frequently see a coyote that will greet us with the most unearthly howls, and will sometimes follow carriages, howling all the time. But everyone looks upon him as a pet. Those big, gray timber wolves are quite another animal, fierce and savage. Some one asked me why I screamed, but I could not tell why. Perhaps it was to urge the horse—perhaps to frighten the wolf—perhaps to relieve the strain on my nerves. Possibly it was just because I was frightened and could not help it!

FORT SHAW, MONTANA TERRITORY,
May, 1888.

SUCH upheaval orders have been coming to the post the past few days, some of us wonder if there has not been an earthquake, and can only sit around and wait in a numb sort of way for whatever may come next.

General Bourke, who has been colonel of the regiment, you know, has been appointed a brigadier general and is to command the Department of the Platte, with headquarters at Omaha, Nebraska. This might have affected Faye under any circumstances, as a new colonel has the privilege of selecting his own staff officers, but General Bourke, as soon as he received the telegram telling of his appointment, told Faye that he should ask for him as aide-de-camp. This will take us to Omaha, also, and I am almost heart-broken over it, as it will be a wretched life for me— cooped up in a noisy city! At the same time I am delighted that Faye will have for four years the fine staff position. These appointments are complimentary, and considered most desirable.

The real stir-up, however, came with orders for the regiment to go to Fort Snelling, Minnesota, for that affects about everyone here. Colonel Munson, who relieves General Bourke as colonel of the regiment, is in St. Paul, and is well known as inspector general of this department, which perhaps is not the most flattering introduction he could have had to his new

24

regiment. He telegraphed, as soon as promoted, that he desired Faye to continue as adjutant, but of course to be on the staff of a general is far in advance of being on the staff of a colonel. The colonel commands only his own regiment—sometimes not all of that, as when companies are stationed at other posts than headquarters—whereas a brigadier general has command of a department consisting of many army posts and many regiments.

The one thing that distresses me most of all is, that I have to part from my horse! This is what makes me so rebellious, for aside from my own personal loss, I have great sorrow for the poor dumb animal that will suffer so much with strangers who will not understand him. No one has ridden or driven him for two years but myself, and he has been tractable and lovable always. During very cold weather, when perhaps he would be too frisky, I have allowed him to play in the yard back of the house, until all superfluous spirits had been kicked and snorted off, after which I could have a ride in peace and safety. Faye thinks that he is entirely too nervous ever to take kindly to city sights and sounds—that the fretting and the heat might kill him.

So it has been decided that once again we will sell everything—both horses and all things pertaining to them, reserving our saddles only. Every piece of furniture will be sold, also, as we do not purpose to keep house at all while in Omaha. How I envy our friends who will go to Fort Snelling! We have always been told that it is such a beautiful post, and the people of St. Paul and Minneapolis are most charming. It seems so funny that the regiment should be sent to

Snelling just as Colonel Munson was promoted to it. He will have to move six miles only!

We know that when we leave Fort Shaw we will go from the old army life of the West—that if we ever come back, it will be to unfamiliar scenes and a new condition of things. We have seen the passing of the buffalo and other game, and the Indian seems to be passing also. But I must confess that I have no regret for the Indians—there are still too many of them!

FORT SHAW, MONTANA TERRITORY,
May, 1888.

THERE can be only two more days at this dear old post, where we have been so happy, and I want those to pass as quickly as possible, and have some of the misery over. Our house is perfectly forlorn, with just a few absolute necessaries in it for our use while here. Everything has been sold or given away, and all that is left to us are our trunks and army chests. Some fine china and a few pieces of cut glass I kept, and even those are packed in small boxes and in the chests.

The general selling-out business has been funny. No one in the regiment possessed many things that they cared to move East with them, and as we did not desire to turn our houses into second-hand shops, where people could handle and make remarks about things we had treasured, it was decided that everything to be sold should be moved to the large hall, where enlisted men could attend to the shop business. Our only purchasers were people from Sun River Crossing, and a few ranches that are some distance from the post, and it was soon discovered that anything at all nice was passed by them, so we became sharp—bunching the worthless with the good—and that worked beautifully and things sold fast.

These moves are of the greatest importance to army officers, and many times the change of station is a mere nothing in comparison to the refitting of a house, something that is never taken into consideration when the pay of the Army is under discussion. The regiment has been on the frontier ten years, and everything that we had that was at all nice had been sent up from St. Paul at great expense, or purchased in Helena at an exorbitant price. All those things have been disposed of for almost nothing, and when the regiment reaches Fort Snelling, where larger quarters have to be furnished for an almost city life, the officers will be at great expense. Why I am bothering about Snelling I fail to see, as we are not going there, and I certainly have enough troubles of my own to think about.

This very morning, Mrs. Ames, of Sun River Crossing, who now owns dear Rollo, came up to ask me to show her how to drive him! Just think of that! She talked as though she had been deceived—that it was my duty to show her the trick by which I had managed to control the horse, and, naturally, it would be a delightful pleasure to me to be allowed to drive him once more, and so on. Mrs. Ames said that yesterday she started out with him, intending to come to the post to let me see him—fancy the delicate feeling expressed in that—but the horse went so fast she became frightened, for it seemed as though the telegraph poles were only a foot apart. She finally got the horse turned around and drove back home, when her husband got in and undertook to drive him, but with no better success; but he, too, started the horse toward his old home.

Mr. Ames then told her to have Rollo put back in the stable until she could get me to show her how to drive him. I almost cried out from pure pity for the poor dumb beast that I knew was suffering so in his longing for his old home and friends who understood him. But for the horse's sake I tried not to break down. I told her that first of all she must teach the horse to love her. That was an awfully hard thing to say, I assure you, and I doubt if the woman understood my meaning after all. When I told her not to pull on his mouth she looked amazed, and said, "Why, he would run away with me if I didn't!" But I assured her that he would not—that he had been taught differently—that he was very nervous and spirited—that the harder she pulled the more excited he would become—that I had simply held him steady, no more. I saw that Mrs. Ames did not believe one word that I had said, but I tried to convince her, for the sake of the unhappy animal that had been placed at her mercy.

I have often met and passed her out on the road, and the horse she drives is a large, handsome animal, and we had supposed that she was a good whip; so, when Mr. Ames appeared the other day and said his wife had asked him to come up and buy the sorrel horse for her we were delighted that such a good home had been found for him—and for Fannie too. Mr. Ames bought the entire outfit. Fannie is beautiful, but wholly lacking in affection, and can take care of herself any place.

All sorts of people have been here for the horses —some wanted both, others only one—but Faye would not let them go to any of them, as he was afraid they would not have the best of care. Rollo had been gone only an hour or so when a young man—a typical bronco breaker—came to buy him, and seemed really distressed because he had been sold. He said that he had broken him when a colt at Mr. Vaughn's. It so happened that Faye was at the adjutant's office, and the man asked for me. I was very glad, for I had always wanted to meet the person who had slammed the saddle first on Rollo's back. I told him that it was generally considered at the post that I had broken the horse! I said that he had been made cruelly afraid of a saddle, and for a long time after we had bought him, he objected to it and to being mounted, and I did not consider a horse broken that would do those things. I said also, that the horse had not been gaited. He interrupted with, " Why, he's a pacer "—just as though that settled everything; but I told him that Rollo had three perfectly trained grades of speed, each one of which I had taught him.

The young man's face became very red and he looked angry, but I had a beautiful time. It was such a relief to express my opinion to the man just at that time, too, when I was grieving so for the horse. I saw at once that he was a bronco breaker from his style of dress. He had on boots of very fine leather with enormously high heels, and strapped to them were large, sharp-pointed Mexican spurs. His trousers were of leather and very broad at the bottom, and all down the front and outside was some kind of gray fur—" chaps " this article of dress is called—and in

one hand he held a closely plaited, stinging black
"quirt." He wore a plaid shirt and cotton handkerchief around his neck. That describes the man who
rode Rollo first—and no wonder the spirited, high-
strung colt was suspicious of saddles, men, and things.
I watched the man as he rode away. His horse was
going at a furious gallop, with ears turned back, as
if expecting whip or spur any instant, and the man
sat far over on one side, that leg quite straight as
though he was standing in the long stirrup, and the
other was resting far up on the saddle—which was
of the heavy Mexican make, with enormous flaps, and
high, round pommel in front. I am most thankful
that Rollo has gone beyond that man's reach, as everything about him told of cruelty to horses.

Yet, Mrs. Ames seemed such a cold woman—so incapable of understanding or appreciating the affection
of a dumb animal. During the years we owned Rollo
he was struck with the whip only once—the time I
wanted him to run down a wolf up the river.

The Great Northern Railroad runs very near Fort
Shaw now—about twenty miles, I think—and that
will make it convenient for the moving of the regiment, and all of us, in fact. We will go to St. Paul on
the special train with the regiment, for Faye will not
be relieved as adjutant until he reaches Fort Snelling,
where we will remain for a day or two. It will be a
sad trip for me, for I love the West and life at a
Western post, and the vanities of city life do not
seem attractive to me—and I shall miss my army
friends, too!

Perhaps it is a small matter to mention, but since
I have been with the Army I have ridden twenty-two

horses that had never been ridden by a woman before!
As I still recollect the gait and disposition of each
horse, it seems of some consequence to me, for unbroken as some were, I was never unseated—not once!

THE PAXTON HOTEL, OMAHA, NEBRASKA,
August, 1888.

ALMOST five weeks have passed since we left
dear Fort Shaw! During that time we have
become more or less accustomed to the restrictions of
a small city, but I fancy that I am not the only one
of the party from Montana who sometimes sighs for
the Rocky Mountains and the old garrison life. Here
we are not of the Army—neither are we citizens.
General and Mrs. Bourke are still dazzled by the brilliancy of the new silver star on the general's shoulder
straps, and can still smile. Faye says very little, but
I know that he often frets over his present monotonous duties and yearns for the regiment, his duties as
adjutant of the regiment, the parades, drills, and outdoor life generally, that make life so pleasant at a
frontier post.

Department Headquarters is in a government building down by the river, and the offices are most cheer-
less. All the officers wear civilian clothes, and there
is not one scrap of uniform to be seen any place—
nothing whatever to tell one " who is who," from the
department commander down to Delaney, the old
Irish messenger! Each one sits at his desk and busies
himself over the many neatly tied packages of official
papers upon it, and tries to make the world believe
that he is happy—but there are confidential talks,
when it is admitted that life is dreary—the regiment

the only place for an energetic officer, and so on. Yet
not one of those officers could be induced to give up
his detail, for it is always such a compliment to be
selected from the many for duty at headquarters.
Faye and Lieutenant Travis are on the general's personal staff, the others belong to the department. Just
now, Faye is away with the department commander,
who is making an official tour of inspection through
his new department, which is large, and includes some
fine posts. It is known as "The Department of
the Platte."

Everyone has been most hospitable—particularly the
army people at Fort Omaha—a post just beyond the
city limits. Mrs. Wheeler, wife of the colonel in command, gave a dancing reception very soon after we
got here, and an elegant dinner a little later on—both
for the new brigadier general and his staff. Mrs.
Foster, the handsome wife of the lieutenant colonel,
gave a beautiful luncheon, and the officers of the regiment gave a dance that was pleasant. But their orchestra is far from being as fine as ours. In the city
there have been afternoon and evening receptions, and
several luncheons, the most charming luncheon of all
having been the one given by my friend, Mrs. Schuy-
ler, at the Union Club. One afternoon each week the
club rooms are at the disposal of the wives of its
members, and so popular is this way of entertaining,
the rooms are usually engaged weeks in advance.
The service is really perfect, and the rooms airy and
delightfully cool—and cool rooms are great treasures
in this hot place.

The heat has been almost unbearable to us from the
mountains, and one morning I nearly collapsed while

having things " fitted " in the stuffy rooms of a dress-
maker.   Many of these *nouveaux riches* dress elegantly, and their jewels are splendid.   All the women
here have such white skins, and by comparison I must
look like a Mexican, my face is so brown from years
of exposure to dry, burning winds.   Of course there
has been much shopping to do, and for a time it was
so confusing—to have to select things from a counter,
with a shop girl staring at me, or perhaps insisting
upon my purchasing articles I did not want.   For
years we had shopped from catalogues, and it was a
nice quiet way, too.   Parasols have bothered me.   I
would forget to open them in the street, and would
invariably leave them in the stores when shopping, and
then have to go about looking them up.   But this is
the first summer I have been East in nine years, and
it is not surprising that parasols and things mix me
up at times.

Faye has a beautiful saddle horse—his gait a natural single foot—and I sometimes ride him, but most
of my outings are on the electric cars.   I might as
well be on them, since I have to hear their buzz and
clang both day and night from our rooms here in
the hotel.   The other morning, as I was returning
from a ride across the river to Council Bluffs, I heard
the shrill notes of a calliope that reminded me that
Forepaugh's circus was to be in town that day, and
that I had promised to go to the afternoon performance with a party of friends.   But soon there were
other .sounds and other thoughts.   Above the noise
of the car I heard a brass band—and there could be
no mistake—it was playing strong and full one of
Sousa's marches, " The March Past of the Rifle Regi-

ment "—a march that was written for Faye while
he was adjutant of the regiment, and " Dedicated to
the officers and enlisted men " of the regiment. For
almost three years that one particular march had been
the review march of the regiment—that is, it had been
played always whenever the regiment had passed in
review before the colonel, inspector general of the
department, or any official of sufficient rank and au-
thority to review the troops.

The car seemed to go miles before it came to a
place where I could get off. Every second was most
precious and I jumped down while it was still in motion, receiving a scathing rebuke from the conductor
for doing so. I almost ran until I got to the walk
nearest the band, where I tagged along with boys,
both big and small. The march was played for some
time, and no one could possibly imagine how those
familiar strains thrilled me. But there was an ever-
increasing feeling of indignation that a tawdry
coated circus band, sitting in a gilded wagon, should
presume to play that march, which seemed to belong
exclusively to the regiment, and to be associated only
with scenes of ceremony and great dignity.

The circus men played the piece remarkably well,
however, and when it was stopped I came back to the
hotel to think matters over and have a " heart-to-
heart " talk with myself. Of course I am more than
proud that Faye is an aide-de-camp, and would not
have things different from what they are, but the detail is for four years, and the thought of living in this
unattractive place that length of time is crushing.
But Faye will undoubtedly have his captaincy by the
expiration of the four years, and the anticipation of

that is comforting. It is the feeling of loneliness I mind here—of being lost and no one to search for me. I miss the cheery garrison life—the delightful rides, and it may sound funny, but I miss also the little church choir that finally became a joy to me. Sergeant Graves is now leader of the regimental band at Fort Snelling, and Matijicek is in New York, a member of the Damrosch orchestra. It is still something to wonder over that I should have been on a street car that carried me to a circus parade at the precise time the Review March was being played! It seems quite as marvelous as my having been seated at a supper table in a far-away ranch in Montana, the very night a number of horse breakers were there, also at the table, and one of them " put up " Rollo and me to his friends. I shall never forget how queer I felt when I heard myself discussed by perfect strangers in my very presence—not one of whom knew in the least who I was. It made me think that perhaps I was shadowy—invisible—although to myself I did not feel at all that way.

Faye wrote to Mr. Ames about Rollo, thinking that possibly he might buy him back, but Mr. Ames wrote in reply that Rollo had already been sold, because Mrs. Ames had found it impossible to manage him. Also that he was owned by the post trader at Fort Maginnis, who was making a pet of him. So, as the horse had a good home and gentle treatment, it was once more decided to leave him up in his native mountains. It might have been cruel to have brought him here to suffer from the heat, and to be frightened and ever fretted by the many strange sights and sounds. But I am not satisfied, for the horse had an awful fear of men when ridden or driven by them, and I know that he is so unhappy and wonders why I no longer come to him, and why I do not take him from the strange people who do not understand him. He was a wonderfully playful animal, and sometimes when Miller would be leading the two horses from our yard to the corral, he would turn Rollo loose for a run. That always brought out a number of soldiers to see him rear, lunge, and snort; his turns so quick, his beautiful tawny mane would be tossed from side to side and over his face until he looked like a wild horse. The more the men laughed the wilder he seemed to get. He never forgot Miller, however, but would be at the corral by the time he got there, and would go to his own stall quietly and without guidance. Poor Rollo!

CAMP NEAR UINTAH MOUNTAINS, WYOMING TERRITORY,
August, 1888.

TO be back in the mountains and in camp is simply glorious! And to see soldiers walking around, wearing the dear old uniform, just as we used to see them, makes one feel as though old days had returned. The two colored men—chef and butler —rather destroy the *technique* of a military camp, but they seem to be necessary adjuncts; and besides, we are not striving for harmony and effect, but for a fine outing, each day to be complete with its own pleasures. It was a novel experience to come to the mountains in a private car! The camp is very complete, as the camp of a department commander should be, and we have everything for our comfort. We are fourteen miles from the Union Pacific Railroad and six from Fort Bridger, from which post our tents and supplies came. Our ice is sent from there, also, and of course the enlisted men are from that garrison.

The party consists of General and Mrs. Bourke, Mrs. Hall, Mrs. Bourke's sister, Mrs. Ord of Omaha, General Stanley, paymaster, Captain Rives, judge advocate—both of the department staff—Lieutenant Travis, junior aide-de-camp, Faye, and myself. Mrs. Ord is a pretty woman, always wears dainty gowns, and is a favorite with Omaha society people. I know her very well, still I hesitated about wearing my short-skirted outing suit, fearing it would shock her. But a day or two after we got here she said to me, " What are we to do about those fish, Mrs. Rae? I always catch the most fish wherever I go, but I hear that you are successful also! "

So with high spirits we started out by ourselves that very morning, everyone laughing and betting on our number of fish as we left camp. I wore the short skirt, but Mrs. Ord had her skirts pinned so high I felt that a tuck or two should be taken in mine, to save her from embarrassment. The fishing is excellent here and each one had every confidence in her own good luck, for the worning was perfect for trout fishing. Once I missed Mrs. Ord, and pushing some bushes back where I thought she might be, I saw a most comical sight. Lying flat on the ground, hat pushed back, and eyes peering over the bank of the stream, was Mrs. Ord, the society woman! I could not help laughing—she was so ridiculous in that position, which the pinned-up dress made even more funny—but she did not like it, and looking at me most reproachfully said, " You have frightened him away, and I almost had him." She had been in that position a long time, she said, waiting for a large trout to take her hook. The race for honors was about even that day, and there was no cause for envy on either side, for neither Mrs. Ord nor I caught one fish!

Our camp is near Smith's fork of Snake River, and not far from the camp is another fork that never has fish in it—so everyone tells us. That seemed so strange, for both streams have the same water from the stream above, and the same rocky beds. One day I thought I would try the stream, as Smith's fork was so muddy we could not fish in that. There had been a storm up in the mountains that had caused both streams to rise, so I caught some grasshoppers to bait with, as it would be useless, of course, to try flies. I walked along the banks of the swollen stream until I saw a place where I thought there should be a trout, and to that little place the grasshopper was cast, when snap! went my leader. I put on another hook and another grasshopper, but the result was precisely the same, so I concluded there must be a snag there, although I had supposed that I knew a fish from a snag! I tried one or two other places, but there was no variation—and each time I lost a leader and hook.

In the meantime a party had come over from camp, Faye among them, and there had been much good advice given me—and each one had told me that there were no fish ever in that stream; then they went on up and sat down on the bank under some trees. I was very cross, for it was not pleasant to be laughed at, particularly by women who had probably never had a rod in their hands. And I felt positive that it had been fish that had carried off my hooks, and I was determined to ascertain what was the matter. So I went back to our tent and got a very long leader, which I doubled a number of times. I knew that the thickness would not frighten the fish, as the water was so cloudy. I fixed a strong hook to that, upon which was a fine grasshopper, and going to one of the places where my friends said I had been " snagged," I cast it over, and away it all went, which proved that I had caught something that could at least act like a fish. I reeled it in, and in time landed the thing— a splendid large trout! My very first thought was of those disagreeable people who had laughed at me— Faye first of all. So after them I went, carrying the fish, which gained in weight with every step. Their surprise was great, and I could see that Faye was delighted. He carried the trout to camp for me, and I went with him, for I was very tired.

The next morning I went to that stream again, taking with me a book of all sorts of flies and some grasshoppers. The department commander went over also. He asked me to show him where I had lost the hooks, but I said, " If you fish in those places you will be laughed at more than I was yesterday." He understood, and went farther down. The water was much more clear, but still flies could not be seen, so I used the scorned grasshopper. In about two hours I caught sixteen beautiful trout, which weighed, *en masse,* a little over twenty-five pounds! I cast in the very places where I had lost hooks, and almost every time caught a fish. I left them in the shade in various places along the stream, and Faye and a soldier brought them to camp. A fine display they made, spread out on the grass, for they seemed precisely the same size.

The general caught two large and several small trout—those were all that day. It was most remarkable that I should have found the only good places in the stream at a time when the water was not clear. Not only the right places, but the one right day, for not one trout has been caught there since. Perhaps with the high water the fish came up from Snake River, although trout are supposed to live in clear water. We can dispose of any number of birds and fish here, for those that are not needed for our own large mess can be given to the soldiers, and we often send chicken and trout to our friends at Fort Bridger. The farther one goes up the stream the better the fishing is—that is, the fish are more plentiful, but not as large as they are here.

About sixteen miles up—almost in the mountains—was General Crook's favorite fishing ground, and when he was in command of the department he and General Stanley, who also is an expert fisherman, came here many times, consequently General Stanley is familiar with the country about here. The evening after my splendid catch, General Stanley said that he would like to have Mrs. Ord and me go with him up the stream several miles, and asked if I would be willing to give Mrs. Ord the stream, as she had never used a fly, adding that she seemed a little piqued because I had caught such fine fish. I said at once that I would be delighted to give her the lead, although I knew, of course, that whoever goes second in a trout stream has very poor sport. But the re-

25

quest was a compliment, and besides, I had caught enough fish for a while.

The next day we made preparations, and early on the morning of the second we started. The department commander had gone to Omaha on official business, so he was not with us, and Faye did not go; but the rest of the party went twelve miles and then established a little camp for the day, and there we left them. Mrs. Ord and I and General Stanley, with a driver, got on a buckboard drawn by two mules, and went five miles farther up the stream, until, in fact, it was impossible for even a buckboard to go along the rocky trail. There we were expected to take the stream, and as soon as we left the wagon, Mrs. Ord and I retired to some bushes to prepare for the water. I had taken the " tuck " in my outing skirt, so there was not much for me to do; but Mrs. Ord pulled up and pinned up her serge skirt in a way that would have brought a small fortune to a cartoonist. When we came from the bushes, rods in hand, the soldier driver gave one bewildered stare, and then almost fell from his seat. He was too respectful to laugh outright and thus relieve his spasms, but he would look at us from the side of his eye, turn his face from us and fairly double over—then another quick look, and another double down again. Mrs. Ord laughed, and so did I. She is quite stout and I am very thin, and I suppose the soldier did see funny things about us. We saw them ourselves.

I shall never forget my first step in that water! It was as chilling as if it had been running over miles of ice, and by comparison the August sun seemed fiery; but these things were soon forgotten, for at once the excitement of casting a fly began. It is almost as much pleasure to put a little fly just where you want it, as it is to catch the fish. My rod and reel were in perfect condition—Faye had seen to that —and my book of flies was complete, and with charming companions and a stream full of trout, a day of

"We were obliged to wade every step."

unusual pleasure was assured. We were obliged to wade every step, as the banks of the stream had walls of boulders and thick bushes. Most of the stream was not very deep, but was a foamy, roaring torrent, rushing over the small rocks and around the large ones, with little, still, dark places along the banks— ideal homes for the mountain trout. We found a few deep pools that looked most harmless, but the current in them was swift and dangerous to those who could not always keep their balance. It was most difficult for me to walk on the slippery stones at first, and I had many a fall; but Mrs. Ord, being heavy, avoided upsets very nicely. At times we would be in water above our waists, and then Mrs. Ord and I would fall back with General Stanley for protection, who alternately praised and laughed at us during the whole day. Mrs. Ord was very quick to learn where and how to cast a fly, and I was delighted to let General Stanley see that grasshoppers were not at all necessary to my success in fishing.

We sat upon a big, flat rock at luncheon, and were thankful that General Stanley was a tall man and could keep the box of sandwiches from getting wet. When we toppled over he always came to our assistance, so at times his wading boots were not of much use to him. Mrs. Ord was far ahead of me in number of fish, and General Stanley said that I had better keep up with her, if I wished. The stream had broadened out some, so finally Mrs. Ord whipped the left side, which is easier casting, and I whipped the right. We waded down the entire five miles, and Mrs. Ord, who had the stream most of the time, caught sixty-four trout and I caught fifty-six, and General Stanley picked up fourteen, after our splashing and frightening away the fish we did not catch. The trout were small, but wonderfully full of fight in that cold water. Of course General Stanley carried them for us. The driver had been ordered to keep within call on the trail, as General Stanley thought it would be impossible for Mrs. Ord and me to wade the five miles; but the distance seemed short to us; we never

once thought of being tired, and it was with great regret we reeled in our lines.

There was a beaver dam above the picnic camp,
and before we came to it I happened to get near the
bank, where I saw in the mud the impression of a
huge paw. It was larger than a tea plate, and was
so fresh one could easily see where the nails had been.
I asked General Stanley to look at it, but he said,
" That? oh, that is only the paw of a cub—he has
been down after fish." At once I discovered that the
middle of the stream was most attractive, and there
I went, and carefully remained there the rest of the
way down. If the paw of a mere " cub " could be that
enormous size, what might not be the size of an ordinary grown-up bear, paws included! Mrs. Ord
declared that she rather liked little bears—they were
so cunning and playful—but I noticed she avoided the
banks, also.

We had left dry clothing at the small camp, and
when we returned we found nice little retreats all
ready for us, made of cloaks and things, in among
the boulders and bushes. There were cups of delicious hot tea, too; but we were not cold, and the most
astonishing thing about that whole grand day is, we
did not feel stiff or the slightest discomfort in any
form after it. The tramp was long and the water
cold, and my own baths many. I might have saved
myself, sometimes, from going all the way down had
I not been afraid of breaking my rod, which I always
held high when I fell. The day was one to be remembered by Mrs. Ord and me. We had thought
all the time that General Stanley was making a great
sacrifice by giving up a day's sport for our amuse-

ment, and that it was so kind of him, for, of course he could not be enjoying the day; but it seems that he had sport of which we knew nothing until the following day—in fact, we know nothing about it yet! But he began to tell the most absurd stories of what we did, and we must have done many unusual things, for he is still entertaining the camp with them. He was very proud of us, nevertheless, and says so often. The ride of twelve miles back to camp seemed endless, for as soon as the excitement of the stream was over we found that we were tired—awfully tired.

We have only a few weeks more of this delightful life. The hunting is excellent, too, and Faye and Captain Rives often bring in large bags of mountain grouse and young sage hens. The sage chicken are as tender and delicious as partridge before they begin to feed upon wild sage in the fall, but one short day in the brush makes them different birds and wholly unpalatable. We often send birds, and fish also, to friends at Fort Bridger, who were most hospitable the day we arrived, and before coming to camp.

I had quite forgotten the wedding yesterday! It was at Fort Bridger, and the bride, a daughter of the post trader, is related to several families of social position at Omaha. We put on the very prettiest gowns we had with us, but the effect was disappointing, for our red faces looked redder than ever above delicate laces and silks. The ceremony was at noon —was very pretty—and everything passed off beautifully. The breakfast was delicious, and we wondered at the dainty dishes served so far from a caterer. The house was not large, and every bit of air had been shut out by darkening the windows, but we were

spared the heat and smell of lamps on the hot day
by the rooms being lighted by hundreds of candles,
each one with a pretty white shade. But some of us
felt smothered, and as soon as the affair was over,
started immediately for the camp, where we could
have exhilarating mountain air once more.

It was really one whole day stolen from our outing!
We can always have crowded rooms, receptions, and
breakfasts, wherever we happen to be in the East,
but when again will we be in a glorious camp like
this—and our days here are to be so few! From here
we are to go to Salt Lake City for a week or two.

THE WALKER HOUSE, SALT LAKE CITY, UTAH.
September, 1888.

THE weather is still very warm, but not hot enough
to keep us from going to the lake as usual this
morning. The ride is about eighteen miles long, and
is always more or less pleasant. The cars, often long
trains, are narrow gauge, open, and airy. The bathing
is delightful, but wholly unlike anything to be found
elsewhere. The wonderfully clear water is cool and
exhilarating, but to swim in it is impossible, it is so
heavy from its large percentage of salt. So every
one floats, but not at all as one floats in other waters.
We lie upon our backs, of course—at least we think
we do—but our feet are always out of the water, and
our heads straight up, with large straw hats upon
them.

They have a way of forming human chains on the
water that often startles one at first. They are made
by hooking one's arms close to the shoulder over the
ankles of another person, still another body hooking

on to you, and so on. Then each one will stretch his or her arms out and paddle backward, and in this way we can go about without much effort, and can see all the funny things going on around us. As I am rather tall, second position in a chain is almost always given to me, and my first acquaintance with masculine toes close to my face came very near being disastrous. The feet stood straight up, and the toes looked so very funny, with now and then a twitch back or front, that soon I wanted to laugh, and the more I tried not to the more hysterical I became. My shoulders were shaking, and the owner of the toes—a pompous man— began to suspect that I was laughing and probably at the toes. Still he continued to twist them around —one under the other—in an astonishing way, that made them fascinating. The head of the chain—the pompous man—became ominously silent. At last I said, almost sobbing, " Can't you see for yourself how funny all those things are in front of us? They look like wings in their pin-feather stage—only they are on the wrong side—and I am wondering if the black stockings would make real black wings—and what some of us would do with them, after all! " After that there was less pompous dignity and less hysteria, although the toes continued to wigwag.

It is a sight that repays one to watch, when dozens of these chains—some long, some short—are paddling about on the blue water that is often without a ripple. It is impossible to drown, for sink in it you cannot, but to get the brine in one's nose and throat is dangerous, as it easily causes strangulation, particularly if the person is at all nervous. We wear little bits of cotton in our ears to prevent the water from getting in, for the crust of salt it would leave might cause intense pain.

Bathing in water so salt makes one both hungry and sleepy, therefore it is considered quite the correct thing to eat hot popcorn, and snooze on the return trip. We get the popcorn at the pavilion, put up in attractive little bags, and it is always crisp and delicious. Just imagine a long open car full of people, each man, woman, and child greedily munching the tender corn! By the time one bag full has been eaten, heads begin to wobble, and soon there is a " Land of Nod "—real nod, too. Some days, when the air is particularly soft and balmy, everyone in the car will be oblivious of his whereabouts. Not one stop is made from the lake to the city.

Faye and I were at the lake almost a week—Garfield Beach the bathing place is called—so I could make a few water-color drawings early in the morning, when the tints on the water are so pearly and exquisitely delicate. During the day the lake is usually a wonderful blue—deep and brilliant—and the colors at sunset are past description. The sun disappears back of the Oquirah Mountains in a world of glorious yellow and orange, and as twilight comes on, the mountains take on violet and purple shades that become deeper and deeper, until night covers all from sight.

There was not a vacant room at Garfield Beach, so they gave us two large rooms at Black Rock—almost one mile away, but on the car line. The rooms were in a low, long building, that might easily be mistaken for soldiers' barracks, and which had broad verandas with low roofs all along both sides.

That queer building had been built by Brigham Young for his seven wives! It consisted of seven apartments of two rooms each, a sitting room and sleeping room; all the sitting rooms were on one side, opening out upon the one veranda, and the bedrooms were on the other side and opened out upon the other veranda. These apartments did not connect in any way, except by the two porches. Not far from that building was another that had once been the dining room and kitchen of the seven wives. These mormon women must be simply idiotic, or have their tempers under good control!

It was all most interesting and a remarkable experience to have lived in one of Brigham Young's very own houses. But the place was ghostly—lonesome beyond everything—and when the wind moaned and sighed through the rooms one could fancy it was the wailing of the spirits of those seven wretched wives. When we returned at night to the dark, unoccupied building, it seemed more spooky than ever, after the music and light at Garfield Beach. Our meals were served to us at the restaurant at the pavilion. I made some very good sketches of the lake, Antelope Island, and a number of the wonderful Black Rock that is out in the lake opposite the Brigham Young house.

About two miles from the city, and upon the side of the Wasatch Mountains, is Camp Douglas, an army post, which the new department commander came to inspect. The inspection was in the morning, and we all went to see it, and were driven in the post with the booming of cannon—the salute always given a brigadier general when he enters a post officially. ˙ It was pretty to see the general's wife partly cover her ears,

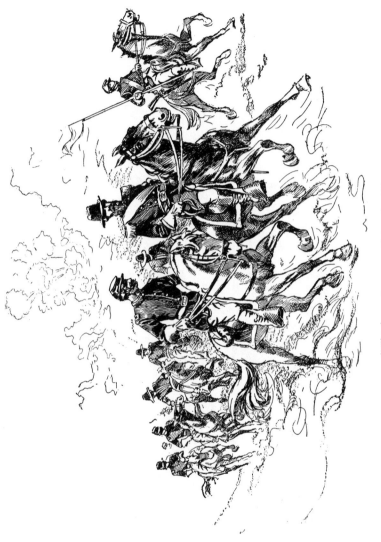

"The inspection was all too short."

and pretend that she did not like the noise, when all
the time her eyes were sparkling, and we knew that
every roar of the big guns added to her pride. If
all those guns had been for Faye I could never have
stayed in the ambulance.

It is charming up there—in the post—and the view
is magnificent. We sat out on a vine-covered porch
during the inspection, and watched the troops and the
review. It made me so happy, and yet so homesick,
too, to see Faye once more in his uniform. The inspection was all too short, and after it was over, many
officers and their wives came to call upon us, when
wine and delicious cake was served. We were at the
quarters of the colonel and post commander. That
was the second post we had taken Mrs. Ord to,
and she is suddenly enthusiastic over army people,
forgetting that Omaha has a post of its own. But
with us she has been in the tail of the comet—which
made things more interesting. Army people are nice,
though, particularly in their own little garrison
homes.

There is only one mormon store here, and that is
very large and coöperative. Every mormon who has
anything whatever to sell is compelled to take it to
that store to be appraised, and a percentage taken
from it. There are a few nice gentile shops, but mormons cannot enter them; they can purchase only at
the mormon store, where the gentiles are ever cordially welcomed also. Splendid fruit and vegetables
are grown in this valley—especially the fruit, which
is superior to any we ever saw. The grapes are of
many varieties, each one large and rich with flavor,
and the peaches and big yellow pears are most

luscious. Upon our table down in the dining room there is always an immense glass bowl of selected fruit —peaches, pears, and grapes, and each time we go down it seems to look more attractive.

We have been to see the tabernacle, with its marvelous acoustic properties, and the temple, which is not yet finished. The immense pipe organ in the tabernacle was built where it now stands, and entirely by mormons. From Brigham Young's old home a grand boulevard runs, through the city, across the valley, and over the hill far away, and how much beyond I do not know. This road, so broad and white, Brigham Young said would lead to Jerusalem. They have a river Jordan here, too, a little stream that runs just outside the city.

There are grand trees in every street, and every old yard, and one cannot help feeling great indignation to see where in some places the incoming gentiles have cut trees down to make space for modern showy buildings, that are so wholly out of harmony with the low, artistic white houses and vine-covered walls. It is such a pity that these high, red buildings could not have been kept outside, and the old mormon city left in its original quaint beauty.

We will return to Omaha soon now, and I shall at once become busy with preparations for the winter East. I have decided to go home in October, so I can have a long, comfortable visit before going to Washington. Faye wishes me to join him there the last of December. I am not very enthusiastic over the prospect of crowded rooms, daily receptions and "teas," and other affairs of more formality. But since I cannot return to the plains, I might as well go to the city, where we will meet people of culture, see the fascinating Diplomatic Corps, and be presented to the President's beautiful young wife.   Later on there will be the inauguration—for we expect to pass the winter in Washington.

(1)

THE END